CRASHES

CRASHES
Robert Beckman

Why They Happen –
What To Do

SIDGWICK & JACKSON
LONDON

TO THE SOVEREIGN OF MY REALM
MISTRESS OF MY HEART
APPLE OF MY EYE
AND SUNSHINE OF MY LIFE
A CONSTANT SOURCE OF INSPIRATION . . . MY WIFE
   PENELOPE

First published in Great Britain in 1988
by Sidgwick & Jackson Limited

ISBN 0-283-99673-0

Typeset in Linotron 202 Sabon by
Rowland Phototypesetting Limited
Bury St Edmunds, Suffolk

Printed in Great Britain by
Mackays of Chatham PLC
for Sidgwick & Jackson Limited
1 Tavistock Chambers, Bloomsbury Way
London WC1A 2SG

Contents

Introduction
by Lord Rees-Mogg

After the October 1987 crash, investors have been forced to think about long cycles and historic panics. There is in fact no certainty that such a thing as the Kondratiev long wave cycle exists. There is a certainty that market bubbles occur, and that market panics occur. This book is a history of some of the more notorious bubbles and some of the more catastrophic panics.

The bubble and panic do in fact have a mathematical shape, familiar to aeronautical engineers and other scientists. The bubble follows the line of an explosive curve; the panic usually shows a vertical drop at some point in its development. In aircraft this is the pattern of the stall, which killed so many of the pioneers of aviation. Panics finished off many of the pioneers of investment. The aircraft's rate of climb rises, passes beyond the point at which it can be sustained, the nose goes up and the plane falls. Many early aircraft fell right into the ground.

The pattern occurs in markets because psychology can change very rapidly from a situation in which there are no sellers – a one-way market going up – to one in which there are no buyers – a one-way market on the way down. Both selling and buying are driven by expectation. So long as expectation is that there will be higher prices, it is rational to buy. Once expectation changes, it ceases to be rational to buy, and it only becomes rational to buy once again when the price has fallen sufficiently far for the next expectation to be of a price rise. This is the reason why markets are usually much more volatile than the economies which underlie their values.

The history of the bubbles is also very instructive to all investors. Some of them have been deliberately blown up, as in nineteenth-century American railroad finance. Some of them have seemed literally insane, as in seventeenth-century Dutch Tulipomania. But all of them have shown the same pattern of a relatively long climb to unsustainable heights, a point of failure and disastrous losses in the decline. It is common for values to fall from the peak by 80–90% and sometimes more.

In all these catastrophes excesses of credit have played a very important role. Credit is easy, so people borrow in order to invest in the new fashion. Prices rise, so people have more security to offer their bankers. More is borrowed; more is invested; prices rise still further. Each turn of this screw pushes the market up. But a point is reached at which borrowers become frightened. The credit screw goes into reverse. Credit inflation moves to credit deflation.

Bob Beckman's book gives an account of some of the most famous of these episodes. As one would expect from them, they are colourful stories; as one would expect from him, they are colourfully told. The lust for money in a rising market can drive people to the most incredible follies – the despair of losses in a falling market has an equally dramatic effect.

But basically this book offers a warning. These bubbles spring from weaknesses in man himself, and particularly on the human alternation of exaggerated hope and exaggerated despair. They have happened repeatedly, they will happen again. So long as investors think that an investment should be bought because it has already risen, they will drive investments up. So long as panic affects human conduct, they will panic. The warning is against irrational investment. Buying real value is the only rational investment policy to follow.

1

The Crash of Tulipomania

How the collapse in the price of tulip bulbs in the
seventeenth century brought the Dutch economy
to its knees while penury and destitution ravaged
the land

The Status Symbol from Turkey

'I'd walk a mile for a Camel!' is the slogan on the display advertising
Camel cigarettes that dominates Times Square in the bustling theatre
district of New York. Against a background of gleaming sands, sprawling
pyramids and the flavour of the Nile, a hidden machine behind the
massive signboard drives puffs of steam through a huge mouth-shaped
opening in the face on the display, emitting giant smoke-like rings of
vapour above the heads of the madding crowds night and day.

Although in various corners of the globe Americans have a reputation
for harbouring certain eccentricities, it is most unlikely that any American
would actually be willing to walk a mile for a cigarette in spite of the
addictive nature of nicotine. It's all a bit of promotional licence from the
advertising copywriters. Yet during the mid-seventeenth century a phenomenon gripped the Dutch people in a bizarre self-propelling promotion
that would have been the envy of any twentieth-century ad man.

Tulpewoerde, Tulipomania or Tulip Madness, as it has since been
referred to, is the very first crash that appears to have been extensively
documented. Smokers might not be willing to walk a mile for a cigarette,
but ordinary people were actually willing to sell their homes, livestock,
farms and businesses to buy tulips. They were mesmerized by a sociologi-
cal delusion whose effects were to reach far beyond that which the most
creative ad man could possibly conceive. At the peak of Tulipomania
family fortunes were squandered for a single tulip bulb. When the price of
tulip bulbs crashed, the same fortunes were lost along with the wealth of a
nation.

The tulip, a native of southern Europe and the Middle East, derives its
name from the Turkish word *dulban*, signifying a turban – a reference to

1

the shape of the flower. According to the evidence that can be pieced together, the first tulips to arrive in northern Europe came from Turkey during the middle of the sixteenth century. They attracted the attention of the Swiss naturalist Conrad Gesner who subsequently brought them into repute, never realizing the commotion that they would ultimately cause. Gesner is said to have been enchanted by these novelties from Asia Minor during a visit to the gardens of the learned Councillor Herwert in Augsburg, who was renowned throughout western Europe for his collection of rare and exotic plants. Herwert claimed to have acquired the bulbs as a gift from a friend in Constantinople.

Following Gesner's introduction of the tulip to Vienna, an increasing number of travellers were struck with its beauty, and for the next three decades its role steadily increased in stature. Within a few years the bulbs were being grown and cultivated in Germany and the Netherlands. Then in the late 1570s the tulip reached England, where the new flower immediately became immensely popular in court circles. By the early seventeenth century tulips had captured the imagination of the French, who seemed to be willing to pay ever-increasing prices for the bulbs. It was in France that the early traces could be seen of what was subsequently to become a madness.

The Fashion Takes Off

Initially, the price of a tulip bulb was only marginally higher than that of other rare plants. But it is always the way with fashion that, if anything captures the imagination of the public and achieves popular acclaim, its price level goes up. The price of tulips began to rise . . . and rise . . . and rise. What price can actually be assigned to the perception of beauty that rests solely in the eye of the beholder? The amount of money that an individual or group of individuals may be willing to pay for a status symbol – especially if status is questionable – cannot be quantified. It is in this limitless region of price – assigned to the intangibles that have no intrinsic or utility values – that the seeds of a speculative mania are sown.

Public attention was understandably focused upon the tulip, which was novel, interesting and seemingly capable of ever-increasing value. During the early stages of its rise in popularity the aristocracy of Germany and the Netherlands were the principal buyers, ordering direct from Constantinople. Culturally and economically, at this moment in history the Netherlands reigned supreme – this was her Golden Age. Her vast merchant fleet, one half of the merchant shipping of the entire world, enabled her to dominate the East Indies trade, and to establish colonies in Asia and the Americas. At home, artists such as Rembrandt, Vermeer and Rubens celebrated the way of life that this new-found wealth made possible. A collection of tulips, on display for all to see, became one of the most

2

desirable status symbols that any family of good taste could acquire. Likewise, no self-respecting man of means could afford to be without an ostentatious display of fine tulips. With the passage of time the craze spread throughout the entire social spectrum, and butchers, bakers and candlestick-makers wanted tulips too.

As the collections grew more refined and the collectors more discriminating, it was the rare specimens that attracted the most attention and commanded the highest prices. Red tulips with black dots, for instance, were felt to be of greater value than red tulips that didn't have any black dots. Premiums were paid for the tulips which had their black dots in the centre. Soon, comparisons were being made with regard to the density of the dots and their placement. A grading system for tulips was developed.

Cultivated tulips can occasionally produce striking and colourful mutations, with ragged petals and flushes of other colours, which are caused by a virus contracted from the soil. In the seventeenth century tulips of this type were nowhere near as abundant as those of a single colour having regular petals. Growers would anxiously scan their gardens hoping for what was described as a break – not unlike a strike at an oilfield or a goldmine. If a tulip grower was lucky enough to have a break, the bloom could then be rectified, which was the term used for the process of tulip propagation. In the event of a particularly unusual or beautiful bloom, the grower could expect to find ready buyers for his rectified discovery. Middlemen would continue propagating, in the hope of marketing the new blooms at a substantial profit. A bulb producing a yellowish stem (referred to as a 'stained bottom'), or a badly formed flower would be discarded. It was only the bulbs that could produce consistently perfect flowers that were rectified and chosen to become breeder bulbs.

The Tulip as the Hub of Industry

As a result of the growth in popularity of tulips during the 1620s new industries were born, especially in the Netherlands where growers seemed to proliferate on a larger scale than elsewhere. Apart from the obvious wealth and status-consciousness of the Dutch, this could have had something to do with the nature of the soil and climate, which was apparently more conducive to bulb growing than elsewhere in western Europe.

Speedier methods for tulip picking and harvesting had become essential, as prices were advancing faster than the tulips could be grown. Packaging techniques had to be developed, since a bulb that might have cost thousands of gilders could fail to grow if it was damaged. New and quicker methods of transportation became necessary, so that these perishable items could be traded internationally in good condition. There were also storage and security problems to be overcome in the bulbfields

3

themselves since, as prices advanced for the rarer species, it was no longer prudent for owners to allow tulips and tulip bulbs to lie unguarded in a glasshouse.

One inventor who had made a study of Egyptian technology attempted to market a tulip-mummifying machine in order to give permanent protection to the plant. The contraption seemed to offer great possibilities, but unfortunately during the course of a demonstration the inventor fell into his machine, leaving his work incomplete.

Tulip growers needed protection against adverse weather conditions affecting their produce. Some bright spark in the Netherlands devised the pluvious policy – the first recorded instance of this type of policy being issued – and as a result the Dutch insurance industry flourished.

Amsterdam was the Wall Street of the early seventeenth century, and banking institutions were naturally also involved. Some collectors held tulips as investments and wanted either to keep them out of harm's way or simply to lodge them as security against loans. As a result the nation's bankers made large-scale investment in the installation of specially designed tulip vaults. Banking took on a new dimension in the Netherlands: there were those who challenged the gold standard in favour of a 'tulip standard'.

All these people and organizations, and many more, reaped enormous profits from the growth of the new industry, and the Dutch nation soon became totally dependent on the tulip bulb. It was to be an ill-fated dependence.

The Nature of Greed

Some are born greedy, some achieve greediness, and some have greediness thrust upon them. But few people are greedy because of what has been done to them by either their ancestors or their contemporary environment. For the majority, greed is primarily a hard-won self-accomplishment. People make greedy fools of themselves by themselves – indeed, some perfectionists have made perfectly greedy fools of themselves. They are often the last to know, and one almost hates to tell them. The ignorance of greed is certainly bliss.

It is difficult to determine at precisely what point the desire to acquire tulips as a collector's item or status symbol was overshadowed by the greed associated with rampant speculation. What is known is that, in the time-tried fashion, greed suppressed reason and the desire for amassing wealth in the tulip market of the Netherlands became the primary purpose of tulip trading. *Tulpewoerde*, the name the Dutch gave to the phenomenon of tulip trading, became synonymous with easy money and get-rich-quick schemes.

In the hands of the profiteers and promoters the tulip became a speculative vehicle, not unlike gemstones, rare coins and stamps in modern society. Until the 1970s their desirability was basically confined to a relatively small number of collectors for whom these somewhat esoteric 'collectables' had a special appeal. But during the heyday of inflation in the mid-1970s, what had previously been the domain of the specialist collector suddenly acquired an 'investment' status and then a speculative status, along with used motor cars of dubious pedigree and a whole range of garbage-bin produce which had never before – and has never since – been considered worthy of any particular investment of speculative merit.

Every Dutch businessman had a tulip broker who would send a messenger with any relevant changes in the price of the leading tulips

---

It was this type of mania that attached itself to the tulip in the mid-1630s. To those who question the sanity of the Dutch people at the time I pose the question: 'Who is to say that a peridot or a Penny Black has any greater intrinsic value than a tulip?' At first, as is the case with all speculative manias, confidence was at a pinnacle. Everybody won. Nobody lost. It all seemed so easy. The rage to possess tulips was so great at all levels of society in the Netherlands that the ordinary industry of the country was completely neglected and fell into decay. Speculating in tulips became the preoccupation of the day, a situation frighteningly similar to the mania for BP shares that mesmerized even the lowest-paid workers in Britain in the mid-1980s.

Tulip jobbers, ever on the alert for new speculative possibilities, made use of all the methods they could in order to gain from fluctuations in price. They accrued huge profits by buying massive quantities each time there was a fall in price and rapidly selling out on every rise. This always prevented prices from falling too far, keeping confidence on the boil. Many individuals who were once collectors of tulips suddenly found they had amassed wealth beyond their wildest dreams of avarice, not unlike their contemporaries of the twentieth century. But many of these individuals were quick to abandon the idea of maintaining a tulip collection in favour of hard cash.

A golden bait hung temptingly before the Dutch public in the form of speculative profits. One after the other, people of modest means rushed to the Tulip Exchanges like flies to a honey pot, tempted by the lure of quick profits without having to work for them. Noblemen, citizens, farmers, mechanics, seamen, footmen, maidservants, chimneysweeps and even rag and bone men had a flutter in the tulip market. 'Do you know the price of a Royal Queen Magenta?' one housemaid could be heard asking another. The average footman might come home bitterly dejected because his investment in Ocolulu Rex had dropped three gilders that day. Every Dutch businessman had a tulip broker who would send a messenger with any relevant changes in the price of the leading tulips as they took place. People of all classes converted their property into cash and invested that cash in tulips. Houses and land were sold to raise cash or were assigned in payment for bargains that were struck on the Tulip Exchanges. Pawn-brokers were deluged with gold, silver, jewellery and various personal possessions from those desperate to raise cash to pay for their tulip transactions. Even unemployed Dutchmen with no visible means of support were known to be earning a living by speculating in tulips.

As the price sky-rocketed, virtually every home had its own tulip field, and such fields occupied nearly every available inch of the country's land surface at the time. The conservatory became the showplace of the home and often assumed the role of sitting room, dining room and bedroom rolled into one. Tulip parties, at which the newest and most exotic acquisitions were put on display for guests to admire and envy, were the rage of the day among the wealthy. Parents would name a child after the kind of tulip most popular at the time of its birth. Certain eccentrics even declared that daily worship of the tulip would ward off the evil that would befall mankind at the coming of doomsday.

The tulip affected the lives of the Dutch people in a way that no one could have believed possible . . . unless he had lived through the Great Crash of '29. But that's the story of a different speculative chapter in history. It was, however, from this simple bulb that the precedents for speculation were established, laying the foundation for the multitude of speculative booms, busts and panics that were to punctuate the financial history of the centuries to follow.

The Tulip Futures Market

By 1636 regular markets for the sale of tulips had been established on the Exchanges of Amsterdam, Rotterdam, Leyden, Alkmaar, Hoorn and other towns where most of the world's business in tulip trading was transacted. But before this time tulip sales were generally held only during the winter months before the planting season. Speculators might gather together a few blossom specimens and a supply of bulbs to engage in barter at one of the inns frequented by the local tulip traders. During his sojourn at the accepted tulip trading pitch of the day, a trader might exchange his Admiral Tromp specimen, which he had purchased for 200 florins in cash, for a General Bol which he would hope to sell in a few days for 1000 florins as the rising price of bulbs accelerated. The trade became so profitable that many felt it far too limiting to restrict these activities to the winter months. Soon a futures market, that could be conducted all year round, developed for tulip bulbs. Traders would issue contracts in the spring, summer and autumn promising the delivery of specified tulip bulbs during the following winter, in the same way as contracts are now issued in actively traded commodities. The aim was to sell the contract – at a profit, of course – before the tulips actually arrived.

The first futures market was followed by an option market, in which traders could purchase 'puts' and 'calls' on their favourite tulip. The call option would give the speculator the right to buy a certain quantity of tulips within a specified time, and the put option gave him the right to sell a quantity of tulips under the same conditions. In essence, call options were wagers based on the assumption that tulip prices would go up over a relatively short period, while put option holders were gambling on the price going down.

Speculators who dealt in tulip futures and options never had any intention of actually acquiring tulips. The true speculator was concerned only with the price movement of his contracts, which he hoped to resell at a profit to some later enthusiast. This was called *Windhandel* – trading air.

As the mania continued to gather pace, prices rose to levels which no one believed would have been possible in a rational environment. At one stage, prices were doubling nearly every day. Thus the Greater Fool Syndrome was born. A tulip trader would often pay any price that was asked for whatever tulips were in popular demand on the assumption that there would be a greater fool than he was, ready, willing and able to pay a still higher price a short time afterwards. Of course the story ends when the greatest fool of all appears, who has no one to sell to at a higher price. But in the Netherlands at this time the story continued to unfold. The greatest fools of all were yet to make an appearance.

Prices Can Go Down as Well as Up . . .

The Dutch genuinely believed that the passion for tulips would last for ever and that the wealthy – and even the not-so-wealthy – would come from all parts of the world and pay whatever prices they asked. Indeed, investors from countries far and wide were frenziedly pouring money into the Netherlands. As a result inflation became rampant and the price of the necessities of life rose sharply, along with the price of houses, land, horses and carriages and luxuries of all kinds.

Chroniclers of the period were quick to provide a vast array of reasons why the price of tulips would continue to rise and never fall, in much the same manner as estate agents now give potential buyers similar reasons why house prices will rise and can never fall. No one could envisage any set of circumstances in which the price of tulips would fall, since it was perceived that all tulips would be subject to limited supply, and that demand would always exceed supply. It was inconceivable that tulips could be anything but undervalued, selling at a mere fraction of the future prospective prices.

Career Opportunities for Tulip Analysts

Alongside the practice of tulip jobbing, a further field of expertise emerged whose function was to analyse the intrinsic value of the various species of tulips and attempt to estimate a future prospective price in the market. This field of endeavour was soon divided into two camps – those who argued that the value of a tulip related solely to what the market was willing to pay for it, and those who felt that careful study of petal formation, angle or length of stem, density of colour, soil ingredients and so on were the elements that would have a direct effect on the future price of that particular tulip. The appearance of the tulip analysts gave the price of the more static, sluggish tulips a fillip.

Huge public demand developed for those tulips deemed by the analysts to be the market's leaders, such as Kauffmanniana, Viridiflora, Keizerskroon, Fosteriana Hybrid and Flora Semper. Speculators seeking maximum capital gain were directed towards the lesser-known secondary tulips. Demand always exceeded supply while the tulip growers toiled in their glasshouses, developing new varieties, only to find that each new tulip issue was oversubscribed long before it reached the market, necessitating a system of quotas (or should I say allocations?) for favoured clients of the tulip broker.

Within hours of their appearance on the Tulip Exchange high-fliers like Admiral Liefken, Admiral Van Der Eyck and Semper Augustus were traded at astronomical multiples of the analyst's intrinsic worth projections. A certain merchant traded two lasts (about four tons) of wheat, four lasts of rye, four fat oxen, eight fat swine, twelve fat sheep, two hogsheads of wine, four tuns of beer, two tuns of butter, 1000 lb of cheese, one complete bed, one slightly used suit of clothes, and one tarnished silver drinking cup – all in exchange for a bulb of Viceroy, which was rated as one of the tulips likely to experience outstanding growth in the years ahead.

The tulip rigger was the seventeenth century's version of the insider dealer

---

By the mid-1630s, in this atmosphere of giddy optimism and supreme confidence, it was felt that poverty would soon be permanently banished from the shores of the Zuyder Zee. People believed that the riches of all Europe would in due course be concentrated in the Netherlands, in much the same manner as, a few years ago, people envisaged that the rising price of oil would lead to Middle Eastern ownership of most of the wealth on this planet. Dutch economists predicted that the perpetual rise in value of the tulip would ensure a continual increase in the gross national product of their country for at least twenty to thirty years, and that the Dutch standard of living would ultimately be the highest in the world.

Tales of Innocence and Gullibility

Whenever there is fortune, there is also misfortune and folly, such as that illustrated by the tulip breeder-grower whose entire stock was consumed by a cow, driving him into bankruptcy and subsequent suicide. Needless to say, the cow did not prosper from the exercise, although attempts were made to create a speculative market in the milk from cows which ate tulips. The problem was the unwillingness of the average speculator to let his tulips be eaten by cows on the off-chance that there might be equal speculative demand for 'tulip cow milk', 'cow tulip milk', or something like that.

There were also incidents of the kind related in *Blainville's Travels*. A wealthy merchant who prided himself on his ability to discover under-priced tulips ordered a consignment from the Levant. When it arrived, it was delivered to the merchant at his counting house by the sailor who had been in charge of the shipment. As a reward for his efforts, the merchant gave the sailor a herring to eat for his breakfast. It seems the sailor had a great penchant for onions. Lying on a counter was an object which seemed to be an onion. The sailor slily slipped it into his pocket as a relish for his herring and left the counting house, proceeding along the quay to eat his breakfast.

Hardly was the sailor down the quay when the merchant suddenly discovered that his valuable Semper Augustus, worth at least 3000 florins, was missing. The entire staff of the counting house was instantly in an uproar. An immediate search was carried out for the precious root, but it was nowhere to be found. Someone then thought of the sailor.

The merchant dashed into the street, followed by other members of his staff. The sailor – simple soul that he was – made no effort whatever to conceal the pilferage. He was found quietly sitting on a coil of rope, chewing the last morsel of his 'onion'. Little did he dream that he had been eating a breakfast whose cost might have fed a whole ship's crew for twelve months; or, as the plundered merchant himself expressed it, 'He might have sumptuously feasted with the Prince of Orange and the whole court of the Stadtholder.' The most unfortunate part of the affair was the fate of the poor sailor, who was imprisoned for several months on a charge of felony.

To illustrate the temper of those days here is a story about a shoemaker in The Hague, who like many others at the time had a small plot of land dedicated to tulip growing. This modest grower had a strike and managed to grow a black flower. The news travelled quickly. Before long the shoemaker was visited by two of the major tulip traders in Haarlem, who purchased the treasure for 1500 florins. Upon completing the transaction, one of the traders immediately dropped the bulb and stamped on it until it was ground to a pulp. The cobbler was aghast. The traders explained that they too possessed a black tulip and had destroyed his in order to protect the uniqueness – and price – of their own. They would have paid anything – 10,000 florins if necessary. The heartbroken cobbler is reputed to have died of chagrin a short time after his strike.

Dirty Dealing

The stories of the ill-fated sailor and the destroyer of the black tulip were innocent enough. But for every tale of misfortune and folly there were several instances of malfeasance, the usual by-product of unrestrained greed. Manipulators of the tulip market trained animals to dig up and devour bulbs for the purpose of creating a scarcity of selected strains, thus forcing prices higher. Dogs, cats, ducks, geese, pigs, chickens and various other household livestock were turned loose on the multifarious tulip patches to create havoc for the tulip breeder-grower and profits for their owners.

As Tulipomania propelled the Dutch people into a state of temporary insanity a new method of malfeasance appeared. The tulip rigger was the seventeenth century's version of the insider dealer, and the practices used were devious and imaginative. There were those riggers who – in order to increase their profits – would start a rumour that a specific tulip field had been destroyed by a chicken invasion. The rumour would send the price of tulips from that region to astronomical heights in anticipation of a permanent shortage of the species destroyed. Needless to say, the rigger responsible for all this would first have purchased large quantities of bulbs from the supplier who was the subject of the rumour. He would then sell his bulbs – at two to three times the price he had originally paid – to unsuspecting buyers who were expecting further and further price rises.

Other tulip riggers would form a pool and choose a particular species of tulip that was out of favour as a vehicle for manipulation. By buying and selling among themselves – not unlike the practices of the auction saleroom of today – the riggers would make it appear that the selected species was suddenly in demand. Uninformed buyers among the financially unwashed and financially unwashable, who knew little of the factors determining the price of tulips, would then come into the market, effecting their purchases from the riggers at over-inflated prices.

The Party's Over

Eventually, the lone voice of prudence that had been echoing in the wings managed to make itself heard. Those who had somehow maintained a semblance of business acumen during the tulip craze became progressively more aware that such folly certainly could not last indefinitely, regardless of what the economists and tulip analysts had to say. The recognition of financial reality began to spread, slowly at first but then with hairraising momentum. Prices dipped, then fell, then plunged . . . never to rise again. Confidence was shattered and a universal panic ricocheted through the land, reaching into the deepest financial recesses from the local merchant to the government itself.

When the merry-go-round came to a stop, somebody had to lose, and the time-honoured pattern which has dominated speculative markets for centuries descended upon the Dutch people. Trader A might have agreed to purchase from Trader B ten Semper Augustus at an agreed price of, say, 10,000 florins. A few weeks after the contracts were signed Trader B

For any investor, 252 years is a long time to wait to get your money back

would have been ready to make delivery of the tulips and receive payment. But during those few weeks the price of Semper Augustus might have fallen by 30–40%. As often happened, Trader A was unable or unwilling to pay the originally agreed price, which was far higher than the market price at the time of delivery.

Defaulters were announced day after day in the townships of the Netherlands. Thousands of Dutch citizens suddenly found themselves the possessors of a few bulbs representing their entire life savings, but nobody wanted to buy them even though they were being offered at a quarter of the original price. The cry of distress became a scream as each man accused his neighbour, attempting to ease the personal burden of his own folly and stupidity. The few who had contrived to enrich themselves by selling out before the collapse were forced to hide their wealth from their fellow citizens. Some had emerged for a brief period from the humbler walks of life to become wealthy and successful tulip traders, and were now plunged back into their former obscurity. The majority, though, suffered far worse than this. Many a scion of a noble line saw the fortunes of his estate ruined beyond redemption. Substantial businessmen worth millions of florins before they became transfixed by Tulipomania were reduced to near beggary. The average Dutch citizen who saw his wealth wither and dry if it was stored in tulips, or simply disappear if held by one of the many banks that failed, was plunged into penury and destitution.

As tulip prices plummeted and conditions deteriorated, the tulip holders in several towns held meetings to discuss what measures should be taken to restore public credit. The government would not intervene, merely advising the tulip holders to agree some plan amongst themselves, but no measure could be devised that was likely to give satisfaction to the deluded people or repair even a slight portion of the mischief that had been done. Still the government steadfastly refused to intervene, having its hands full with banks, companies and individuals who were going into bankruptcy by the thousand, along with the problem of starvation and poverty as the numbers of unemployed increased.

Lawsuits were so numerous that the courts were not able to handle the deluge, but no Dutch court was able to enforce payment of debts incurred in tulip trading. It was deemed that they fell into the category of gambling debts, and when the question was referred to the government in Amsterdam the judges unanimously agreed that such debts were not recoverable in law.

Dutch commerce was decimated by Tulipomania, for the country had been starved of other investment while the wealth of the nation was being solely directed towards the tulip trade. The Netherlands was plunged into a depression and its financial credibility obliterated in international markets. It was many decades before the Dutch authorities and merchants were able to hold their heads high in the world again.

Those who believe that the price of investments may fall, but always recover, should consider the plight of the Dutch. If they were alive today, Dutchmen who had invested in tulips during the seventeenth century would still be waiting to see the value of their bulbs return to the levels of 1636. For any investor, 252 years is a long time to wait to get your money back.

The experience of the Dutch who ruined themselves speculating and gambling on the tulip market should be an example to the rest of the world when it comes to the perils of speculation. Those who refuse to learn the lessons of history are condemned to repeat them. What we do learn is that no one appears to want to profit by any of the lessons of history. Greed and avarice seem to have no boundaries and a most defective memory. Less than a century after the experiences of Tulipomania Britain embarked upon its own version of the affair, involving one of the most monumental and irrational speculative follies of all time . . . which led to yet another fateful crash.

2

The Crash of the South Sea Bubble

How the collapse of the eighteenth-century version
of privatization brought the entire British nation
into disrepute and to the edge of financial ruin

Plus Ça Change

Privatization – the sale of companies owned by the state to members of the private sector – is a phenomenon associated with the Thatcher administration of the 1980s. Yet although this method of mobilizing small investors as a means of increasing government revenues and reducing the national debt may seem like a modern device, it's not a new trick at all. In fact it's over 270 years old. . . .

At the beginning of the eighteenth century Britain was the master of Europe – or at least her politicians claimed that she was. London was the bustling trade centre of the world. Citizens throughout the land were enjoying the good things of life with plenty of extra spending money in their pockets. True, there were certain structural weaknesses in the British economy, but nobody was worried about that. In other words, the Britain of the early eighteenth century was in several respects somewhat like the Britain of the 1980s.

During the early eighteenth century a great hi-tech boom was underway in the areas of construction and transportation, and promoters in these fields were reaping fortunes. A get-rich-quick atmosphere was in the air, not unlike the current atmosphere of post-Big Bang, in which twenty-five-year-old hot-shot City gunslingers are being offered astronomical salaries for the purpose of helping the big brokers fleece the lambs. But in those far-off days there was no multiplicity of companies in which people could invest their money. What might be considered the London Stock Exchange listings consisted of no more than three investments – stock in the Bank of England, the East India Company and the South Sea Company.

The Bank of England needs little explanation. The East India Company was the most successful and best-known of the various companies – such as the West India Company and the Hudson's Bay Company – set up by

13

the British in foreign parts, originally to obtain trading concessions and ultimately to acquire political ascendancy and even colonial rule. From such humble beginnings the East India Company became a great enterprise that promoted the development of the Indian sub-continent and made great fortunes for those who served it. The South Sea Company, on the other hand, was a comet that shot across the financial skies for a brief ten years, subsequently disappearing into nothingness.

The Lure of Untold Riches

The commercial basis for the Company was claimed to be the exploitation of the monopoly of trade in the South Seas, which embraced a vast area including the whole of South America, the West Coast of North America and points westward until it met the boundaries of the East India Company's monopoly in the Far East. This certainly appeared to be a ripe, juicy plum of the first order. Britain ruled the seas. Her military and commercial powers were unchallenged. How could the venture fall?

Unfortunately, the British government of the early eighteenth century was prone to the same kind of cosmetic manoeuvring as Mrs Thatcher's government. In reality, the South Sea Company was formed not for commercial exploitation but for the purpose of restoring public credit and of providing for the discharge of the army and navy debentures – paying off money borrowed to finance the forces – along with other parts of the national debt. In other words, Britain was in financial difficulties due to a burgeoning Public Sector Borrowing Requirement.

Taxes were high at this time because of heavy government spending: there were repeated increases in the duties on wines, vinegar, Indian goods, woven silks, tobacco, whalebone and other articles. The authorities felt that if further taxation was imposed they would be faced with anarchy. The formation of the South Sea Company – as a kind of eighteenth-century privatization scheme to raise money to finance the country's debts – was considered a brilliant solution. Its creator, the Tory leader, took great credit for it and his flatterers called the scheme 'the Earl of Oxford's masterpiece' (whether the current British Personal Equity Plan will ever be called Chancellor Lawson's masterpiece remains to be seen). In 1711 the Company received a royal warrant, and no less a personage than King George I became its Governor.

Not surprisingly, the South Sea Company got off to an auspicious start. In a rather high-handed manoeuvre the holders of £9.5 million worth of British government securities were forced to exchange these low-risk government securities for shares in the new South Sea Company at par. In other words, every £100 worth of interest-bearing British government securities were exchanged for a hundred £1 shares in non-interest-bearing equity of the South Sea Company. Not unlike the vast promotion that

14

accompanied the British Telecom flotation, reams of material were issued by the government outlining the glowing prospects of the South Sea Company. People were told of the great gold and silver mines of Peru and Mexico, which were believed to be inexhaustible. All that was necessary was to finance the exports of British manufacturers to the South American coast, where Britain would be repaid by the natives a hundredfold in gold and silver ingots.

A 'leak' claiming that Spain, whose sphere of influence included most of South America, was willing to concede four ports on the coasts of Chile and Peru for the purposes of trade, was industriously spread just when the authorities were about to effect the swop of the South Sea Company shares for government securities. This increased general confidence in the shares and the Company had a successful launch. It was later disclosed that Philip V of Spain had never had any intention of allowing Britain free trade with the ports of Spanish America. Negotiations had been started, admittedly, but were subsequently neutered by some hefty demands from the King of Spain.

Shortly after the launch the share price sank from 100 to 77½, and for several years they showed no better performance. It soon became clear that the promoters of the South Sea Company had no interest whatever in its commercial potential, nor had the investors who had been seduced by royal decree. In harmony with the times, investors were out for a quick profit, just like the purchasers of the various 1980s' privatization issues. When the prospects of a quick profit faded, so did demand for the shares and so did the government's chances of improving its finances.

The King's speech at the opening of Parliament in 1717 made pointed allusion to the state of public credit in Britain, and recommended that proper measures be taken to reduce the growing national debt. The South Sea Company and the Bank of England proposed that the Company's £10 million capitalization should be increased to £12 million, by subscription or otherwise. An Act of Parliament called the South Sea Act was passed,

---

Investors were out for a quick profit, just like the purchasers of the various 1980s' privatization issues

---

enabling the Company to increase its capital stock to this amount in exchange for the sum of £2 million, which would be paid by the Company towards discharging the principal and interest on the debt due by the state for the lottery funds from the reign of Queen Anne, who had died in 1714.

The name of the South Sea Company was once again thrust upon the British. Although the Company itself produced little profit through its trading activities, it began to flourish as a monetary vehicle due to the continual hype created by the authorities and its directors.

By 1719, things had begun to look up again as a new wave of speculation swept the country. The artificial stimulation for shares in the South Sea Company started to produce results, and demand improved considerably. The directors were so encouraged that new ideas were sought for the purpose of expanding their influence. The Mississippi scheme of John Law (see Chapter 3), which had so dazzled and captivated the French people, came to mind: it was envisaged that something similar could be set up in England. The anticipated collapse of the John Law scheme in no way diverted the directors of the South Sea Company from their intentions. Wise in their own conceit, they imagined they could avoid all Law's mistakes and carry on the scheme forever, stretching the cord of credit to its limit without causing it to snap.

Treachery and Skulduggery

Sensing that the time was right, the directors of the South Sea Company put together a plan which would make it the most influential corporation in the country and even relegate the Bank of England to second place. The proposal was to pay off the entire national debt in one swoop by incorporating it with the Company's shares. The sum involved was £51,300,000 – a massive undertaking at the time. The government loved the idea. The national debt had originally been contracted during a period when interest rates were at historically high levels, and the South Sea Company were planning to take it over in return for a mere 5% per annum interest, falling to 4% by 1727. The Company also offered to pay the government £3.5 million immediately 'for the privilege of taking over the national debt'. The scheme may appear treacherous and reek of skulduggery, but is it really all that different from a scheme which encourages the purchase of government assets that pay a piddling dividend while the authorities discourage, through punitive taxation, the purchase and issue of low-risk fixed-interest-bearing government stock?

The final proposals for the takeover of the national debt were introduced to the House of Commons in January 1720. The directors of the South Sea Company assured the government that, if the scheme were approved, the national debt would be eradicated within twenty-five years. At the same time rumours were circulating from 'sources close to the government' that prominent politicians and courtiers were busily buying shares in the Company, anticipating an explosive rise in the price when the government approved the scheme. In fact John Aislabie, then Chancellor of the Exchequer, was supposed to have purchased no less than £27,000 worth for himself, raising all he could beg, borrow and steal to effect the purchase. A member of the Opposition was quick to point out that the entire arrangement appeared to benefit only a chosen few friends of the government – shades of British Telecom! To counter what was deemed an unfair advantage to a privileged small group, it was proposed that the transaction be thrown open to public bids. With visible chagrin Aislabie was compelled to agree to receive further proposals.

The Bank of England Fights Back

The Bank of England immediately saw that its key role in British financial affairs was being threatened. The 'public bid' allowed the Bank to defend its position. The South Sea Company had offered the government £3.5 million for the privilege of taking over the national debt, so the Bank made a counter-bid of £5 million. The directors of the Company quickly came through with a higher bid of £7,565,000. The Bank was not willing to better the cash sum offered by its rival, but asserted that the Bank had performed great service to the state in the most difficult times. It should be the Bank of England, it declared, which should receive preferential treatment, rather than a company that had never contributed anything to the nation.

The Whig leader, Robert Walpole, was the chief speaker in the Commons in favour of the Bank of England, while the Chancellor, John Aislabie, was the principal advocate on behalf of the South Sea Company. The House began to debate the two contenders' proposals.

Sowing the Seeds for a Bitter Harvest

While we're waiting for the result of the deliberation, let's look closer at the structure of the deal. Exactly what did the Chancellor of the Exchequer and the directors of the South Sea Company intend to accomplish by taking over the national debt? Taking over a debt of that magnitude seemed like a pretty weird transaction. It wasn't. The South Sea Company proposition was merely one of thousands of share promotion schemes that were to follow over the centuries. The directors wanted more than anything to catch the public eye in an unprecedented fashion, in much the same way as any other company that wants to promote its share price when the public has a lot of disposable income. The directors wanted the South Sea Company to be seen as the world's first super-conglomerate that had government blessing, after which they would make a public offering of the shares amidst fanfares not unlike those which accompanied the British Telecom privatization. This massive share promotion operation would then enable it to offer its private holdings at a fantastic premium after the issue had been oversubscribed in precisely the same manner as British Telecom. In other words, the directors of the South Sea Company were setting a pattern which was to be followed by countless promoters since . . . including the British government of today.

17

On 22 February 1720 it was resolved that the proposals of the South Sea Company were likely to be the most advantageous for the nation. The Company was duly authorized to create £1 of new stock for every £1 of national debt it took over. The next step was to distribute those newly issued shares to a more than willing market. The directors, highly optimistic, saw a chance to raise enough money immediately to pay the multi-million pound 'privilege' kicker to the authorities and still have plenty left over to make profits and cover further necessary expenses. The latter consisted of bribes promised to politicians and courtiers, including the King's mistress. Unfortunately, the South Sea Company was not in a position to offer knighthoods to mitigate its expenses.

The Voice in the Wilderness

When the passage of the Bill was announced, Exchange Alley in the City of London was in a fever of excitement. Shares in the Company, which had been quoted at 130 before the announcement, rose steadily, reaching 300, and continued to rise with the most astonishing speed during the entire time that the Bill was in its various stages. Robert Walpole, a voice in the wilderness, was the only statesman in the House of Commons not caught up in the wave of speculative euphoria and greed. Only he was willing to speak out against the 'privileges' granted to the South Sea Company:

> It countenances the dangerous practice of stock jobbing and would divert the genius of the nation from trade and industry. It would hold out a dangerous lure to decoy the unwary to ruin, by making them part with the earnings of their labour for a prospect of imaginary wealth. The great principle of the project was an evil of first rate magnitude; it was to raise artificially the value of the stock, by exciting and keeping up a general infatuation, and by promising dividends out of funds which could never be adequate for the purpose.

To this statement he added in a prophetic spirit that, if the plan succeeded, the directors of the South Sea Company would become the masters of the government. They would probably go on to form a new and absolute aristocracy in the kingdom, leading to control of the legislature. If the scheme failed, which he was convinced must happen, there would be general discontent and the country would be ruined. It was Walpole's belief that when the bubble finally burst the nation would suddenly awake as if from a dream, and people would begin to ask themselves how they could possibly have chosen leaders who would expose them to such a heinous catastrophe.

But all his eloquence was in vain, as the eloquence of all those who followed him down the centuries was used in vain against any crowd that had tasted the flavour of easy money. They were all looked upon as false prophets, their warnings compared to the omens of evil croaked by hoarse ravens. Although in former times the House had listened with the utmost attention to every word that fell from Walpole's lips, during the two months that the Bill was in progress the benches were deserted when it was known that he was going to speak on the South Sea Company question. Walpole's friends, however, compared him to Cassandra, the prophetess who foretold the fall of Troy, predicting evils which would be believed well enough when they came home to men's hearts and stared them in the face.

Leaks and Rumours from the City

While the Bill was being debated in the House the most extravagant rumours were being circulated through the City PR machine, as they had at the time of the Company's original flotation. News of treaties between England and Spain was spoken of as being leaked by 'informed sources'. A rumour was spread that Spain was going to grant free trade to all her colonies. It was whispered that the rich produce of the great silver mine in what is now Bolivia was to be brought to Britain, and that silver would become as abundant as coal and iron. A report was issued predicting potential demand from Mexico for cotton and woollen goods made in Britain. Presumably the Mexicans were to empty their goldmines in payment for these cheaply manufactured goods, which would be sold at several hundred times their manufacturing cost. It was generally felt that British merchants trading in the South Seas would become the richest the world had ever seen, and the broking fraternity predicted that every £100 invested would produce thousands of pounds per annum return to the investor.

As a result of the tireless efforts of the propaganda machine, directed by Sir John Blunt, the chairman of the Company, the shares reached 400. Then there was some profit-taking, which brought the price back to 350. Here it remained when the Bill was finally passed by the House of Commons with a majority of 172 to 55.

In the Lords the Bill was hurried through all its stages with unprecedented rapidity. Several members spoke against the scheme during its shotgun passage, but their warnings went unheeded since many peers were busy trying to get the latest price on the South Sea shares – the speculating frenzy knew no social boundaries. Lord North and Lord Grey said the Bill was unjust by nature and could prove fatal in its consequences; it was calculated to enrich the few while exposing the many to ultimate impoverishment. Earl Cowper compared the Bill with the famous horse of the siege of Troy: like the Trojan horse, he warned, the Bill had been ushered in and received with great pomp and exclamations of joy, but within rested the means of destruction and treachery.

Hubble, Bubble, Toil and Trouble

On 12 April, five days after the Bill had become law, the directors opened their books for a subscription of a million shares at 300 for every 100 nominal value. The new stock was heavily oversubscribed, as they had anticipated. Of course, the entire scheme was going to stand or fall according to the Company's ability to generate a large and constant influx of funds from the investing public. The initial offering was in 'partly paid' form. Investors could pay in five instalments of 60 each for every 100 in capital that was purchased at 300. In just a few days the shares advanced from 350, with the initial offering being sold at double the subscription price of the first payment. Does it all sound familiar?

When the market for the shares began to lag, in order to furnish fresh funds and to provide a new incentive the Company offered to lend money at a low 5% interest rate against shares that were deposited. The investor who held South Sea stock, or who would subsequently buy it, was allowed a loan of 250 for each 100 in capital he held. With the shares standing at 400 there was a margin of 150 – provided, of course, the stock maintained its price. So successful was the new loan gimmick that the South Sea Company repeated the offer no fewer than three times.

For the purpose of keeping the share on the boil, on 21 April the directors declared a midsummer dividend of 10% – double what had been anticipated – to which all holders were entitled. The directors opened their books for yet another subscription of stock: one million was offered at 400. Such was the eagerness of people from every walk of life to get in on the speculative boom that in the course of just a few short hours the shares were oversubscribed one and a half times.

'A company for carrying on an undertaking of great advantage, but nobody to know what it is'

The expansion of credit and the rise of speculation go hand in hand. In a typical bandwagon frenzy characteristic of speculative booms, innumerable companies of a similar structure to the South Sea Company started to spring up. Regardless of the legal restrictions, which normally made it extremely difficult to form new companies, ventures in which members of the public could buy shares – primarily on credit – emerged in multiplicity day after day. They were soon being called 'bubbles', the most appropriate name that could ever have been devised. Simultaneously stockbroking became all the rage. Everybody wanted to get in on the act. The overall result was a transformation of British society almost overnight, as Robert Walpole had predicted.

Some of the 'bubble companies' were plausible enough. If they had been floated when the public was in a more rational state of mind, their shares might have been pursued to the advantage of all concerned. But while some could have been viable, a large number had lunacy written all over them. Most were formed with only one purpose: the promoters simply took the first opportunity of any rise in the share price to grab their profits and run.

One company was formed, with one million capital, for a 'wheel of perpetual motion'. Another had the declared purpose of 'encouraging the breed of horses in England and improving of glebe and church lands, and repainting and rebuilding parsonage and vicarage houses'. But the most absurd and preposterous of all, the one which revealed more completely than any other the utter madness of people at that time, was a company started by an unknown adventurer who didn't even take the trouble to invent a scheme. In the share prospectus it was called 'a company for carrying on an undertaking of great advantage, but nobody to know what it is'. The promoter promised that every subscriber 'who deposits £2 per share is to be entitled to £100 per annum'. Within five hours he had attracted over £2000 to the company's 'head office' in London. In the sixth hour he was comfortably on his way to the continent and was never heard of again. Remember Keith Hunt and the promises he made to those whom he was able to seduce into commodity trading under his discretionary authority in 1987?

It was estimated that the sums sought by all these multifarious speculative undertakings amounted to about £300 million (think of it as representing more than six times the Thatcher government's current debt). This, of course, posed a severe threat to the harbinger of the whole affair, the South Sea Company. Obviously, every pound that went to another company's share subscriptions would be lost to the South Sea Company, which desperately needed a continual flow of money to keep its financial machine going. You can compare the problem to what would happen today if there was a sudden fall in the stock market and the redemptions of units in unit trusts exceeded sales.

When in Doubt, Legislate

In an effort to get South Sea Company shares on the move again, the directors went back to their friends in high places, cash in hand, to try and get some legislation enacted. On 11 June 1720 George I published a proclamation declaring that all of these 'unlawful bubble companies' should be deemed public nuisances, and that anyone dealing in their shares would be prosecuted and liable to a £500 fine. This was considered a small price to pay for dealing in 'bubbles', so the con men continued.

The directors of the South Sea Company now had to add a bit more pressure in more far-reaching circles – which, of course, was paid for with shareholders' money. Very quickly the so-called Bubble Act was passed, which made illegal all companies that had not obtained a royal charter. The 'bubble companies' that had obtained anything at all in terms of formal permission were few and far between – the directors of the South Sea Company had paid handsomely to see to that. As a result no fewer than eighty-six were now declared illegal and put out of existence. This was just the tonic that the South Sea Company needed, and its shares started to rise: on 10 July the price hit 1000.

In the background was a double-edged sword of unrest. In the first instance, the Bubble Act proved counter-productive in certain respects. Investors had no way of knowing who was legal and who would be declared illegal under the Act. Accordingly, indiscriminate selling of shares in all companies began, since only the South Sea Company was above suspicion. It only took a few days for the market to dry up completely, and no buyers could be found at any price.

Investors were suddenly alerted to the fact that share prices can fall as well as rise, and that when they fall they fall faster than they rise. Even the 'insider dealers' in the South Sea Company started to become apprehensive, and all too soon the general atmosphere of panic began to affect these shares too. After they reached 1000 the opinion was widely held that they would rise no further. The market had contracted 'roundophobia' – the fear of round numbers. So many sellers and so few buyers of South Sea shares appeared in Exchange Alley that they dropped from 1000 to 896 on one day and down to 640 on the next, creating the typical pattern of a crashing market that was to be repeated over and over again throughout history.

Desperate Measures

Against all logic, the Company tried a fourth flotation of shares, accompanied by the usual fanfare. Its efforts appeared to be successful for a short time, but in the end the flotation failed – too few shares were bought. The news spread like wildfire and the market price of the shares started to fall . . . and fall . . . and fall. By mid-September 1720 the price was down to 400, 60% of the value of the shares having been lost in just over two months.

Most investors are unwilling to admit that the losses they suffer are primarily the result of their own greed and stupidity. The tendency is to abdicate responsibility to a stockbroker, investment adviser, tip sheet or whatever. In this case, the loss of money and face were laid at the door of the directors of the South Sea Company. Investors were infuriated when they learned that Sir John Blunt and several of his personal acquaintances had sold their own shares near the top of the market just a few weeks earlier.

The state of affairs became alarming, and in desperation the directors tried a further ploy. During the autumn of 1720 they announced that at Christmas the Company would pay a 30% dividend, to be increased to 50% in subsequent years. But the big question in the minds of those investors who were beginning to think more logically was: 'Where is the money going to come from to pay these grandiose dividends?'

The directors saw the writing on the wall. In a panic they turned to their arch-enemy, the Bank of England, and proposed that the Bank take over some blocks of shares at 400. But the Bank dreaded the idea of being involved in a calamitous situation and rejected the various overtures that were made, including those of Robert Walpole. It was later reported that the directors of the Company and of the Bank had agreed to circulate six million South Sea Company bonds, and as a result the share price began to rise again. When the rumour was denied, South Sea Company shares plummeted. The directors could now no longer appear in public without being insulted and abused, and riots were beginning to break out in the City as irate shareholders gathered to voice their disapproval.

The Bubble Bursts

Finally the Bank acquiesced, but it was all to no avail. When it issued the bonds they were received with such discredit that a run began on the leading British goldsmiths and banks – everyone wanted their money back at once – since it was believed that several had lent out large sums, accepting South Sea stock as security. Many bankers closed their doors and absconded. The chief cashiers of the South Sea Company stopped making payments. This caused a run on the Bank of England itself, which suddenly found itself paying out more money than it was taking in. Discovering, as it had suspected, that it was not able to restore public confidence and stem the tide of disaster without exposing itself to ruin, the Bank withdrew its support for the South Sea Company. The entire system of credit in England was brought to the brink of total collapse as company after company went under.

An inquiry was made the following year as to the cause of the disaster. The affair was attributed to the nefarious practices of the Company's directors, who were all leading members of the Establishment. Charles Blunt, brother of Sir John and an 'insider' of the South Sea Company, had cut his throat in September 1720. Robert Knight, who had doctored the books, had escaped to the continent. In the House of Commons it was said that Parliament should declare the directors of the South Sea Company guilty of parricide and subject them to the ancient Roman punishment for that transgression – to be sewn into sacks, each with a monkey and a snake, and drowned.

In their inimitable way the authorities found sufficient scapegoats to appease the angry masses, but the real cause of the South Sea calamity rests with the primitive instincts of politicians themselves, who habitually exploit human weaknesses. At the time of the inauguration of the scheme, politicians eager for power and public recognition agreed to the hare-brained idea even though it was fairly obvious that it was dangerous because the Company would be no more than a vehicle of financial manipulation. Nothing was done to develop the potential of the great territory over which the Company had a trading monopoly. Throughout its life it had very little current income and enormous expenses, especially directors' fees and some hefty 'unidentifiable' costs. The politicians supported the folly and subsequently agreed to one inept measure after the other in order to keep that folly afloat and postpone the inevitable evil day of reckoning. The acts of these politicians, who later turned their backs on the scheme that they had once so vigorously supported, brought the entire nation into disrepute and to the edge of financial ruin. As with the Netherlands a century earlier, it was to be many decades before credibility was restored and even longer before Britain was once again considered a trustworthy nation.

3

The Crash of the Mississippi Bubble

How John Law persuaded the French government
to print the money used to finance one of the most
bizarre speculative follies of all time

The Splendour of the Sun King

It is beyond dispute that Louis XIV was a man of exceptionally extravagant tastes, and that he presided over a realm with equally inflated
running costs. The seemingly endless series of wars, the grandeur of his
colossal palace at Versailles with its interminable parties and extravaganzas, the vast endowments granted to his court favourites, his mistresses
and his royal bastards, are just a few of the many excesses that devoured
the wealth of France under the Sun King.

Louis craved splendour for himself as monarch in an effort to eclipse
the outmoded feudal hierarchy that had prevailed prior to his reign. At the
same time, it was his genuine desire to establish France as the principal
country of Europe through her victories on the battlefield, the high living
standards of her people and her contribution to the arts. But that kind of
ambition demands immense financial resources. Even the indefatigable
Colbert, the man responsible for devising Louis' centralized fiscal and
administrative system, was unable to satisfy his master's unlimited appe-
tite for money to finance what were considered necessary indulgences.

When the King died in 1715, after a reign of seventy-two years, his
successor, Louis XV, ascended the throne as a five-year-old child. His
father, mother, brothers and sisters had all been dispatched by the
wretched Madame de Pompadour, Louis XIV's highly influential mistress. The boy's uncle, Philippe, Duc d'Orléans, was made Regent. In this
capacity he also took on the responsibility of the national debt, amount-
ing to over 3 billion livres – in twentieth-century terms even more
staggering than the colossal 200 billion dollar deficit which has been
borne by the United States throughout the 1980s. There was no way that
France could repay this debt; the interest alone absorbed the major part of
the national income. France was rapidly becoming impoverished – during

25

the winter of 1709 it had been reported that people had been driven to eating human flesh – the corpses found lying on the streets of Paris. Among the few available options even national bankruptcy was being considered . . . until John Law made his appearance.

History relates that the collapse of the South Sea Bubble in 1720 left the average Englishman with a very deep suspicion of all joint stock companies and anything remotely involving investment for many years to come. On the other side of the English Channel, in July of that same year, the collapse of John Law's Mississippi Bubble was to implant an even deeper mistrust in the minds and hearts of most Frenchmen for anything resembling a *banque* for an even more enduring period.

Why was control of the entire French economy ever allowed to fall into the hands of this middle-aged gambler and adventurer? How was it this Scottish commoner was made first Duc d'Arkansas? And why, only six months before the Mississippi Bubble burst, had this out-and-out adventurer been made Comptroller General – which put him virtually in charge of the entire fortunes of France? You may find some of the answers when considering the character and background of John Law; recognizing at the same time that both the South Sea Bubble and the Mississippi Bubble shared the same common denominator – the national debt. However, while the South Sea Company was a swindle, the Mississippi Company was not. Indeed, John Law's efforts actually started out with the noblest of intentions.

A Gambler and Ladies' Man

To begin with, John Law was no ordinary adventurer. He was born in Edinburgh in 1671, the son of a goldsmith, the great-great-nephew of the Archbishop of Glasgow. His father had prospered sufficiently to acquire the Lauriston estate near Cramond, and young John was brought up in a comfortable home, equipped in every way to take his place in Edinburgh society. Moreover, the 'making and contracting' of loans and the wide range of banking business – then still carried out by goldsmiths like his father – were part and parcel of his natural childhood environment.

The 1670s saw England and France, former enemies under the Commonwealth, move together again; Charles II received 500,000 crowns from Louis XIV in 1675, and a secret treaty between the two countries was concluded the following year. Except at times of war, until the French Revolution a century later any Englishman or Scotsman who wished to be considered fashionable and cultured was bound at some time or other to enter Parisian society. Most Frenchmen of rank and position, too, would expect to visit England or at least to speak the language of their near neighbour.

Trade was at this time developing rapidly throughout the world.

During John Law's formative years the French East Indies Company had established its factory at Chandanagore. France was also investigating opportunities in the New World, where the French explorer Jacques Marquette reached the headwaters of the Mississippi. Another pioneer, La Salle, ventured further and, having explored the Mississippi from source to mouth, he claimed in the name of France all the territory between the Mississippi and the Rockies. It was to be called Louisiana, and included the vast area drained by three great rivers – the Mississippi, the Missouri and the Ohio.

Law's command of mathematics helped him devise a winning system during his early ventures at the tables

---

From an early age John Law demonstrated a considerable aptitude for arithmetic and algebra, and took an almost precocious interest in financial matters. At the age of fourteen, as the eldest son, he was taken into the family business, his father's counting house. For three years he worked feverishly to acquire an insight into the principles of Scottish banking. By the age of seventeen he was tall, strong and of imposing stature. Although his face was deeply scarred from smallpox which he had suffered as a child, there remained an agreeable expression along with an air of authority and intelligence. And he had an astute command of financial jargon. He was also a ladies' man. With a keen interest in fashion, he wore only the most stylish attire and women often referred to him as 'Beau Law'. Most men, however, despised him and gave him the unflattering nickname of 'Jessamy John'.

Not surprisingly, Law was as reckless as the spirit of his age. After the death of his father in 1688 he decided to abandon his desk at the counting house, which by then had become irksome. Being a young man of reasonably independent means, he decided to leave Edinburgh and go to London to seek his fortune. When he arrived – very young, very vain, good-looking and tolerably rich, with the spirit of adventure running through his veins – he was immediately attracted to the high life and used London's gaming houses to finance his extravagances. His command of mathematics helped him devise a system by which he was able to amass considerable sums of money during his early ventures at the tables. Many seasoned gamblers envied his good fortune and studied his method of play very carefully. Soon he had attracted a wide following at the casinos, where other gamblers would attempt to emulate his methods and stake their money on whatever bets he made. Law was no less fortunate in affairs of gallantry: the most noble of ladies would smile graciously at the handsome Scotsman whenever he appeared.

But the same success that was to bring about his good fortune also acted to bring about his misfortune. After nine years in London Law had become an inveterate gambler, and as his bravado at the gaming tables increased so his prudence diminished. He was ultimately forced to mortgage the family estate in order to repay his mounting gambling debts. At the same time he quarrelled with Edward 'Beau' Wilson, the talk of fashionable society in London, who challenged him to a duel to the death with swords.

The precise reason for the quarrel has never been established, although it was certainly about a woman. It is widely supposed to have arisen when 'Beau' Wilson removed his sister from the house where Law's mistress lodged. Wilson, older than Law, was a generous host; but where his money came from was something of a mystery. One explanation was that he was kept as a secret lover by Elizabeth Villiers, mistress of William of Orange. Another was that 'Beau' had robbed the Holland Mail – a crime for which (according to the story) an innocent man had been hanged. Whatever the truth of the matter, Edward Wilson was regarded by most people as 'civil and well natured', although he was not considered to be among the brightest.

As for Law's part in the affair, he always maintained that he had no grudge against Wilson, who was supposed to have sent him a number of threatening letters. It is even more unlikely that, as some suggested, Law had been hired as an assassin by Elizabeth Villiers to remove 'Beau' once he had become an embarrassment. It is more commonly accepted that the Scotsman was drawn against his will into the quarrel, which flared up at the Fountain Inn in the Strand.

'Beau' Wilson, accompanied by his friend Captain Wightman, demanded satisfaction; and the parties left almost at once for nearby Bloomsbury Square. It was the briefest of encounters. 'Beau' Wilson made a pass; then Law, who was by far the better swordsman, parried and riposted . . . thrusting his blade deep into his opponent's stomach. In the time it took

---

In less than ten days Law was charged with murder, and subsequently convicted and condemned to death

---

Law to withdraw his blade, the duel was over. 'Beau' Wilson lay dying at his feet. Law realized he would now be arrested on the capital charge of having killed his opponent in a premeditated duel. In less than ten days he was charged with murder, and subsequently convicted and condemned to death.

Law pleaded benefit of clergy, and the offence was reduced from murder to manslaughter – for which he faced a heavy fine. At this point, 'Beau' Wilson's relatives lodged an appeal against the reduction of the charge and Law was re-arrested. This time, he was taking no chances.

28

While waiting for the appeal to be heard, Law's friends helped him to escape from Newgate jail. A reward of several hundred pounds was offered by the High Sheriff for information leading to his capture, but the prisoner had already left on the morning tide, bound – it was believed – for Brest in Brittany.

A Prophet Without Honour in His Own Land

Over the next two or three years John Law travelled widely, taking an increasing interest in international economic and financial matters. For a time he became confidential secretary to the English resident in the Netherlands, where he took the opportunity to study closely the operations of the Bank of Amsterdam, then the most important financial establishment in Europe.

When he returned to Scotland in 1700, John Law was dismayed by the havoc wrought on the Scottish economy by a colonization scheme devised by the same William Paterson who had set up the Bank of England. The idea had been to raise funds for an expedition to the Isthmus of Panama, then known as Darien, where it had been proposed to establish a colony called New Caledonia. The territory was inhospitable and conditions were hard; as a result the venture failed and the great majority of the would-be colonists, including most of Paterson's family, died. Meanwhile many thousands of investors lost every penny they had put into the project, bringing Scotland to a state of near-collapse.

Law was deeply moved by what was taking place in his native land. After studying conditions in Scotland for twelve months he felt he could offer some solutions based on his banking experience and what he had learned during his travels. As he saw it, Scotland would best be served by abolishing the farming of revenues; instead, he proposed the introduction of a simple system of direct taxation. The revenue raised could be used to establish nationalized industries which could undertake the 'needful' branches of production, most of which were being neglected by private enterprise at the time. Additional elements of John Law's scheme for the salvation of Scotland involved the abolition of trade monopolies, the freeing of raw materials from import duties and a programme designed to provide work for the unemployed. In 1701, John Law arranged for the publication of an anonymous pamphlet entitled *Proposals and Reasons for Constituting a Council of Trade in Scotland*. It was John Law's dream that his far-reaching approach to mitigating the problems in his homeland would achieve immediate recognition, after which he could come forward as its author. Unfortunately for him, its suggestions were dismissed out of hand. After waiting four years to see at least part of his plan adopted, Law accepted defeat. Feeling thoroughly dejected, Law left Scotland in 1705 to take up his travels on the continent again.

Economic Wizardry

For the next four years he gained more banking experience while earning a living at the gaming tables. At the same time he did his best to gain audiences with European monarchs and ministers, in an attempt to persuade them to experiment with his highly original theories on money and banking. The handsome Law, now well travelled and a good conversationalist, was welcomed everywhere he went. Although he was later proved to be thoroughly reckless, most of his friends and acquaintances agreed with the assessment made by the French historian Saint-Simon, who considered Law to be 'completely innocent of any element of greed or knavery'.

In 1709, still striving for recognition, John Law published a second pamphlet – again anonymously. Its title was *Money and Trade Considered with a Proposal for Supplying the Nation with Money*. The new paper was far more comprehensive than his first effort. Law argued that the more money in circulation in any country the more prosperity that country would enjoy: 'Domestic Trade depends upon money. A greater quantity employs more people than a lesser quantity. An addition to the money adds to the value of the country.'

At that time, 'money' meant a limited supply of gold and silver bullion in which debts – such as government bonds – ultimately had to be repaid. A dilemma that puzzled many policy-makers was how to introduce into a system based on silver and gold bullion currency the flexibility needed for a series of credit-based transactions. Paper currencies had not yet been dreamed up in Europe. Yet the Venetians of the fifteenth and sixteenth centuries were fully conversant with the methods required. As Tommaso Contarini, an eminent sixteenth-century Venetian banker, stated, it was not difficult for the banker to 'accommodate friends without the payment of money' by doing no more than 'writing a brief entry of credit'. How to

---

Law argued that the more money in circulation the more prosperity the country would enjoy

---

escape the straitjacket imposed by a gold and silver coinage was still seen as a major problem in Europe during the eighteenth century, especially since the coin of the realm held in a nation's treasury owed more to the skill of that nation's sea captains and the accuracy of its naval gunners than to the strength and needs of the national economy.

John Law covered the problem in depth in his tract. He firmly believed that paper money should be introduced as standard currency, and that the practice of using bullion for the settlement of all debts should be abandoned. Law insisted that not only was paper money more convenient to handle than gold and silver coinage; it could be supplied in such quantities as would truly represent the demands of the economy, backed by the value of the nation's real assets – principally the land itself, rather than sterile gold and silver held in a vault.

It was Law's contention that, instead of relying on a given quantity of gold or silver in the treasury, the actual amount of paper money required by the economy could be issued as and when needed. As a result, interest rates could fall and the production and profitability of the nation would be expanded and enhanced. Law's objective was to induce members of the public to accept in repayment merely another kind of paper money and, ideally, be willing to exchange their bullion for that paper. Specifically,

---

In essence, John Law was laying the foundation of the banking principles used as standard practice today

---

Law urged the creation of a central bank which, by incorporating a liberal lending policy, would permit the supply of credit to be expanded at will.

In essence, John Law was laying the foundation of the banking principles used as standard practice among virtually all of today's central bankers. We will soon see the mischief that these principles have caused, and the total failure of the international banking community to learn anything at all from the experiences of the eighteenth century.

Following the publication of his first paper in Scotland during 1701, Law had urged the Scottish and English authorities to establish a state bank that would control credit and issue paper money. At the time he had been unable to convince them of the importance of his proposals. In 1705 the Scottish Parliament resolved that 'the forcing of any paper credit by an Act of Parliament is unfit for this nation'. In 1711 Law tried again, this time with much more detailed suggestions. Once more he was refused. He then decided to approach another monarch who was having financial difficulties at the time, and a scheme along the lines of the one submitted to the Scottish authorities was placed before the Kingdom of Savoy in 1713. But once again Law's proposals were rejected. It has been said that his scheme was rejected not on economic grounds, but more because the landed gentry would in time become beholden to government if his methods were ever implemented. It was not the actual monarchs who were against Law's principles, but those with vested interests who exerted pressure on the authorities – in much the same way that self-interest groups still impose their influence on politicians today.

Be that as it may, John Law was not a man to give up. Travelling to Brussels, Vienna, Rome and elsewhere, he continued to put forth his ideas on banking and finance to whoever would listen. At the same time, he prospered through gambling and speculation. By the time of Louis XIV's death in 1715, Law is reputed to have amassed at the tables a fortune of some 114,000 livres – equivalent to about £2,500,000 in today's money. More important, so far as Law was concerned, he seemed at last to be gaining support from men in high places.

During the last days of the old King, John Law had tried to persuade the French government to try his prescription to cure France's deep economic malaise. For some time national expenditure had been double the country's revenues; and the so-called farmers-general of the taxes were doing little but line their own pockets. In his memoirs, the Duc de Saint-Simon wrote despairingly of the state of the French economy: 'People never ceased wondering what had become of all the money of the realm. Nobody could any longer pay, because nobody was paid: the country-people . . . had become insolvent: trade no longer yielded anything – good faith and confidence were at an end.' The troops were neither paid nor fed, and as a result they were always defeated in battle.

The money was recoined, Saint-Simon recorded. Increased to

a third more than its intrinsic value, [it] brought some profit to the King, but ruin to private people; and a disorder to trade which completed its annihilation. Samuel Bernard, the banker (reputedly the richest man in Europe), overthrew all Lyons by his prodigious bankruptcy. . . . The discredit into which paper money had fallen, was the cause of its failure. . . . In the spring so many disorders took place in the market of Paris, that more guards than usual were kept in the city.

Such was the mood in Paris that a nobleman returning from the opera 'was assailed by the populace and by women in great numbers crying, "Bread! Bread!". . . . He got away by throwing money to the people and promising wonders: but as the wonders did not follow, he no longer dares to go to Paris.'

Had Law confined himself to what he had already accomplished, he would have been remembered as one of the great benefactors of France

---

Later, Saint-Simon admitted that, when the Duc d'Orléans offered him the Presidency of the Council of Finance, he declined because 'I had good reason for shrinking from this office. I saw that disordered as the finances had become there was only one remedy by which improvement could be effected; and this was National Bankruptcy . . . but it was a responsibility I did not wish to take upon myself before God and man.'

Yet try as he might, John Law could not convince the Council of Finance or the dying King that he had a formula which could help rescue France from its penury. In fact, Louis XIV refused to receive Law. But Law did make his mark with the Duc d'Orléans, who remembered how impressed he had been with Law on an earlier occasion when they had met at the gaming tables. Their friendship was fortuitous, and the Duc's appointment as Regent to the young Louis XV marked the turning point for John Law.

Success At Last

The new Regent hoped that Law's economic propositions would in some way be a reflection of his skills at the tables. What honours would be bestowed upon the Duc by a grateful nation if he discovered a means to relieve the destitution being endured by the French people! Once again John Law formally approached the Council of Finance, and once again they rejected his plans. But the Regent was in a position to act regardless of what the economic advisers approved or disapproved, and he gave Law permission to set up a private bank.

In May 1716 Law, by then a French subject, was empowered to open the Banque Générale, of which he was to be chief executive. It was located on the ground floor of his magnificent home on the Place Louis-le-Grand, now the Place Vendôme, and its capital was 6 million livres, payable one-quarter in cash and the balance in *billets d'état* – promissory notes of the government, selling at the time for 25% of their face value.

From then on, John Law was able to deploy the outstanding financial skills for which he had become renowned. He convinced the Duc d'Orléans that all citizens should be required to pay their regional taxes in the form of Banque Générale notes. In this way the bank would be assured of a steady inflow of funds for its operations and thus its success.

On Law's suggestion the bank was authorized to issue notes which were redeemable on demand in silver coin at the same value as the silver coinage on the date the note was issued. Since the national currency – the livre – was often subject to sudden changes in value, French citizens discovered it was far safer to hold their savings in banknotes issued by the Banque Générale than in the coinage of the realm with its fluctuating purchasing power. The banknotes, since they paid interest and were more convenient to hold than silver or gold bullion, came to sell at a premium over their face value in bullion. As the notes gained increasing acceptance, Law was able to lower interest rates from 30% to 6% and then 4%, driving the usurers out of business. Less than a year after the launch of the Banque Générale with its 6 million livres of capital, there were 60 million livres of notes outstanding.

As Law had predicted, the mood of the nation improved dramatically, the pulse of trade and industry quickened and the French economy surged. Had he confined himself to what he had accomplished up until then, no doubt he would have been remembered as one of the great benefactors of France and the creator of a miraculous system of credit. But Law was not content to stop at that point. He wanted to expand his talents. Branches of the bank were opened in Amiens, La Rochelle, Lyons and Tours. The Banque Générale became a public company much along the lines of today's major banking institutions, and the stage was set for the next act of the extravaganza.

The Master-stroke of an Opportunist

Law envisaged a method by which he could induce the French people to exchange their gold for paper on an even more immense scale than hitherto. He introduced an ambitious plan intended to exploit the full resources of France's Louisiana Territory, which stretched from the Gulf of Mexico in the south-east to the Rocky Mountains in the west and the Great Lakes to the north, including thirteen of the states that now comprise the United States. It was a master-stroke on Law's part to persuade the Regent to give him control over the vast landmass of the Louisiana Territory and the Mississippi, the last of which gave the scheme its name.

Make no mistake, the region was certainly not without its problems. Settlement in the New World was arduous, to say the least. By the beginning of the eighteenth century, virtually all the early Spanish colonies on the south-western coast of North America had become extinct. Only half the settlers who arrived on the *Mayflower* in 1620 actually managed to survive the first Massachusetts winter. In 1699 some 750 French pioneers attempted to settle in the Mississippi delta region; six hundred were stricken by yellow fever or malaria and perished within the year. It is not surprising that the last act of *Manon Lescaut* has Manon and her lover wandering aimlessly over the sinister landscape of the Louisiana Territory, waiting to succumb to disease and starvation.

Still, there were many who were wildly enthusiastic about the prospects offered by the Louisiana Territory. The *Nouveau Mercure* referred to the area as 'one of the most beautiful and fertile countries in the world, with gold, silver, and emeralds in great quantities'. According to John Law, his scheme would give France the benefit of the vast gold deposits which – it was thought – lay beneath the soil of Louisiana and could be panned from the banks of the Mississippi. Besides, Law and his associates were absolutely convinced that the Mississippi project – 'The System', as it was called – would in due course become a formidable rival to the British East India Company, which attracted wealthy investors from all over the world.

Law was granted a charter for a Mississippi development company during August 1717. The company, called the Compagnie de la Louisiane ou d'Occident, received by royal decree a twenty-five-year lease and all sovereign rights for the territory. The company was obliged to transplant a minimum of six thousand French citizens to the Louisiana Territory along with three thousand slaves, and was permitted to raise and maintain its own militia. The French government was by now in full approval of the scheme and discouraged any sceptics. When the explorer Cadillac began spreading stories about the difficulties and hazards of establishing a colony in the Louisiana Territory, he was arrested and quickly hustled off to the Bastille.

The political opposition was not so easily silenced as Cadillac. There was an angry reaction from the *Parlement* of Paris – one of the superior courts in the country that was beginning to assume a quasi-political role. Its members, along with many leading Parisians, thought it inexcusable to hand over valuable privileges and territory to a foreigner who was a Protestant into the bargain!

Like most successful opportunists, John Law moved with the speed of greased lightning and the cunning of a Cheshire cat. The Compagnie de la Louisiane ou d'Occident quickly obtained a monopoly on the growing and selling of tobacco to be used in the manufacture of snuff, which was in wide use at the time. This caused public uproar and the wildest of rumours began to gain momentum in the French capital. One included a story to the effect that the *Parlement* of Paris planned to arrest Law, try him and string him up.

The protest reached a new crescendo when Law and his associates were given the trading rights for all ships and merchandise of the Company of Senegal, which would also assure a supply of slaves for future settlements of the Compagnie de la Louisiane ou d'Occident. The opposition to this latest manoeuvre became so severe that the Regent was forced to intervene or risk the entire project falling into disrepute. Turning the tables on his – and Law's – critics once again, the Regent decided, through another royal decree, to transform the Banque Générale into the Banque Royale. The Banque Royale, which would be a state bank, would absorb all the

---

The Banque Royale was the world's first central bank, not unlike the Federal Reserve Bank or the Bank of England

---

assets of John Law's Banque Générale and have a nine-year monopoly on minting the royal coinage, thus giving the bank total control over the nation's money supply. In essence, the Banque Royale was the world's first central bank, not unlike the Federal Reserve Bank or the Bank of England. John Law's fondest ambition had finally been realized. Exactly in accordance with his original design, a central bank had been created which would finance schemes that private entrepreneurs were unable or unwilling to undertake – like the risky venture in the Louisiana Territory.

Unfortunately for all concerned, there was a serious flaw in this plan. It would not now be John Law who would handle the issue of banknotes, but the King of France – or, for the moment, the Regent. Law would merely act as Director General to His Majesty. The danger lay in the fact that Law would no longer have control over the quantity of notes in circulation, upon which his original scheme was based. It would be the Regent who would decide how many notes were to be printed and how often, including whatever sums were required to support his own extravagant lifestyle. And repercussions of an even more serious magnitude were yet to come.

Control of the entire non-European trade of France had now been placed in the hands of John Law and his associates

---

In March 1719 the Compagnie de la Louisiane ou d'Occident, after acquiring control of the Senegal Company, was allowed to absorb the French East Indies Company and the China Company, subsequently assuming the new title of Compagnie des Indes; in June the Africa Company was absorbed. Control of the entire non-European trade of France had now been placed in the hands of John Law and his associates. On paper, this prodigious structure was one of the greatest enterprises in the world.

But the public was still sceptical. Many were frightened by the South Sea Bubble, whose financial gymnastics were causing concern on the other side of the English Channel. The shares in the Compagnie des Indes were originally issued in a block of 200,000 at 500 livres a share. By late 1718 they had lost 50% of their value and were standing at 250 livres per share.

It was in early 1719, before the Compagnie de la Louisiane ou d'Occident changed its name to the Compagnie des Indes and before the Banque Générale was transformed into the Banque Royale, that John Law had put into play a practice that would form the basis of artificial fiscal stimulus for centuries to come. On his advice, the Regent pumped up by 30% the supply of paper notes, which were then circulated. As a result, people suddenly found themselves with more money in their pockets. They now had disposable income, and disposable income is the fodder for speculation. It was used for the purchase of shares in the Mississippi enterprise, just as John Law had planned. The shares of the company began to take on a new life – and afterwards, a life of their own.

In July that year the last financial bastion of the state was to fall when the Compagnie des Indes acquired the Royal Mint, along with the lease held by the Banque Royale for minting the royal coinage. Although John Law was no longer in charge of issuing notes, he was able to manipulate the metallic coinage without impediment – which to some extent gave him more control than the Regent had. The Regent could have paper money printed, but it was redeemable only by John Law's coinage.

In August the Compagnie des Indes had another coup, acquiring the right to act as the national tax collector for nine years. This move successfully quashed a rival company which had been trying to develop an 'Anti-System'. At the same time, exciting reports were being circulated from unknown sources claiming new acquisitions for the Compagnie des Indes, new contracts, and greatly enhanced prospects in the Louisiana Territory and elsewhere. Members of the public with money to burn, courtesy of the Banque Royale, suddenly became increasingly interested in the shares of the Compagnie des Indes. Law himself, it was revealed, had bought futures contracts in it, which gave him the right to purchase the shares at their existing price at some time in the future. He was reputed to have paid double the normal market value for these contracts. The market became intrigued, then excited. The share price of the Compagnie des Indes soon recovered to the original price of 250 livres per share, then doubled, and soon doubled again. The doubters were silenced. Visions of vast, productive Mississippi savannahs, of huge goldmines, of the fur trade, the tobacco monopolies and the massive banking profits – in addition to the wealth of the Orient to be gleaned by the East India and China Companies, along with the fantastic natural resources being exploited by the Africa Company – served to dazzle speculators beyond all reason.

A Licence to Print Money

Then Law revealed another element in his plan, which he had no doubt learned from the innovators of the South Sea Bubble scheme. His idea was to become a national hero by using the shares of his Compagnie des Indes to assist in repaying the national debt of France. Law called for the government to issue 3% notes to its creditors. At the same time, the Compagnie des Indes would issue shares which the state creditors could purchase with the notes that were issued. There were few other securities available, and since the price of the Compagnie des Indes shares continued to rise, Law was confident that the holders of banknotes would be eager to exchange their banknotes for shares.

The price of shares in the Compagnie des Indes rose and rose and rose. Each new issue of shares was matched by the printing of more and more banknotes, which fuelled the rise in the shares. By the spring of 1719, some 100 million notes had been issued by the Banque Royale. By midsummer the amount had nearly quadrupled and the price of shares in the Compagnie des Indes had soared to 5000 livres, ten times the original issue price. By October the shares had reached 8000 livres and a further 800 million banknotes had been issued. The creditors of the state were actually having a great deal of difficulty in obtaining the number of shares they wanted.

Even though the price of the shares had risen by more than fifteen times their original price a few years earlier, during the autumn of 1719 the speculative frenzy seemed to be just getting underway. The succession of privileges granted to the Compagnie des Indes fanned the excitement.

Ultimately the speculative stampede in France became contagious, attracting followers from other parts of Europe. The mother of the Regent, the Duchesse d'Orléans, estimated that more than three hundred thousand people flooded into Paris in the hope of climbing aboard the share-buying bandwagon and thus making their fortune. The Rue Quincampoix, a narrow street near the Hôtel de Ville, which housed the

Indians bedecked with gold were paraded through the streets of Paris

administration, became the focus of intense activity. In cafés, in restaurants and in the street, operators established themselves as traders in the shares of the Compagnie des Indes, buying and selling shares to whoever might come along, clearing huge daily profits in the rising price of the shares. Cobblers and itinerant tradesmen found they could make more money by renting out the stalls and benches to which they had laid claim than they could through any other form of work. The going rate for a park bench was 200 livres a day to a stock jobber. A stall would fetch 300 livres a day. Property in the vicinity of the Rue Quincampoix, which had originally been let at 40 livres a month, was now fetching 800 livres a month! In one account of the era it was claimed that a hunchback who pushed his way up and down the teeming Rue Quincampoix gave up begging and was able to gain a good living by furnishing cramped speculators with a space on his back so they could record their share transactions.

Law continued to advertise the shares of the Compagnie des Indes with flamboyant and ingenious displays: Indians bedecked with gold were paraded through the streets of Paris; engravings were published showing mountains of silver and cliffs of emeralds in Louisiana. Individual fortunes – quite immense considering that at the outset the Mississippi scheme had only been capitalized at 100 million livres – mounted as the price of the shares soared. The killings made in just a few short months included those of a chimney sweep who made 40 million livres and of a waiter who made 30 million livres in six weeks. There was a beggar who seemed to have emptied his tin cup in the right place at the right time and who was reported to have made a 30 million livre killing which would buy him a mansion with farmland to which he could retire for the rest of his life.

Law found himself the most popular man in all Europe. Since he and he alone had the power to issue shares in the Compagnie des Indes whenever he pleased, and below the prevailing price level if he chose, he could immediately enrich anyone to whatever grandeur they wanted, at will. In his memoirs, Saint-Simon noted: 'Law, besieged by applicants and aspirants, saw his door forced, his windows entered from the garden, while some of them came tumbling down the chimney of his office.' He was eagerly sought after by social-climbing women, but, a happily married man, he resisted with valour the advances and temptations offered by a variety of *femmes fatales*. Yet, wrote the Duchesse d'Orléans, who knew him well: 'Law is so run after that he has no rest, day or night. A Duchess kissed his hand before everyone, and if a Duchess kisses his hands, what parts of him won't ordinary ladies kiss?'

John Law had just about everything a man could want, with one exception – he did not have a title, which by then he desperately wanted. A major impediment for Law was that, although he was a citizen of France, he was not a Catholic; he was a Protestant at a time when religious controversy and persecution were rife. He adopted the Abbé Tencin as his spiritual adviser, and a series of satisfactory meetings ensued . . . which also involved the transfer of several thousand shares. In September 1719 Law renounced his Protestant faith and was received into the Catholic Church during a splendid ceremony at Notre Dame. This automatically cleared the way for his appointment as Contrôleur des Finances of France.

The Completion of Law's Grand Design

A few weeks later the powerful Compagnie des Indes was merged with the Banque Royale. John Law's 'System' – and his personal triumph – gave him control over all France along with a sizeable chunk of world trade. Just twelve months had seen the development of his confidence and a sense of security that wiped out all memory of the despair and desperation of his earlier years.

At the same time, however, cracks were beginning to show in Law's empire, which at the time, engulfed in his new-found self-esteem, he didn't seem to notice. J. K. Galbraith summed up the scenario most succinctly, along with the prospects that lay ahead for Law: 'The miracle of money created by a bank, as John Law showed in 1719, could stimulate industry and trade, give almost everyone a warm feeling of well-being. . . . And as Law also showed, the further result could be a day of reckoning.' During the early months of 1720, that 'terrible day of reckoning' was not far off.

An Accident Waiting to Happen

A further incentive offered to shareholders was that of dividends, which were anticipated to be 'very substantial'. When the promised dividend was declared – at 40% – the share price staged an explosive rise, reaching the incredible level of 20,000 livres, which was forty times the price the shares had been offered at three years earlier. At that share price the value of the entire company was put at 12 billion livres, compared with the original value of less than 100 million livres. Anyone with an abacus – the eighteenth-century equivalent of a pocket calculator – could easily see that the profits from the various monopolies held by the Compagnie des Indes could not possibly maintain a dividend of 40%, regardless of how encouraging the prospects were. Based on what could be determined in terms of the prospective profitability of the company in 1720, it would take many, many years before the earnings from the various enterprises would be able to produce a reasonable return on the 20,000 livre share price. The whole affair had turned into one gigantic bubble – inviting a puncture. When the time is ripe, the needle is never remote. The Compagnie des Indes became an accident waiting to happen!

Stories began trickling through the Mississippi delta of extreme difficulties and heavy losses incurred in several ventures: they were a powerful warning to those prepared to listen. According to the reports and rumours, all was not well in the process of colonization. The campaign to induce Frenchmen to move to the Mississippi region was becoming less and less effective. An increasing number who had planned to go started to have second thoughts, especially since they could make so much money trading in shares at home. If there were too few people to colonize the Louisiana Territory, the dream could never be fulfilled. Law resorted to engaging blue-uniformed gangs who were instructed to kidnap reluctant unfortunates right off the streets. Judges were encouraged to sentence thieves, prostitutes and other undesirables to deportation, all in the interests of colonizing the New World. But the solid merchant venturers and skilled artisans – those who were desperately needed to make the colonization scheme function – were conspicuous by their absence, unwilling to spend years of their lives among the dangerous and unreliable riff-raff that comprised the new settlers.

Stories began trickling through the Mississippi delta of extreme difficulties and heavy losses: they were a powerful warning

Another underlying weakness of the scheme suddenly began to attract attention as many professional operators began to look beyond the mere escalation of the share price. A number became quite concerned at the discovery that very little of the funds being raised for the Mississippi venture was actually moving beyond Paris. Indeed, much of the money was being siphoned off at source to defray the expenses of the French government, which included the costly lifestyle of the Regent.

Yet when these rumours and stories first began circulating, for many –

40

if not most – who were speculating in shares the gossip was only a minor consideration. Of paramount importance was that more and more shares and notes should continue to be issued; and that the price of the shares and the value of the notes should go on rising at the previous breakneck speed, if not faster!

Another Bubble Bursts

Like the manias we have seen before, the phenomenon may have been rooted in the greed of ordinary people. But it also owed a great deal to the fact that notes issued by the Banque Royale would be paid to the government in taxes, who in turn would pay the dividends due on these notes to investors; the investors in their turn would hurry along to buy more shares and notes which they would pay for with the dividends they had received, in a seemingly perpetual eighteenth-century 'daisy-chain'. It was not what John Law had planned. It was the manner in which the Duc d'Orléans influenced the affair that made this situation inevitable from the moment Law's private bank had been transformed into the combined casino and printing press called the Banque Royale.

Amplifying the potential for disaster was the fact that most of the frenetic trading in shares involved very little cash payment, not unlike the markets of the twentieth century. Investors were only required to make a 10% deposit as initial payments for their shares, and even then that could be put up in *billets d'état*, which always sold at a deep discount. Also acting to blow up the bubble still further was the steady issue of notes by the Banque Royale. At one point the notes in circulation were only covered by one-tenth of the gold and silver into which those notes were supposed to be redeemable on demand.

In early January 1720 the share price began to falter. The unthinkable had begun to happen. Somebody, somewhere, began selling and others followed. At first, although the transactions were sufficient to call a halt to the rising share price, selling was not particularly heavy. It wasn't until late January 1720 that the potentially catastrophic nature of the bubble was revealed. Two princes close to the throne sought cash payment in silver and gold for a huge block of several thousand shares. This was the first genuine test of the 'System', and it didn't pass!

Law was suddenly faced with the problem of finding the massive quantities of gold and silver required to meet the redemption pledge of the mountain of notes involved. J. K. Galbraith tells the story: '[The princes] sent a bunch of the notes to the Banque Royale to be redeemed in hard currency . . . three wagons were sent to carry back the gold and silver.' On hearing the news of this massive share sale, many thousands of people began to sell and ask for payment in hard currency. The Banque Royale was steadily drained of its coin.

Law appealed to the Regent, who insisted that the princes return 'a considerable share of the metal' to the Banque Royale. But the amount returned did not suffice to stem the rot. In order to replace the loss of purchasing power caused by the bullion that was being paid out to meet redemptions, Law turned to printing more currency! Nine presses churned for weeks, producing over 1.5 billion new paper livres.

According to the laws of supply and demand – which also applies to currency – if supply exceeds demand the value falls. The supply of new livres exceeded the demand for them. Law had hoped that the massive injection of new money would be used to purchase shares in the Compagnie des Indes, as before, causing the share price to rise, thus restoring confidence. He was wrong. People wanted hard cash more than ever after the issue of the new paper money. The value of the livre slipped as people scrambled to exchange their notes for hard currency. Law made the fatal error of attempting to control the price of Compagnie des Indes shares by issuing what is called fiat money, the same kind of funny money governments print today. In the end, yet another of his schemes proved counterproductive.

Rapidly running out of options, Law appealed once more to the Regent, successfully, urging that a law be passed forbidding people to possess more than 500 livres in gold or silver. Those who violated this order would be liable to a stiff fine and confiscation of their hoard. But for frightened people, where there's a will there's a way. Suddenly, a black market began to flourish in gold and silver coin. To reinforce the new regulations, the French authorities empowered a state militia to institute house raids, and recruited paid informers who were willing to denounce their friends and neighbours. The safest thing was to take one's bullion out of the country.

One bright spark thought he had found a way round the legislation. He began buying silver plate and jewellery with the notes he had received from his share sales, encouraging others to do the same. The scheme he had devised was quickly stamped on. Further legislation was enacted banning the manufacture of gold and silver plate and jewellery. In addition, strict controls were placed on the purchase and sale of second-hand plate and jewellery.

Suddenly, a black market began to flourish in gold and silver coin

---

Amidst the chaos, the price of Compagnie des Indes shares fell sharply, dropping from the peak of 20,000 livres to 9000 livres by the end of April 1720. At the same time, the amount of gold that could be redeemed in exchange for paper notes steadily diminished.

Law felt that confidence must quickly be restored at all cost, so he turned to chicanery. According to one popular story he hired a collection of beggars who were sent down to the Marseilles docks, picks and shovels on their shoulders, masquerading as workmen on their way to dig more Louisiana gold out of the mountains. But the ruse was uncovered, the story leaked back to Paris and confidence in the shares sustained an even harder blow.

Next, a plan was set into motion by the French authorities to bring about a series of wild and violent fluctuations in the currency, in order to discourage people from exchanging Law's comparatively safe banknotes for the King's manifestly unstable gold and silver coin. This move also failed. Despite all these manoeuvres, pressures on the Banque Royale and the 'System' continued to increase.

Saint Simon wrote: 'Every rich man thought he was ruined; every poor man believed himself reduced to beggary'

As a final alternative, Law decided he would try to encourage gold and silver into France by making French goods more competitive in foreign markets. On 21 May 1720 a decree was issued calling for a phased reduction in the value of the notes of the Banque Royale until two notes were the equivalent of one. In other words, the currency was to be devalued by no less than 50%. For six days, panic reigned all over France. The decree was quickly cancelled, but withdrawal of the proposal failed to stabilize the situation and the panic caused the share price to fall further. Between April and early June the price fell from 9000 to 5000 livres per share.

To the investor or speculator of the time, it mattered little that the shares had risen from an issue price of 500 livres per share to 5000 livres per share. What mattered more was the fall from its peaks of 20,000 livres in January 1720 to 5000 livres in just five months. Obviously, if the price could fall from 20,000 livres to 5000 it could also fall from 5000 to 1250, and so on – and the shares of the Compagnie des Indes could ultimately end up valueless. Saint-Simon wrote: 'The uproar was general and frightful. Every rich man thought he was ruined; every poor man believed himself reduced to beggary.'

Law, who had once been fawned upon by royalty and hoisted to one of the most exalted positions in the land, supported by the Church of Rome, became the object of national examination. Without a doubt he was the most hated man in all France, possibly all Europe. The masses who had lost fortunes on their ventures with the Compagnie des Indes blamed it all on John Law, never considering their own naïvety and stupidity. He became the focal point of indignation, ridicule and public insult. The mob took over. His offices were attacked. Guards were needed to protect him from the furious crowds who tried to break into his home to injure him, when previously they would have been overjoyed simply to have attracted his notice. He was stripped of his position as Contrôleur des Finances, and reduced to a notorious, titleless foreigner who had managed to gain French citizenship. The Regent, once his friend, refused to see him.

Yet Law was still chief executive and principal shareholder of the Compagnie des Indes, a post from which he could not be ousted. In order to maintain the 'System' for as long as feasible and in the most gallant manner possible, Law continued to redeem shares and notes from his own resources of silver and copper, ceremoniously burning the banknotes he had redeemed. On one particular occasion, it was reported that no fewer than fifteen thousand desperate souls thronged before his offices, spilling over on to the pavements and streets outside in the hope of exchanging their paper for something tangible. According to public records, sixteen of those people died of suffocation in the process.

The End of the Affair

On 10 October 1720, the Banque Royale suspended payments and closed its doors forever. All hope had vanished. Commerce slowed to a standstill. France had to survive on the basis of barter. As the distribution of food and various other goods faltered, talk of starvation was commonplace.

Law, his life in constant danger, is believed to have fled to South America – a pauper. What he had left after redeeming the notes of the Banque Royale from his own resources was heavily invested in a number of French estates. These were confiscated by the French authorities, along with the rest of the assets he had to leave behind.

There is a somewhat piquant sequel to Law's story, revealing that the greatest of the great may find it difficult to absorb a very simple lesson. In December 1720 an envoy was sent to locate Law by Tsar Peter of Russia – one of the most powerful men in the world at the time. He travelled for three months through Amsterdam, Brussels and Paris in search of the destitute financier, and when he finally found Law he explained that he had been asked to invite him to come to St Petersburg. The Tsar desired Law's assistance in helping solve some of Russia's economic problems. John Law, we are told, had the grace to refuse – politely, of course!

For a time Law was able to sustain himself, essentially through gambling, while travelling from country to country. He finally settled in Venice where he died, alone, impoverished and forgotten.

Epilogue

Even after the collapse of the Banque Royale and the Mississippi conglomerate – along with the entire French economy – Saint-Simon still

44

maintained that Law's imaginative ideas and skilful approach to international finance and banking would have been successful if employed in another country. But it would have had to be a country where those in charge of the nation's purse strings – unlike the authorities in France – were capable of exercising a degree of restraint. As Saint-Simon saw it, the principal fault of Law's 'System' was the flimsy and dangerous superstructure that the Duc d'Orléans had encouraged him to balance on top of his original creation, the Banque Générale: 'If [to] the solid merits of such a bank are added . . . the mirage of a Mississippi scheme, a joint stock company, a technical language, a trickster's method of extracting money from Peter in order to pay Paul, the entire establishment, possessing neither gold mines nor the philosopher's stone, [it] must necessarily . . . [leave] a tiny minority enriched by the total ruin of all the rest of the people.'

There are many similarities between the ascent and collapse of Tulipomania, the bursting of the South Sea Bubble and the self-destruct mechanism of the Mississippi scheme. There are also many differences. Yet one common denominator links all three together – the function of debt and credit, fully endorsed by the government of the day's monetary policy.

Over the centuries, since the pitiful tale of John Law virtually every country in the world, from the tiniest to the most prodigious, has embraced a 'bank of issue' – a central bank. It is intended to be the lender of last resort, responsible for saving a country from whatever mess it gets itself into. But who can claim that any of these central banks may not ultimately suffer a catastrophe similar to that of the Banque Royale?

As you will see in Chapter 10, in 1974 the Bank of England came close to such a disaster when it became immersed in the rescue of the second-line banking sector. It has been rumoured that the social security system in the United States is bankrupt, along with the Federal Deposit Insurance

---

Who can claim that any central bank may not suffer a catastrophe similar to that of the Banque Royale?

Corporation. If all of the calls on the Federal Reserve were made at once, the central bank could not survive. Notions of that nature have been circulating in America for quite some time. The element of truth is not quantifiable. But who is to say?

You could certainly be forgiven if a chill now runs down your spine when you think of the 200 billion dollar deficit in the United States, along with the billions which have been lent to bankrupt third world countries that will never be repaid. Debt and credit have once again kept the wheels of the Western world turning down one of the longest orgies of debt creation in world history – just like in John Law's day. How long can the wheels of commerce run on a path of shaky credit? When a debt structure has been stretched to its absolute limits – such as it is now – as with a knitted jumper, if one single thread is unravelled just a bit too much, the whole garment unravels.

Karl Marx was adamant when he insisted that the capitalist system was a destructive organism. It was his firm belief that ultimately the system must self-annihilate, as debt creation caused business cycles to become more unstable and explosive. You may now reflect on Tulipomania, the South Sea Bubble and the Mississippi Bubble, comparing them with the events of the twentieth century which already include one major crash and the implications of a second. Do you begin to cringe at the thought that perhaps Marx could be right?

4

The Crash of Crashes

How a series of financial calamities during the
second half of the nineteenth century brought about
the longest depression the world has ever known

Look Back in Horror

If our contemporary society were to look back into history for the single
most devastating crash it can think of, there is really no contest. Without
hesitation, the Crash of '29 springs to mind along with the agonizing
Great Depression that followed. But what was it like from the vantage
point of the 1920s? Again, there is no contest. Those enjoying the
prosperity of the Roaring Twenties would immediately recall the final
quarter of the nineteenth century, when markets, investments and the
world as a whole fell into an abyss of futility and despair.

Today, the Great Depression is synonymous with the soup kitchens,
unemployment, business collapses, bank failures and hunger marches
that followed the Crash of '29, often referred to as the Great Crash. But
before then the phrase 'Great Depression' was used with reference to the
series of bubbles and crashes that began in 1873 and continued for
twenty-four years until the world's markets and the economy hit rock
bottom in 1897. Even after 1929, historians continued to refer to the
period 1873–97 as that of the Great Depression. In 1893 the historian
D. A. Wells, for one, viewed the two decades that had passed as a series of
financial calamities 'unparalleled in the history of the world. . . . It has
been continuous during all these twenty years,' he wrote. In 1897
Professor J. W. Jenks of Cornell University saw the preceding era as one of
repeated great waves of financial and economic catastrophe, 'covering a
score or more years bearing the panic fluctuations on their surface as mere
ripples'.

The New World – the Americas both North and South – was a key
source of growth for Britain and the rest of Europe throughout the first
half of the nineteenth century. The whole of the American continent was
prone to running exceptionally large deficits, providing ready markets for

47

Europe's exporters. These deficits – which allowed the Americans to purchase large quantities of goods manufactured in Europe – were financed by loans from European bankers. As the century progressed, the fate of the American continent and of Europe became ever more closely intertwined.

The Nineteenth-century Boom

Since the Crash of '29 and the Depression of the 1930s, even the gloomiest among us have been conditioned to assume that increasing prosperity is the normal order, having experienced over five decades of post-war expansion. So it was in the early 1870s – the years of the railway boom and the property boom, and the heyday of the Industrial Revolution. Yet every crash is firmly rooted in the boom that precedes it; there can be no crash without a boom.

The early nineteenth century saw the opening up of the American Mid-West and its agriculture. It saw the birth of great new cities like Chicago, built on the Great Lakes where the development of the canal system facilitated the industrial growth of Ohio, Michigan, Illinois, Pennsylvania and northern New York State.

The 1830s and 1840s heralded the expansion of America's mighty cotton industry in the South. The demand for cotton had taken a quantum leap with the spread of textile machinery, particularly in Britain, France and Belgium, and the effect was immense economic expansion in the USA. Between 1819 and 1837 wealth in America, along with commerce, nearly doubled.

The Cotton Slump

The boom that began in the 1820s was soon accompanied by generally rising prices, massive borrowings and heavy speculation in shares, particularly in land. By 1827 a speculative orgy was in full swing, with all that that implied, and the crash came in the form of a collapse in the price of cotton. The huge losses suffered on the London market, where there had been excessive speculation in cotton, left the Bank of England in the humiliating position of having to turn to France for help, and US President Jackson deplored the plight in which Britain and the United States found themselves: '. . . two nations, the most commercial in the world, have now been plunged into embarrassment and distress with the same difficulties and reverences and, at length, the same overwhelming catastrophe'.

The slump of the 1830s, which also engulfed Belgium, France and Germany, brought the boom of the early nineteenth century to a temporary halt. A wide range of other speculative favourites apart from cotton suffered sharp setbacks. Shares continued to fall for seven years until, on average, they had lost more than three-quarters of their previous values. While the slump of the 1830s was severe, it only represented one of several minor punctuation marks in the nineteenth-century boom compared to what lay in store at the end of that boom.

In spite of the heavy losses suffered by cotton speculators in London and the embarrassment of the Bank of England, this slump was actually less severe in Britain than elsewhere. The reason could have been the rapid expansion of the railways in Britain at the time, which was more advanced than in other countries. The economic activity thus engendered was able to offset the slack in other areas of the economy.

'Two nations, the most commercial in the world . . .
have been plunged into embarrassment and distress'

While Britain's cotton industry was passing through hard times, the slowly developing engineering industry helped to soften the impact of recurring waves of recession. Her iron foundries were set on a course which, by 1870, would see them responsible for half the world's output. Already by the 1830s there were two Englands – though not the Two Nations of Disraeli. In the Midlands, bounded by Birmingham and Stoke-on-Trent in the west and Sheffield, Nottingham and Leicester in the east, industry and populations moved easily, served by the network of canals. Also well served were South Wales and parts of Lancashire. But in the North of England, from Yorkshire to the Scottish border, the hilly countryside was unsuited for canals; and there were few navigable rivers. That was one great reason, wrote G. D. H. Cole, 'why railway development began in the North – with the Stockton and Darlington Railway . . . chiefly designed to open the inland coalfield of South Durham'.

By 1836 the climate in Britain was just right for expansion. Speculators and investors were beginning to recover from the cotton fiasco. Commodity prices began to recover, and far-sighted businessmen were quick to realize that raw material prices were too tempting to pass by. In 1837, although pockets of recession remained in several areas of the economy, the seeds of speculation in the railroad sector began to germinate, first in Britain, then elsewhere.

In the United States, railroads enabled a comparatively small and scattered population to develop the country as nothing else could have done. Railroads opened up the West, linking the new, developing cities of the Middle West with the established industrial complex of the Eastern seaboard. One of the most important developments was the construction of the rail link between New York with Chicago, which had been incorporated in 1834 when Chicago had a population of no more than four thousand. It was to take another sixteen years for the rail link to be completed. The new network of railroads linking the active and enterprising cities of the rapidly developing Mid-West further speeded the exploitation of the vast agricultural potential of the Great Plains, which had begun with the canals.

The Panic of 1857

It is often the case that while new vehicles for expansion and speculation are being introduced, others are in their death throes, heading for extinction. The embers of the property and canal speculation of the earlier part of the century had barely cooled when the Panic of 1857 struck, following on the heels of the Crimean War. The Panic was endemic to the build-up of speculation around the world, fuelled by a period of economic boom and buoyed by new gold supplies from California and Australia. Britain was at the height of its powers, leading the Industrial Revolution and dominating world trade. Germany was just beginning to assert its industrial leadership in continental Europe. In the USA, the West was being opened up.

The target of speculative mania during the 1850s were the shares of railway companies. From less than 110 miles of track in 1850 the extent of the railways had soared in seven years to 2867 miles. But on 24 August 1857 the boom in railway stocks in both Britain and America was pricked and yet another bubble burst. This was a Grade A panic in every respect.

The first warnings came when the New York branch of the Ohio Life Assurance Trust Company was unable to meet its obligations and had to suspend all payments. The *New York Herald* predicted that the company's financial difficulties were widespread and would soon assume the proportions of a major crisis. The *New York Herald* was absolutely correct in its judgment. Countless American investors who had put their savings into railroads were ruined; so were the banks from which the railroad companies had been borrowing so freely. When investors were squeezed, the banks they had borrowed from also failed.

In the northern states the Panic came as an exceptionally severe blow. It brought considerable distress to the industrial cities, exposing the sheep farmers of Ohio to extreme hardship. Fortunately – for the cities as well as for the farmers – the productivity of the wheatlands was scarcely affected at all, a factor that was to play a major role in the rapidly approaching Civil War.

On the far side of the Atlantic investors in London and other European cities, who had also been speculating heavily in US railroad stocks, sustained very heavy losses. In Britain the affair was known as the Crisis of 1857, and it was the most severe that Britain, or any other nation, had encountered up until then. Financial shocks and failures spread like a forest fire from America to England, on to France, then to Germany and Scandinavia.

The Indian Cotton Crash

The result of the events of 1857, however, was a recession but not a depression. It served merely as an interruption to the underlying economic boom. The Panic and many of its side effects were all over by 1859. By 1860, the wheels of prosperity were rolling again.

After the slump, the character of boom conditions began to change. The seeds of monetary inflation that had been used so effectively by John Law – for a time – had been planted with the discovery of gold in California and the famous Gold Rush of 1849. Twelve years of inflationary expansion followed, and now all that was needed to make these seeds mushroom was a full-blooded war. Wars that occur at the mature stages of an expansion are economically deadly. Such a war will take the inflationary cycle to its final frenetic peak while inducing intense waves of speculation as money is pinpointed to finance the war.

Price inflation is not merely confined to food, clothing, goods and services. When intense inflation occurs, it permeates society in every area, particularly – in the later stages – in financial assets such as works of art, antiques and Stock Exchange investments. Unlike the previous periods of boom during the nineteenth century, there was a dangerous inflationary element in the boom that began in 1859. It was when the United States gave birth to the war between the states – the Civil War – in 1861 that the Sword of Damocles was placed over the future of the world's economy and financial markets. It would hang there for decades to come.

The formula for a speculative mania – the last hurrah – was firmly in place. All speculative manias have a star performer. The star performer of the one that began in 1861 was a country that seems an unlikely contender from the viewpoint of the twentieth century. It was India.

It would be a mistake to overlook the impact which the Civil War in America had on other nations. Like most wars, it caused an immediate increase in the demand for raw materials – particularly cotton to clothe

---

All speculative manias have a star performer

---

the armies. Cotton production in the Southern states of America was diverted to wartime use and was no longer exported. The need to keep the mills of Lancashire supplied with cotton meant that mill owners turned to India, a major producer at the time. As with most commodities during wartime, the price of cotton rose and rose and rose. In India the reaction was predictable, as reported by the Bank of Bombay: 'The great and sudden wealth produced by the rise in the price of cotton shortly after the commencement of the American Civil War [led to] excessive speculation. From this period, everyone in Bombay appears to have become wild with the spirit of speculation.'

51

In a near carbon copy of the South Seas Bubble, speculation spread like wildfire, and, according to the Bank of Bombay, 'companies were started for every imaginable purpose'. Although the enterprises were multi-farious, they all rested on top of an inverted pyramid of cotton. After reaching dizzy heights in 1865, the price of cotton collapsed and took the Indian economy and the various hosts of speculation along with it.

The Crash in India was truly a crash in the best tradition. The Bank of Bombay, whose shares were a principal target for speculators, slumped from their peak of 2850 rupees in 1865 to 87 rupees over the next two years, representing a fall in value of 97%. Bank of Bombay reclamations plunged from 55,000 rupees to 1750 rupees by 1865, the year the American Civil War ended. The President of the Bank, Premchand Roychand, with his wild lending policies reminiscent of the Duc d'Or-léans, was made the scapegoat and accused of single-handedly causing the mania. He was dismissed and publicly ostracized, not unlike John Law. It seems that people find considerable comfort in abdicating responsibilities for their follies to those in authority. Prime Ministers and Presidents should take note.

The Overend Gurney Collapse

Thanks to the rapid development of communications technology during the first half of the century – from the telegraph to the sub-marine Atlantic cable, from the telephone to Exchange Telegraph's ticker-tape machines – all the major markets of the world were now becoming one. Better communications made the transaction of international business readily accessible to all who were prepared to make the effort. When a leading American railroad company manipulator learned from the 'wire' that a stockbroker in Amsterdam was holding shares that he wanted, he simply crossed the Atlantic, saw the broker, purchased the shares and returned home. The downside of better communications was that it was more difficult to keep a secret – especially if it was calamitous news. When Overend Gurney, a respected London discount house, failed on Black Friday in May 1866, the news sent shock waves around the world within minutes. The *Annual Register* reported 'the wildest agitation that has ever been known in the City, and the Government was compelled, as in 1847 and 1857, to authorise the Bank of England to issue notes beyond the legal limit'.

There is little doubt that it was the bursting of the bubble in India that paved the way for this crisis, whose impact, in a highly unstable inflation-ary world, was in turn felt in markets all over the world. In June Aagra and Mastermans Ltd failed, followed by the Royal Bank of Scotland. As observed by the *Annual Register*, the financial holocaust of 1866 demons-trated 'the peculiar risks of banks administered by traders, whose intent in obtaining undue accommodation is likely to prevail over their regard to the protection of their shareholders'.

The shock to the system that had begun in India was widely felt, spreading from London to Paris, Amsterdam and Wall Street. Yet, at the early stages of the financial massacre, ordinary investors still seemed to be so mesmerized by the hope of gains that they tended to overlook the high level of risk inherent in their activities. It was said they had been programmed to heed only good news – never bad news. At the same time, many who dabbled in speculative markets were – as Alan Jenkins points out – misled into believing that 'with all these improved communications, theoretically, rumour and fraud would gradually cease to exist. But, then . . . the Devil is always winning.'

The Devil certainly had plenty of scope in the US financial markets of the mid-nineteenth century, dominated as they were by thrusting, often ruthless men with names like Fisk, Gould, Astor, Harriman, Rockefeller and Vanderbilt. The market was open, ebullient, reckless and dangerous. At the same time there were no Anti-Trust laws to guard against monopolies, and no Securities and Exchange Commission to keep an eye on the way Stock Exchange dealings were conducted. Politicians were corruptible and labour was cheap. There was virtually no labour legislation: labour – and life – were considered expendable. Taxation for all was low, and there was no excess profits tax. Banks, numerous and of every kind, were subject only to a modicum of legislation. Large or small, the banks were anxious to lend on almost anything before the boom times ended. Most stock markets operated on very small margins: in the United States you only had to make a down payment of 10% of the cost of the shares you wanted to buy.

Crisis on the Boulevards

The French markets operated on a pattern similar to that of the American markets. For a considerable time, as a result of the John Law experience, the French were suspicious of anything resembling the practice of banking. This was all to change under Napoleon III, who became Emperor in 1851. Under the Second Empire he pursued a deliberate policy of allowing full rein to financiers and entrepreneurs. Unlike John Law, the Emperor firmly believed that the entrepreneurs of his day would complete railway construction and public projects faster and more efficiently than the public authorities could – provided, of course, the capitalists could see a profit in it for themselves.

Under his patronage two brothers, Emile and Isaac Périre, established the Crédit Mobilier bank, which created a number of businesses under its banking umbrella and was willing to finance projects refused by other bankers. Crédit Mobilier also had the backing of Baron Georges Eugène

Haussmann, financier, town planner and another of the Emperor's favourites. Haussmann was commissioned by him to rebuild Paris, ridding the city of its slums and giving the capital the same character as London, which Napoleon III so admired. When the Baron tried to raise the necessary funds, he found the public was responsive but not the bankers, in spite of the insistence of the government. In 1855 Crédit Mobilier duly obliged and financed Haussmann's grandiose scheme, incurring the displeasure of other bankers including the great House of Rothschild.

The rebuilding was to cost 2500 million French francs, which would be about 80 billion French francs today. That sum was forty-four times the city's normal annual budget. The Baron, with the approval of the Emperor, had ridden roughshod over – and around – all of the legal restrictions that should have applied to the scheme.

There was much work for all aspects of the building trade, and no less than 20% of the entire workforce of Paris was engaged in executing the scheme. Contractors – and sub-contractors – grew rich. Despite the fact that there was a financial crisis at the time, Paris had an air of prosperity.

By 1867 most of Haussmann's grand design had been completed, and in 1868 Crédit Mobilier collapsed. When the results of excessive spending and speculation began to take their toll and Crédit Mobilier found itself in difficulties, the House of Rothschild gave vent to its implacable hostility and effectively administered the *coup de grâce*, calling in outstanding loans which they were fully aware Crédit Mobilier could not repay at the time.

Millions of Frenchmen and the bulk of the financial institutions in France had committed vast quantities of money to the Périre brothers on the basis of Napoleon III's support. When Crédit Mobilier failed, the entire financial establishment of Paris suffered an excruciating shock, promoting further failures throughout the country.

The Robber Barons

Four years after the formation of Crédit Mobilier in France, a similar company was established in the United States, ostensibly to raise funds for the Union Pacific Railway. In reality, Crédit Mobilier was set up in the United States merely to assist in building a fortune for the Massachusetts industrialist Congressman Oakes Ames. For the railroad magnates of the 1860s – the Robber Barons – locomotives and timetables, new routes and drilling stock were never an end in themselves. They were essentially the means to an end, to create more wealth and accumulate more power. Oakes Ames had used the shares of Crédit Mobilier – apart from enriching himself – to 'persuade' members of Congress to give him and his friends the favours they sought in the interest of Union Pacific. Among those who received shares were the Vice-President, Henry Wilson, and a future US President, James A. Garfield of Ohio. As historian Richard O'Connor saw it, viewed from the standpoint of Congressman Ames' contemporaries Crédit Mobilier – American version – was 'a model of efficiency and economy in the field of official corruption. Less than a hundred thousand dollars was paid out to Congressional shareholders . . . in exchange for legislation . . . which enables the financiers to clear upwards of forty million.'

No single individual in American financial history exemplified the Robber Baron to a greater degree than Jay Gould. His operation spanned three decades, from the beginning of the American Civil War through the

---

'the most hated, feared and envied man in America during the second half of the nineteenth century'

Long Depression that began in the 1870s and ended in the 1890s. Ruthlessly flourishing in the speculative heyday of the Robber Barons, Gould amassed a fortune estimated at 77 million dollars – and died without a friend in the world. According to his biographer, William O'Connor, in *Gould's Millions*, he was 'a Napoleonic genius who defiantly strutted through the field of American finance. Between the US Civil War and 1892, the year of his death, Jay Gould conducted a relentless war against the American Government and its citizens. Known as "the little wizard", his contemporaries said he was the most hated, feared and envied man in America during the second half of the nineteenth century.'

At the time of his most notorious endeavours, the slight figure of Jay Gould could often be seen on Wall Street, flitting from one building to the other. He would slink along like an alley cat, expecting someone to kick him as he went along. 'Lucky thing the mob didn't catch Jay Gould on Black Friday, 1873,' said Jess Parker, a Wall Street stockbroker of the time. 'They were going to hang him to a telegraph pole for what he did that day and they would have gotten him if old uncle Russell Sage hadn't hidden him under a boat down on Long Island and carried his meals there for three days.' What appeared to be the door to his office, with his name on it, opened into an empty broom cupboard because too many people had kicked it open in an attempt to shoot him. One of the very few people privy to the secret of where his office was really located was Congressman Oakes Ames. It was Gould whom Oakes had chosen as a bed-fellow for his operation with Crédit Mobilier and the Union Pacific railway.

Virtually from its inception, the Union Pacific railroad was bled white of its funds while they were being channelled through Crédit Mobilier, directed by Oakes Ames and his cohorts. In addition, the railroad company had been saddled with a floating debt of 5 million dollars and another 10 million dollars in income bonds. This, as Gould saw it, was the time to start moving. He began buying Union Pacific shares – but not for the reasons that the railroad builders themselves might have had (wanting to reach the West Coast), nor even to benefit his other railway interests. As his biographer Richard O'Connor put it: 'A railroad to him was a set of books . . . not an engineer pulling down the Johnson bar to outrun an Indian war party. . . . Thus he felt free to use the railroads as pawns, along with its millions of acres of former Government land, coal deposits, mountain timber and the life savings of thousands of stock and bond holders, in a complicated and impersonal chess game.'

As a result of his play for Union Pacific, Jay Gould acquired one-third of the shares of the railroad. He then joined the board and was soon running the whole shooting match. Through a series of clever manoeuvres he transformed the debt into a long-term bond issue and persuaded the holders of the income bonds to accept in their place a flotation of sinking fund bonds. Crédit Mobilier was the financial cesspool for Gould's manoeuvres. And Crédit Mobilier crashed in the same manner as its French counterpart when the speculative bubble of the railways was burst.

The Crash of '73 – the Crash of Crashes

The series of financial dislocations that began in 1865 when the stock market collapsed in India, leading to the Overend Gurney crisis and the collapse of Crédit Mobilier, was unlike any series of financial dislocations earlier in the period, which is why I have described at length the events leading to the longest depression the world has ever known and the Crash of Crashes. What began in 1865 had a very special significance for the bursting of the various speculative bubbles coinciding with the deflation of the most serious speculative bubble of all – the fiat money bubble. The crashes that began in 1865 were certainly nothing like the Panic of 1857. The amount of money that was being printed by the authorities prior to the Panic of 1857 was relatively small compared to what had been taking place following the Civil War. Essentially, the crisis that began in 1866 marked the point where the printing of money ceased to perform its function, as John Law had learned.

The story of the Long Depression and the Crash of Crashes is the story of debt implosion and the destruction of money. Copious amounts of money ended up in money heaven as bankruptcy and the collapse in the value of creditworthy assets suddenly brought to an end the unrestrained creation of money that took the inflationary cycle to its final peak – as it always does. The price that has to be paid for an abandonment of sound monetary principles is indeed a heavy one. It always has been. It always will be.

The Crash of Crashes was long. It was global. It was more intense than

56

most people imagined could ever be possible. Serious problems seemed to be reaching a crescendo in 1872. In the USA, a speculative mania in railroad stocks was continuing, yet the four thousand business failures in 1872 were a third up on those of the previous year, and involved debts totalling 121 million dollars. Liabilities totalled a staggering 228,500,000 dollars, which was nearly twice the level of the previous year. During 1872, eighty-nine railroads defaulted on their bonds. These included the Boston, Hartford and Erie; the Kansas Pacific; the Northern Pacific; the Missouri, Kansas and Texas; and the Rock Island – all considered to be blue chip investments three years earlier. During the latter part of the year the boom in railway shares began to falter. Several shares plummeted. Early in 1873 financial commentators in the United States began issuing warnings that the US banking system could be at risk, due to the highly precarious nature of the railroad industries' debt structure. Railroad companies which had been financing their expansion through the sale of bonds to institutional investors and members of the public began finding it extremely difficult to sell their bonds, if not impossible. Whereas the railroads had been considered the bluest of blue chip securities up to 1872, the sharp fall in many of their shares led to deep suspicion of anything connected with railroads, including railroad bonds – even though the bond guaranteed repayment of the principal.

Adding to the problems of the 1870s were men like Andrew Carnegie, who had decided that America's future required the development of the iron and steel industries. This further increased the competition for both loans and equity capital. All that Carnegie and his like were able to offer in return was a stake in the future prosperity of the nation – which looked less than promising in 1872. The insatiable demand for funds was unrequited: but bankers couldn't lend, and the public wouldn't lend. As it happened, the event that triggered the Crash of 1873, signalling the start of the Long Depression, came from outside. But this was merely fortuitous – any major shock from any source could have sent the fiat funny money house of cards tumbling down at any time.

When the spectre of calamity began to appear, it was as if an elephant had just jumped into your bathtub

---

It was after the opening of the World Exhibition in Vienna on 1 May 1873 that a horrendous crisis of confidence gripped the Austrian capital. Several Viennese banks, caught up in the overspeculation in US railroad shares, came crashing down. Like a fire-storm the panic swept through Germany, where normally the banks tended to be more stable than those of Austria; several German banks were obliged to call a moratorium. Also caught up in the panic were the Belgian, Italian and Swiss banks, which maintained regular, close links with their German colleagues. Next came a number of Dutch banking institutions. Although it took almost four months before the first red glow of panic was seen on the New York Stock Exchange, by then credit was almost at snapping point. When the spectre of calamity began to appear, it was as if an elephant had just jumped into your bathtub.

You could say the Crash of Crashes really began with the hoisting of the storm cones over Wall Street on Monday, 8 September 1873. That was the day the New York Warehouse and Security Co. collapsed. Five days later, a similar fate overtook the US banking firm of Kenyon, Cox. On Wednesday, 17 September there was pandemonium on Wall Street when shares crashed. On Thursday the 18th a well-respected Philadelphia finance house, Jay Cooke and Co., failed. Somehow the stockbrokers and their clients managed to keep their nerve during the morning of Friday, 19 September, when a brief period of tranquillity appeared. But, later in the afternoon of that fateful day, like a bolt from the blue came a series of bear raids on railroad shares. Across the board, railroad shares were crashing as selling orders seemed to come from all corners of the globe at once, forcing prices downwards.

It is suspected that Jay Gould single-handedly engineered the crash of Friday, 19 September, after slowly unloading his railroad holdings beforehand. His objective was to force prices downwards so that at the bottom of the crash he could repurchase them at – hopefully – a fraction of their true net worth.

It was only sixteen years before, on 24 August 1857, that an earlier boom in railway shares had collapsed. One might imagine that such a sharp lesson would be long remembered. But, as history shows, banks, market men and investors have notoriously short memories. When the New York Stock Exchange closed its doors on that nightmarish Saturday in September 1873, most observers looked at the affair as a totally unique

---

Most were unable to grasp the vast difference between the life of a company's shares and that of its function as a productive organism

---

and unprecedented disaster. Surely the railroad companies were too dynamic, too important to be allowed to fail! What most were unable to grasp was the vast difference between the life of a company's shares on the Stock Exchange and that of its entirely separate function as a productive organism. Very rarely do the twain meet.

The public in both the United States and Britain believed in the railways – in their early stages of development, the railways had found no need to turn to the Stock Exchange for finance. Although some companies had issued shares which were dealt on the Stock Exchange, many railways

58

were financed through local industrialists, who had appealed directly to the public. They advertised the shares and held what were called 'enthusiasm meetings'. The banks, too, were tapped for funds.

When the need for financing grew too great for these sources, first the new provincial Stock Exchanges were used to float the shares and bonds of the railways, then the larger exchanges. From the very beginning, railroad shares were looked on as a highly risky investment. There were frequent charges of 'allotment rigging' – some investors were allocated more shares than others – a practice claimed to have been invented by Jay Gould. A large amount of business was done unofficially in the coffee

---

The real problem was not the men who built the railroads, but the money men who manipulated them

---

houses and in the street – literally on 'the kerb', which is the nickname for the US Stock Exchange. Railroad mania also introduced the stag, who, then as now, applied for an allotment of shares, intending to sell them at a profit before the time came to pay for them.

A great deal of the speculation took place in the provinces and small towns, where middle-class merchants, doctors, lawyers and tradesmen were as much attracted to speculating in the railroads as were those of greater means. Money was flowing into the railroads from all sources from the 1860s onwards – the demand for capital was insatiable. While bank deposits in the United States rose by 43 million dollars, during the corresponding period the banks made loans which totalled a colossal 283 million dollars. At the same time, while the circulating capital of the railroads increased by a mere 7.5%, debt increased by 50% – and still the railroad companies clamoured for more and more money. To add to the dangers of the situation, there was a considerable inflow of foreign funds, since investment prospects outside the United States were not considered to offer anything like the promised returns of railroad speculation.

A socio-economic law of C. Northcote Parkinson is that expenditure will always rise to meet and exceed income. So it was with railroad mania. Railroads were being overbought. The railroad mileage doubled. Funds were deployed to translate increasingly ambitious new projects into faster locomotives, more comfortable carriages, more freight-carrying capacity and – above all – more and more bridges, cuttings and miles of track. Wildcat schemes were entered into which would not have been considered viable without the ample funds pouring into the railroads.

The real problem was not so much the men who built the railroads, as the money men who manipulated them, such as Jay Gould. If there was any sign of indignation from bankers or investors, it would be pointed out that hundreds of miles of track were being laid down – throughout the

United States, Britain and South America. 'They're still there,' they'd say. 'They're advancing even further every day.'

The burden of debt which the railroads were accumulating grew constantly heavier, while the ability to pay the interest on that debt became an increasingly serious problem. In 1872, of 364 listed railroads in the United States, only 104 had been able to pay any dividend at all – while 69% of those who were able to pay limited the payment to 10% or less. More and more straws were piled on to the camel's back. Unless the railroad companies could maintain their momentum, there was a constant threat of their not being able to sustain their massive expenditure programmes and service the huge loans to which they were committed. In a sense it was – for investors and banks alike – a case of More or Nothing. It was the manipulators rather than the innovators who called the tune.

Throughout the first half of 1873 the Crédit Mobilier scandal was gathering momentum, demoralizing Congress and accentuating the general distrust of big business. The notorious exploits of Jay Gould were a not inconsiderable influence. Meanwhile, New York had been agitated by news of banking scandals, causing further severe strain on money markets, already under the strain of the too-heavy structure of debt. The crash had to come, but no one expected it to be as long and as devastating as it was.

The Aftermath

As soon as news of the closure of the New York Stock Exchange on 20 September 1873 reached Washington, President Ulysses S. Grant and his Treasury Secretary, W. A. Richardson, hurried to New York. Jay Gould sat on the sidelines, blaming the government for its bad management and the public for their lack of confidence. Having conferred with leading figures in banking and business, the government came to the same conclusions that the Governor of the Bank of England had reached in the Panic of 1857 and that John Law had reached just after the Mississippi bubble burst. The only way to stem the panic and stave off total collapse would be to ease credit. Accordingly, the authorities announced they would buy back government bonds from the banks.

President Grant, Secretary Richardson and other high government officials met various financial leaders including Commodore Vanderbilt at a Fifth Avenue hotel. The bankers pooled their resources, and for the very first time in history issued clearing house certificates as a temporary form of acceptable money; the government released 13 million dollars from the Treasury for the purchase of government bonds.

After ten days, the New York Stock Exchange reopened. The worst fears of the market were allayed by the realization that the collapse of the stock market, the failure of the banks and the closure of the New York Stock Exchange was almost wholly attributable to the crash of the debt-laden railroads. Once the dust seemed to have settled on the September '73 collapse, bands of voluntary workers moved into action on the city streets in an effort to assist those growing numbers of unemployed who had become beggars during the ensuing months. As the *Troy Morning Whig* reported: 'Business at the soup house continues lively . . . the ladies plan to furnish either salt fish, oyster soup or fish chowder for Fridays thereafter.' By the time of the Crash one newspaper had estimated that the unemployed in New York had risen to one worker in every three. Conditions were even harder west of the Mississippi. There, grasshoppers and grubs destroyed many crops. Blizzards were sweeping across the open plains of Kansas and Nebraska.

The reopening of the Stock Exchange brought a sigh of relief, but that minor restoration of confidence was fleeting. What was even worse than the immediate impact of the collapse was the fact that by the end of the year business was still refusing to pick up. The actions of the government had had very little effect. They were short-term measures for a short-term crisis, but the American economy was desperately sick and, as with all patients on the critical list, careful nursing was required and a long period of convalescence before health would be slowly restored. No one at the time was remotely aware of the length of convalescence that would actually be needed.

In 1873 more and more firms failed, while the forces of depression raged with an even greater ferocity. The level of unemployment in the major cities soared to what was estimated as half of the workforce. Railroad building was grinding to a halt. In 1874 only 1940 miles were built – one-third of the average of the preceding five years. All industries connected with railroads – rolling mills, machine shops, foundries and so on – followed suit and either closed down or cut their production drastically.

Business failures during 1874 jumped to 5800; in 1875, 7700; in 1876, 9000; in 1877, 9000 again. Most railroads went into bankruptcy. The continuing increase in the level of unemployment far outstripped the ability of charities to relieve hunger and destitution. Breadlines formed everywhere. Many previously wealthy railroad magnates – Jay Gould excepted – stood in them with other unfortunates. Jay Gould was busying himself with other matters.

Gold – the Manipulated Crash

Not even President Ulysses S. Grant was saved from the treachery of the skunk of Wall Street, as he was aptly known. The idea for one of Gould's most famous financial extravaganzas must have been stirring in his brain for a long time. But it wasn't until he had accumulated a vast fortune through his misdeeds with the railroads that he had sufficient cash to carry out the scheme.

Gould decided he wanted to control the gold market in the same way he controlled the railroads. Gold had a dual role in Gould's operations. The money he was making out of the railroads he held in gold. Ergo, if he could force the price of gold upwards he would increase his profits that much more. Europe was on the Gold Standard at the time. A higher gold price would help American farmers sell their produce abroad. Stimulating the exportation of grain and other farm produce would mean more freight traffic for his railroad – and again, more profit for Gould.

Since early 1869 he had been waiting for an opportunity to enter the gold market and possibly engineer a spectacular price rise which would take it back up to the wartime price level of 241 dollars an ounce. Following the Civil War, trading on the gold market had become dull and listless, with the price settling down to around 131 dollars. Gould believed the time was ripe for some speculative activity. He yielded to the temptation and bought 7 million dollars' worth of gold, which sent the price skyrocketing. There was only 15 million dollars' worth of gold circulating in the United States, and Gould now owned more than half of it. The only snag was the 100 million dollars' worth of gold held in the vaults of the US Treasury, which placed the US President in charge of the gold price. Gould's task was to plug up this safety valve just long enough to push the price as high as he could, selling out before the Treasury got wise and sent the price hurtling downwards again. Somehow Gould had to prevent the Treasury from dumping gold – releasing it on to the market so as to reduce the price – during a crucial week or so of his operations. He also had to know, during his campaign, whether or not the Treasury was hoarding gold or releasing it. To obtain the kind of information he needed, he would have to infiltrate the Cabinet – no easy task, since Gould was *persona non grata* among the higher echelons.

Gould agreed to pay Corbin 15,000 dollars for every one dollar advance in the gold price if he could persuade President Grant not to sell

---

For some time, Gould had been cultivating a grizzled old rascal named Abel Rathbone Corbin, the husband of Jenny Grant, the President's middle-aged sister. Gould, waving the American flag and assuming the role of patriot, managed to convince Corbin that if the US government encouraged the price of gold to rise, American farmers would reap enormous benefits from the higher prices for the expected bumper crop that year. The railroads would also profit from the hauling of grain to market, and the entire economy could be revitalized. Unequalled prosperity for all would result, according to Gould. On the other hand, if the government were carelessly to dump gold, a terrible depression would grip the land and – heaven forbid – another Civil War might break out, for which the President would be responsible.

Corbin, duly impressed, conveyed the programme for additional prosperity to his brother-in-law. When President Grant was in New York in June 1870 Gould was introduced to him at the Corbin household. He briskly took charge of the presidential party's entertainment and travel arrangements, seizing the opportunity not only to bend the President's ear but also to show the speculators in the Gold Room – where gold dealings were transacted – how intimate he was with him. This relationship, greatly exaggerated by Gould, was used as an effective propaganda weapon during his later manoeuvres.

Fisk made an 8 million dollar gold purchase, based on Gould's assurance that all the big-wigs were in on the plot, 'beginning with President Grant'

Gould decided to go for broke and once again began purchasing gold in large quantities. After a few months he owned all the gold then circulating in the United States, while also holding contracts by which he could call upon merchants, bankers, brokers and other speculators to deliver more gold to him – for which, as the only source of supply, he would ask twice the price he had paid. By that time the price was 146 dollars an ounce.

The Gold Room, and all of Wall Street, were quickly alerted to the fact that an unparalleled raid was being conducted. The first symptoms of panic began rumbling through the narrow streets of the financial district. In the meantime, Gould was deviously exerting steady pressure on the government to keep the Treasury's golden sluice gates shut tight. But speculators in gold began to disbelieve the artificial trend Gould was trying to establish. For several weeks the price refused to budge above the 146 dollar level as sellers pounded away. Although they were 'short' – selling, on paper, gold they didn't actually own – it was assumed these positions could be covered when the Treasury started selling gold again.

Gould was under pressure. Unless he could get the price of gold zooming – and quickly – he would lose control, the price would come tumbling down and the brokers would start demanding payment on those rubbery certified cheques issued by Crédit Mobilier, who financed gold purchases in excess of his resources. To complete his plan he somehow had to panic people into buying gold again, then dump all the gold on the market when he judged that the price had reached its peak.

About that time President Grant decided to stop off at the Corbins' on his way to Saratoga. Before his arrival, Gould pleaded with Corbin to convince the President how dangerous it would be to sell any gold at that time – and, to support his convictions, he agreed to pay Corbin 15,000 dollars for every one dollar advance in the gold price if he was successful. When the President arrived, Gould lurked in the hallway outside the dining room while Corbin made his pitch with the President. It worked. President Grant sent a letter to the Secretary of the Treasury advising that it would not be wise to sell large amounts of gold while crops were still in transit to market. European offers could be cancelled.

A further boost was given to Gould's campaign against those who were trying to force the price of gold lower in the form of one Jim Fisk, a less sharp-witted operator than Gould. Gould told him that, in exchange for his support, he would let Fisk in on the ground floor of the most fantastic manipulation in history, which was being supported by none other than the President of the United States. Fisk jumped in whole-heartedly to the extent of an 8 million dollar gold purchase, based on Gould's assurance that all the big-wigs were in on the plot, 'beginning with President Grant and ending with the doorkeepers in Congress'. Fisk was completely unaware that he was buying gold that didn't exist from sellers who didn't have it to sell – Gould still held all the gold in circulation in the United States. Later Fisk was made the principal victim of the Gould–Corbin confidence game.

In order to bolster his relationship with Fisk, Gould gave him complete charge of all purchase operations, along with the responsibility of dis- seminating the latest information to the Gold Room (or should I say disinformation?). With a flourish, Fisk rushed to the Gold Room the following day, placing huge orders while spreading tales of the President's co-operation. 'The President wants to see the gold price at 1000 dollars an ounce,' Fisk claimed.

Perhaps the most bizarre aspect of all this was the willingness of those involved to believe in the extent to which it was claimed the President was willing to co-operate. While rumours of his collusion were being shouted through the Gold Room, the only reaction from the traders was to shift

---

It was a time when everybody was feathering their nest, so why not the President of the United States?

---

their positions in gold accordingly. Everyone was prepared to believe the wild rumours. No one protested. There were no demands for an investiga- tion or congressional inquiry. After all, it was a time when everybody was feathering their own nest, so why not the President of the United States?

On the suggestion that the price of gold could rise to 1000 dollars an ounce, those who were short of it rushed to buy in order to cut their losses. Gould was a supplier, but at steadily higher prices. He had accumulated 40 million gold contracts, representing twice the available supply. Part of his holding was financed from his own pocket, but the majority came from the railroad treasury and the banks controlled by the Gould forces. It would appear that Gould's master plan was in the course of completion as the price of gold steadily advanced.

Now, just as Gould appeared on the brink of his victory, he was summoned to the Corbins' house. It appeared that the sleep-walking President was finally coming to his senses. Corbin's wife had received a letter from her sister-in-law, indicating a realization of how potentially scandalous the President's involvement in the gold ploy had become: 'Tell Mr Corbin that the President is very much distressed by your speculations and you must close them as quickly as you can.'

Ivan Boesky was a small-time piker compared to the nineteenth-century operators, who wrote the rule-book on insider dealing

---

Gould was fully aware of the implications of the letter. The President was about to order the Treasury to start selling gold again from their reserves. The price would plummet. Gould would lose all control. The letter was actually a warning to Corbin, the President's brother-in-law, advising him that the gold bubble was about to be punctured and he'd better liquidate his holdings before he was caught in the crash. Ivan Boesky was a small-time piker compared to the nineteenth-century operators, who wrote the rulebook on insider dealing. Corbin insisted that the account Gould had opened in his name at the Gold Room should be closed forthwith and that Gould pay him 100,000 dollars in accrued profits. Gould objected angrily, but finally agreed. But Gould asked one concession: 'I am a ruined man if the Gold Room ever gets wind of this letter,' he pleaded. 'It must be kept a secret.' By then Gould held 15 million dollars in bullion and another 35 million dollars in contracts. He felt he could not risk the possibility of a leak; nor would the market be able to withstand any sizeable selling order from him and his partner. That night and the next day only the Corbins and Gould knew of the letter. Fat, dumb, jolly Jim Fisk, happy as a pig in swill – anxiously preparing for the next part of the campaign when he would rally the price of gold to greater glory – was not informed.

Gould decided to unload and sell as much gold as he could, as fast as he could, in whatever way he could, without decimating the price structure. There was only one problem. If Jim Fisk did the same, others at the Gold Room would soon realize the Treasury had decided to sell gold. Prices at the artificially manipulated levels would cease. Sellers would return. Gold would plunge before Gould could get out.

Finally, with regret, but without any perceptible twinge of conscience, Gould decided quietly to abandon his sinking ship and pull away in the only available lifeboat rather than risk drowning by rescuing his friend and partner Jim Fisk. He had planned to tell Fisk about the letter, but would instruct him to continue buying gold and encouraging others to do the same none the less. He would sell, while Fisk, his friend, continued to buy. Gould would continue to pretend he was running with the bulls on gold, who believed the price was going to rise to 1000 dollars. In actuality, he was about to assume control as the biggest bear in the cage.

For the next day or so, Gould was to walk on a razor's edge. When the Gold Room opened in the morning, Fisk bellowed, 'I'll bet anyone 50,000 dollars that gold will rise today', while giving orders to his equally excited brokers to buy all the gold they could lay their hands on – 'phantom' gold, as he later referred to it. Gould stayed in his office tearing up the

---

'The terrific yells issuing from a lunatic asylum would not equal in intensity the cries of speculators in the Gold Room'

---

newspapers and keeping several messengers busy running back and forth to the sub-Treasury building. The instant the flash came from Washington ordering the Treasury to sell gold, Gould was to be advised. At that moment it was his intention to sell with a vengeance.

Obviously Gould's bull-in-bear's-clothing façade was bearing fruit, and he persuaded Fisk to keep on buying. But he kept it to himself that it was his gold that Fisk was buying. The atmosphere in the Gold Room was tense. Gould went on selling through another broker, while keeping up the pretence of buying through Fisk. Despite the growing anxiety in the Gold Room, the price kept rising. Up and up it went – 143 ... 155 ... 160. At that point, reported the *New York Herald*: 'The revengeful war whoops of the furious Indians, the terrific yells issuing from a lunatic asylum, would not equal in intensity the cries of speculators in the Gold Room.'

It was a feat of wizardry worthy of the most astute market trader. During the course of eight days, Gould managed to dump most of his gold holdings while the price continued to rise against the massive buying orders of the Fisk regime. After finally unloading all the gold he wished to unload, Gould began a new strategy. He withdrew from the market, causing a temporary artificial shortage which would send the price forging ahead all over again.

It worked like a charm. Jim Fisk, completely oblivious of Gould's role in the affair, offered to bet a further 50,000 dollars that the price of gold would hit 200 dollars an ounce before the end of the day. One stock-broker who thought gold was due for a fall, and who was indebted to the Gould–Fisk duo, when confronted with yet another price rise went home and blew his brains out in traditional Wall Street fashion. But Fisk's brokers shrieked with delirious excitement as the price of gold moved up, up, up.

As a final gesture, and in order to squeeze the very last penny of profit from the operation, Gould went back into the gold market. Since he had no further gold to sell, he started selling gold he didn't have in the knowledge that he would be able to buy it back later on at a price lower than that which prevailed at the time. In other words, Gould started 'selling short'. Soon a messenger from the sub-Treasury secretly brought him the news he had been waiting for. Secretary of the Treasury Butterfield had received firm instructions from President Gould to order the sale of 5 million dollars' worth of government gold the following day. It took fourteen minutes from the time Gould received the tip-off for a Treasury notice giving the information to be tacked on the Gold Room bulletin board. Every minute of that time lag, it was estimated later, was worth about 100,000 dollars to Gould.

Varooom! The price of gold collapsed like a blown-out tyre. Within fifteen minutes the gold price fell from 164 dollars to 133 dollars. One eye-witness account said the spectacle that followed could have been produced only in Dante's *Inferno*. So great was the confusion that at one end of the Gold Room there was a bid of 135, while at the other end brokers were still bidding 160.

Albert Speyer, a broker for Jim Fisk, was quite unable to comprehend the fact that the golden bubble had burst. He was one of the brokers still howling orders to 'buy at 160 for any part of a thousand' after the price had fallen by 30 points. Unbeknown to Fisk or Gould, Speyer had been hiving off some of the purchases for himself, getting into commitments which were well beyond his means as a broker. As the gold price steadily plummeted, it was reported that Speyer went raving mad in the Gold Room, shouting: 'I am Albert Speyer. Some persons have threatened to shoot me. Well, here I am. Now, shoot, shoot!' Dishevelled and ranting, Speyer was finally escorted away from the Gold Room by his friends.

'I am Albert Speyer. Some persons have threatened to shoot me. Well, here I am. Now, shoot, shoot!'

Throughout the period following the Treasury announcement the Gold Room hummed with news and rumours, all of which pushed the price down even further. Supposedly there was a gigantic bear syndicate, organized in Europe, preparing to dump millions of dollars in gold on New York. Fisk was besieged with offers to sell, most of them from the same individuals who minutes before had believed that Fisk's prediction of a 200 dollar gold price might come true. After the Gold Room had closed that day, the Exchange district was still boiling with rumours. Gould reputedly had lost over 30 million dollars and Fisk had been shot dead by a ruined spectator. Toasts were raised to the false reports. Fisk had been nominated the villain of the episode because of his blithe attitude in the face of general mayhem and disaster. 'Can't a fellow have a little innocent fun without raising a hullabaloo and going wild?' was his statement to the *New York Sun*.

The fearsome battle to control gold ended quickly – but months were required to repair the wreckage. Failures of a number of firms, suicides and ruin were the penalties paid. Several of Gould's partners had gone bankrupt, while Gould had become so haggard with the strain of the proceedings – and so frightened by the mobs howling for his life – that Fisk said, 'There was nothing left of him but a pair of eyes and a suit of clothes.'

> *'Can't a fellow have a little innocent fun without raising a hullabaloo and going wild?'*

But I really don't think we need pity Jay Gould: at the end of the exercise he had cleared a profit of 11 million dollars. Many wondered why Big Jim Fisk didn't choke the life out of his little partner when he learned – later, presumably – that Gould had double-crossed him and come out a substantial winner. As it happened, Fisk was in no way affected by the collapse of the golden bubble. He had purchased some 60 million dollars' worth of gold and simply refused to accept the obligations when they came due. All the buying he had done was in the names of other parties; he could not be prosecuted.

Of course, Fisk had reason to protest against Gould's double-dealing by not informing him of the letter received by Corbin's wife. There was also the matter of Gould's heavy gold sales which he was duped into buying as Gould pretended to be a buyer. But Gould somehow managed to talk Fisk into believing it was all the fault of President Grant and that 'frightened and greedy Corbin', both of whom had cut the ground out from under them. Gould also gave Fisk a share of the 11 million dollars in profit he had made, thus salving some of the hurt. Corbin's reward for his efforts turned out to be a big fat zero. But that was better than the fate of most who joined Gould in his escapade, who were then facing ruin.

Fisk and Gould holed up in a derelict building where they remained for a few days until calm had been restored to the Gold Room. A few days after the crash, when the two finally decided it was safe to be seen in public – surrounded by bodyguards, of course – Henry N. Smith, one of Gould's brokers, who had been thoroughly hoodwinked and made bankrupt, ran up to Gould and said: 'I'll live to see the day, sir, when you earn your living by going around with a hand organ and a monkey.'

Gould's penetrating eyes glittered with amusement as he glibly replied, 'Maybe you will, Henry, maybe you will. And when I need the monkey, Henry, I'll send for you!'

The Long Global Depression

Gold crashed. Stock Exchange securities were pummelled. Businesses came tumbling down like an endless parade of fragile Humpty Dumpties. Unlike the earlier part of the century, when it appeared as if commodity prices and prices in general were on a permanently rising trend, for the first time in forty years prices of raw materials and finished products in the shops were also declining. The period from 1865 to 1897 stands out as the most insistent and corrosive period of commodity price erosion in recorded history. Cotton, wheat, grain, beef, pork bellies and all the metals collapsed across the board.

The favourite contemporary explanation for the plunge in the general price level throughout the second half of the nineteenth century was 'mechanization'. But this is a half-cock theory. The explosion of commodity prices, along with the general price level between 1861 and 1864, was clearly due to the American Civil War – just as the earlier period of sharp price inflation had been prompted by the response of the authorities to the Napoleonic Wars in Europe, culminating in the Battle of Waterloo in 1815. The response of the authorities was to print money to finance these wars, fuelling the rise in the general price structure. If there is no money to pay for inflated prices, prices won't rise. Government, following the principles of John Law, provided all the money that was needed.

When prices rose, people begged, borrowed and performed whatever other financial tricks they could muster in order to cash in on the progressively higher price levels which they believed would never end, justifying their reckless commitments. But credit is nothing more than single entry book-keeping. If banks fail, businesses go bankrupt and the value of assets disintegrate, those credits – which represent money – disappear, and there are insufficient funds available to pay for the inflated prices or to cope with the requirements of production and commerce. When that happens, the entire price structure crumbles like the walls of

---

Businesses came tumbling down like an endless parade of fragile Humpty Dumpties

---

Jericho. That's what happened during the period 1873–97. The phenomenon is called deflation. We are all familiar with inflation, which represents rising prices. Deflation is the converse, representing falling prices, and is much more difficult to control. When the deflationary economic monster finally gets out of his cage, destruction runs rampant.

The idea of deflation was discussed at the time in the press, but no one bought the idea. People had been attuned to inflation as a permanent way of life during most of the century. They could not grasp the concept of deflation. In times that were seen as hard, the problem was regarded more as that of a reluctance to borrow – or a desire to pay off debt and reduce outgoings if possible. It was 'a question of confidence and not of capital', as one commentator put it in August 1884.

This attitude is just as difficult to comprehend from the viewpoint of the late twentieth century, which has also been nurtured on a lifetime's experience of inflation in goods and services, share prices and particularly homes. In most people's experience, the only thing that is worse than borrowing too much is borrowing too little. But, unlike the 1980s, in 1867 a piece of legislation was introduced in the USA in which lenders' rights were preserved with almost religious fervour. The horrendous Bankruptcy Act of 1867 provided for the involuntary bankruptcy of any business enterprise on the initiative of a single creditor. It was doubtful if the legislators were fully aware of the far-reaching consequences of this Act. Businessmen quickly became risk-averse, perpetuating the momentum of the deflationary forces that were already in place. An attempt on the part of the authorities to print money in order to stimulate economic activity during hard times can be a matter of trying to put the toothpaste back into the tube or 'pushing on a string', as John Maynard Keynes was to point out.

Historians divide the period of crashes and panics between 1873 and 1897 into three distinct waves of desperation. The first lasted from 1873 to 1879; the second from 1882 to 1886; and the third – and most damaging – from 1893 to 1897. Obviously there was very little room for a sustainable prosperity in between these cataclysms. Only seven of those twenty-five years allowed any relief from desolation. In other words, what took place during the final quarter of the nineteenth century was far worse than the financial and social dislocations resulting from Tulipomania, the South Sea Bubble or the Mississippi Bubble, which were relatively brief and isolated affairs by comparison. The depression into which the United States was plunged *circa* 1873 took the rest of the world with it, hanging like a thick fog over Britain and Europe for a generation.

'Let us have another war; let us be beaten and paid an indemnity and then we shall all be prosperous again.'

Periods of recovery among nations during the twenty-five-year depression were staggered, sporadic and fragmented. In Germany there was a minor recovery in 1877, representing a snap-back reaction to the series of dislocations that started in 1873. A minor recovery in the United States began to take hold in 1879. But Britain at this time was experiencing a deepening slump: unemployment had risen for seven consecutive years, attaining in 1879 a peak of 12½% of the workforce, the highest level reached in the second half of the nineteenth century.

If the slump in France was less marked than elsewhere, there was a very good reason: the massive war reparation payments made to Germany in 1871 after the Franco-Prussian War. The defeated French were compelled to pay a war indemnity of £90 million, in the days when that was real money. The payment helped start a chain of inflation in Germany, contrasting with the strongly deflationary climate in France. An inflationary speculative boom took wing in Austria and Belgium alike, leading to the inevitable panic and culminating in the collapse of the war indemnity payment. France, as the payer, was deflated and thus spared the ensuing panic and slump. 'Let us have another war; let us be beaten and paid an indemnity and then we shall all be prosperous again.' This was a quip in a ruefully sick-joke editorial that appeared in a German newspaper during the slump of the 1870s.

Wall Street was berated as an 'evil in the land'

The depression that began in the United States in 1873 was indeed a strange affair: strangest of all that it should have been so deep and pervasive in America, when that young economy seemed to have just about everything going for it. Most observers were completely nonplussed by the 1873–9 slump. At the start, it was good old-fashioned calamity. Banks were closing. Businesses were failing. People were losing their jobs. Breadlines were forming. But when the panic phase appeared to have spent its force, business remained stagnant like a limp rag. There was no 'technical snap-back'.

Back in Europe, better times did actually come as 1879 turned into 1880; in fact for a few months the recovery was described as 'violent'. But the improvement in business conditions was short and sweet, curtailed by the slump that began in 1882. The Union Générale bank – capitalized at its pinnacle of success at 600 million francs – collapsed, along with the smaller Banque de Lyon et de la Loire. The closures were accompanied by panic on the Paris and Lyon Bourses. This time it was France who experienced the misery of a slump, compounded by an outbreak of phylloxera that annihilated her vineyards.

For America, the recovery that started in early 1880 just petered out on the back of the financial tremors of 1882, and the economy was plunged into a slump again. As financial turmoils go, for most countries the Panic of 1882 was not particularly traumatic, although it was sufficient to put the US Gross National Product on the skids again. During the year it dropped by 25%, while the rise in the stock market that was getting underway quickly evaporated. 'When will business improve?' was the plea that echoed around the world.

During 1883, in an attempt to abdicate responsibility for the further downturn in business conditions and agree a scapegoat, Wall Street was singled out for attack by the politically self-righteous. *The Nation* dubbed the chronic lassitude of the Street as 'one of the strangest phenomena of modern times; restricting consumption and making capitalists timid, resulting in general blueness and despondency'. Wall Street was berated as an 'evil in the land', a danger to private wealth. Then, as now, it was fair game to attack the market for failing to satisfy the insatiable appetites of the gamblers and would-be millionaires whose greed, stupidity and recklessness were responsible for the many unsustainable bubbles in the first place.

'One of the strangest phenomena of modern times
. . . making capitalists timid, resulting in general
blueness and despondency'

During 1884, prices fell on stock markets and commodity markets alike. Speculation was non-existent. It was time to sell, sell, sell! Bankers curtailed loans and rapidly withdrew funds from the highly volatile call market through which most short-term financial transactions were financed. Money shortages grew worse, intensifying the already deep feeling of uncertainty. Desolation, deprivation, anguish and hardship spread like creeping damp through the drab working-class quarters of American cities. In October 1884, a survey carried out by Bradstreet put unemployment in twenty-two north-eastern states at 13%. On average, wages declined by 20–30% throughout the United States during 1884. On the other hand, immigration to the United States was breaking all records. Conditions were bad the world over.

In 1885 Britain was locked into a depression just as obstinate as that of 1873. That year a Royal Commission was set up to deal with the depression in trade and industry. Among its recommendations was a protectionist trade policy aimed particularly at the USA, the decline of whose currency was undermining the sale of British goods in foreign markets.

Yet Britons, Europeans, South Americans, Asians and others were convinced that the United States remained the land of golden opportunity. The only opportunity that the USA had to offer at the time was that of enabling people to experience penury on a larger scale than in their mother country. The inflow of immigrant workers from abroad tended to exert an even heavier downward pressure on wages at a time when the US economy was already engaged in a kamikaze mission.

The Panic of 1884, severe while it lasted, is historically recorded by the failure of Grant and Ward, carrying the General and former President of the United States to financial ruin. Ex-President Ulysses S. Grant at once set about writing his memoirs, which helped him repay the high debt incurred by the failure of his son's firm, in which he was a special partner.

The son of the ex-President was one of the smoothest rascals ever to have set foot in Wall Street. Referred to as the 'Young Napoleon of Finance', Ward spent several years in prison where he doubtless calculated time and again how, if only he had done this or that, he might have escaped detention. Promising huge profits to anyone who invested with the firm of Grant and Ward – after all, the ex-President was a special partner – he sailed along smoothly enough paying Peter with Paul's money, until the wind changed and Paul's ship failed to arrive with any new money! What followed was Ward's exposure, arrest and imprisonment – and heavy losses for those who believed in his skill and the credibility of the ex-President.

The crash of Grant and Ward brought down a number of other banks and brokerage houses. As usual a whole series of high-level thefts, frauds and peculiar speculations were uncovered. Hetty Green, known through-out the financial district as 'the witch of Wall Street', did her bit to help along the debacle of 1884 by suddenly calling for the delivery of 25 million dollars in securities and 475,000 dollars in cash from the prominent firm of J. J. Cisco and Co. The bankers could come up with neither the securities nor the cash. Like others in a similar position at the time, they were forced to close their doors for evermore. The shock to the securities market was severe, but the effect faded comparatively quickly.

The saviour of the period was J. Pierpont Morgan, who had come into financial prominence at about that time. However, failure continued to occur at regular intervals throughout the summer of 1884, culminating in the closing of the Wall Street Bank due to the discovery of costly irregularities by its head cashier.

The second phase of the Long Depression came to an end in 1886. The following two years were prosperous – 'the best since 1880', wrote several commentators – with money pouring into business. Europe invested heavily in US securities; the construction industry and railroad building

---

People took fright as they became aware that all the gold in the Fort Knox might soon disappear

---

picked up. Heavy industry was running at full tilt again. The year 1892 marked the hundredth anniversary of the New York Stock Exchange. But almost before the candles on the birthday cake began to flicker, rumblings of a new storm could be heard. Just as small boats rush to port as clouds gather, so did gold leave the United States for Europe ahead of the storm beginning in 1892. By April 1893, the 100 million dollar gold reserve which was held against the outstanding 346,681,000 dollars in legal tender notes had come under threat.

People took fright as they became aware that all the gold in Fort Knox might soon disappear and their dollars would be worth nothing more than the paper they were printed on. The demand for gold increased. President Cleveland issued a decisive statement that the government would continue to pay gold for Treasury notes, and pointed out that additional gold had been furnished by New York banks. His statement came too late. Shares began falling on the Stock Exchange again and companies began to fail – the bankruptcy of the Philadelphia and Reading Railroad was a notable example. In May 1892 share sales escalated. Europe had been selling securities ever since the Baring Crisis in 1890, and these sales now expanded significantly. To add fuel to the fire, banks in Australia were failing, adding to the worries of London and to its repatriation of funds.

The failure of the National Cordage Company in May 1892 was a particularly severe blow to the US stock market. The company was a favourite among tipsters and was probably the most widely touted share on the New York Stock Exchange, which had seduced large and small investors alike in large numbers. When the company collapsed, failure in the stockbrokerage industry came swiftly as the stock market plunged.

Money became tight, as it always does in critical periods. By 1893, a full-blown panic – to which all involved should have previously been accustomed – was being experienced. The spring and summer of that year witnessed continued declines in share prices and in business. As in the slump of 1880, the US Gross National Product fell precipitously, ending the year with a decline of 20%. Reports from all over the country accentuated the panic. Banks and businesses were failing in frightening numbers. The Erie Railroad, noted for its ups and downs in the hands of Jay Gould, fell down for the last time – into the hands of the Official Receiver. The Long Depression was in full swing anew: failures, unemployment, breadlines, falling shares, credit liquidation, money stringency and the familiar cry for 'more money' to soften the hard times.

At last prices began to recover, and then boomed
like a greyhound out of the trap

Depositors crowded the counting rooms of savings banks. Drained and frightened banks which exercised their lawful privilege of withholding payment only made matters worse. Merchants and manufacturers by the thousand were forced to the wall. With each company failure the ranks of the unemployed swelled that much more. During 1893, over six hundred banking institutions failed, along with seventy-four railroads and fifteen thousand businesses.

At last, from 1897 onwards, most prices began to recover as business picked up – and then boomed like a greyhound out of the trap. McKinley's election as President in 1896 marked the victory of the businessmen's party over liberalism, paving the way for the amazing third of a century that was soon to open. Two years later, the successful termination of the Spanish-American War stimulated the industrial activity of the country, which rose to levels unheard of in recent times. The United States was hailed throughout the world as a leading power and a land of incomparable prosperity. The twenty-four-year Long Depression was over.

A Warning for the Future

The index of industrial share prices ended the quarter-century almost exactly where it began. Its fluctuations in between were smaller than in any similar period since 1800. I've often said that the stock market can do anything it likes any time it likes. That 'anything' also includes doing nothing for long periods – very, very long periods. Try and imagine a period of twenty-five years in which shares made no progress at all, leaving everyone involved in a total state of unreward for two and a half decades. The period in the 1960s and 1970s when the Dow Jones industrial averages in the US got stuck at the 1000 level was only fifteen years long and, besides, that long plateau followed a thirty-year period of unprecedented gains – so a bit of consolidation and recapitulation was called for. Not so in the late nineteenth century. The level of industrial share prices at the trough of 1877 was no higher than it was at its best levels in 1835. After forty-two years investors in the stock market, by and large, were no better than all-square, despite the colossal strides made by the economy over the period. Indeed, the nineteenth century produced in the final analysis a 'profitless prosperity'.

Now let's take a careful look at the economic and financial environment of the 1980s. During the early part of the 1980s, the gold bubble was punctured. After rising to nearly 1000 dollars an ounce at one stage, the price plunged and fell below 300 dollars an ounce. The silver bubble also burst in the early 1980s, bringing about the downfall of the Hunt brothers. Banks have been failing continuously in the USA. The Continental Illinois Bank, the ninth largest bank in the United States, was the subject of a rescue operation by the Federal Reserve. The First Republic Bank Corporation, the largest bank in the state of Texas, also had to be rescued during early 1987.

Along with gold and silver, we've seen the crash in the price of tin and the total collapse of the tin cartel. Similarly the price of oil has plummeted, falling from a peak of 40 dollars a barrel to a mid-1986 trough of under 6 dollars a barrel. The Kuwait Stock Exchange toppled and had to close. The giant Johnson Matthey bank in England failed. At the same time, commodity prices are yet to achieve levels that were reached during the late 1970s, and appear to be trending downwards.

In October 1987 there was a crash on the New York Stock Exchange which was repeated in every major Bourse. During the post-mortems that

75

appeared after the crash, numerous comparisons were being made to the Crash of '29 and the Great Depression of the 1930s. Yet if one were looking for historical precedents, the circumstances of the 1870s–90s provide far more interesting parallels with those of the 1970s–80s. In my view, what lies ahead is far more likely to resemble that particular period than any other.

I'm about to show you why!

5

The Great Property Crash

How the land boom in Chicago and Florida brought
ruin to all those who believed house prices could
only rise and never fall

The Many Forms of Madness

The way the world really works is a very far cry from the way most people
think it works. Pleasant illusions are far more popular than painful facts.
The normal state of affairs is perceived to be one where each of us, as an
individual, has an inalienable right to increase his or her wealth through
time. Your familiarity with crashes so far should tell you that human
beings will go to ingenious lengths to protect and justify their illusions,
postponing the day of judgment for as long as possible. People will do
almost anything to pursue their dreams of future prosperity through their
speculative endeavours. Yet time and again we have witnessed, and
continue to witness, the massive evaporation of speculative fancies when
it is revealed that none of these markets is ever capable of meeting the
demands of the dreamer. Bubbles are the stuff that dreams are made of.

Bubbles burst when there is simply no one left who is willing (or able) to
push the price of the chosen speculative vehicle any higher. That may
appear an oversimplification. But it should make the point. When the lift
operator at your office begins telling you how he bought soya beans for
half of what they are selling at today, you'll know the reservoir of buyers
for soya beans is getting mighty low. When the office cleaners start giving
each other share tips, it's time to take a very close look at the future
prospects of the stock market. When a twelve-year-old boy begins to tell
you why you should be in the option market – as was the case in 1987 –
it's time to head for the exit, but quick! Many did just that during 1987. A
greater number – to their grief – did not.

Cocktail parties can serve a useful function, aside from the chance to
consume cocktails. During the early 1960s, before the stock market blew
itself out on yet another occasion, I was invariably among the most
popular guests at any cocktail party. Men and women would mill around,

77

asking me what was going on 'on the Street'. What did I think of the firm's latest underwriting? Did I have any good inside tips? I'm still fairly popular on the cocktail party circuit – but for a different reason. Very few people will ask me my view on the stock market, because the conversation will invariably drift in a different direction. Joe will be telling Murray about the house he bought for £30,000, which has just sold for £195,000. The old dowager who occupies her time as a dilettante will be discussing 'the wonderful development opportunities in the Hays Wharf area' where the developers are desperately trying to find investors. What was it like at the last cocktail party you went to? Did it make you wonder if there can possibly be anybody left to jump on the residential property bandwagon?

Nothing is immune from becoming the subject of a speculative bubble

---

During the seventeenth century tulips were the chosen vehicle for financial self-immolation. In the early eighteenth century, it was shares in the South Sea Company and the Mississippi Company. In the nineteenth century the selected self-destruct mechanisms for speculators were cotton, wheat, railways, canals and commercial property, along with residential property – the family home!

In a study of crashes there are two lessons of quintessential importance, if you want to avoid becoming a victim of any future crash. The first lesson you must learn is that nothing is immune from becoming the subject of a speculative bubble. Nothing! Intense speculation can break out in any country, and in anything for which there may be a reasonably ready market. The range of items which have succumbed to speculative fever is awe-inspiring: gold, silver, tulips, orange juice, salad oil, ships, railways, crude oil, farmland, building land – the list is endless. The list could also include . . . the family home!

The second lesson you must learn if you would like to become crash-averse is the criteria for the perverse crash vehicles selection process. The ideal host for a potential crash involves whatever most people at the time are willing to believe can never fall in value. This is probably the most difficult of all lessons to learn in crash avoidance therapy. It's also the most important.

In retrospect, when we look at the many people who were victims of previous crashes, we will probably come to the conclusion that these people were naive and primitive – and perhaps a little funny in the head. After all, what well-balanced and emotionally stable individual could ever conceivably stake his entire life savings on a tulip? Let me say it would be most unwise to pre-judge the issue unless you happened to be there at the time! To be objective in the decision-making process, you must be acutely aware that, when these bubbles were being inflated, they looked perfectly

78

normal and respectable to the people inflating them. In fact, the vehicles of speculative manias looked better than just 'safe and respectable'. They looked like an absolutely sure winner, one that could never, ever, fall in value – only rise. At the speculative peak, the reasons given to 'prove' such vehicles could never lose value were unshakable. Otherwise, these vehicles could never have attained the stature of host to a full-scale speculative mania to start with.

Tulips are not in fashion at the moment. Nor are railways, tobacco leaves, canary seed or canals. Is investing in any of those really any less feasible or rational than buying chunks of metal to store in a vault, or to hide under the bed as a safe haven for savings? Yet it wasn't all that long ago that people were readily able to justify investment in gold as a sure thing. Some still believe gold is the best place to keep their savings, even though gold has been relegated to the same league as copper, aluminium, wheat, coffee beans or any other commodity you might care to think of. But, early in 1980, many believed there was some formula, some intrinsic value that would keep the price of gold rising, higher and higher and higher in perpetuity. It was predicted that gold would reach 1000 dollars an ounce. Some frowned and said 2000 dollars an ounce. Two sisters in Costa Rica achieved international fame by predicting that gold would eventually reach 5000 dollars an ounce. What's more, they had a vast array of charts and statistical data to 'prove' it. The price of gold never did reach 5000 dollars an ounce – or 2000 or even 1000 for that matter. In 1981, it reached a peak of just under 900 dollars an ounce and then proceeded to lose nearly two-thirds of its value over the next two years. There was no magic in gold! No intrinsic quality which would ensure further price rises! Gold, like most things, is worth only what someone is willing to pay for it. Like beauty, value is in the eye of the beholder. And that's just as true of the family home!

What happened to gold also happened to silver, with a far greater vengeance. What happened to gold, silver, tulips, 'bubble' companies, railways and canals also happened to shares on the Stock Exchange. There is only one vehicle – we were still told – that appeared to be immune to a speculative bubble. Just about everyone at that cocktail party would agree – and that's the family home!

As Safe as Houses?

It is almost universally accepted that residential property is now the only really sound investment. Most people are 100% certain that if there ever *is* a decline in house prices, it will only be a temporary aberration. Indeed, it is difficult to find anyone of supposedly sound mind who is not totally convinced that their home will be immune not merely to inflation, but to deflation, recession, depression, the deterioration of currencies and any change or calamity that may occur in the political climate. But – guess what? That's exactly how the Dutch felt about their tulips!

There is a plethora of arguments in support of the thesis that house prices will rise forever. 'People will always need somewhere to live,' they say. 'Property is a finite commodity,' they say. 'No government would ever *allow* house prices to fall. They wouldn't dare to – it would lead to political and electoral disaster.' So many similar arguments have been advanced that I could go on for ever! There are almost as many reasons to justify the utter conviction that house prices will rise for ever, as there were for believing that shares in railroad companies would rise and rise in the latter part of the nineteenth century. . . .

The 'pent-up demand' idea is no more than the invention of the real estate salesman or property agent

---

When it comes to residential property we hear countless references to 'pent-up demand'. This is supposed to convince us that the demand for houses is increasing, ready to burst out of its cocoon. Supposedly, the fact that more people are being born than are dying means that the demand for homes must increase; and so must the price. This, as we shall see, is a sheer aberration.

An idea that has yet to make any impact on the media is that just because somebody *wants* something, it does not necessarily mean they're in a position to go out and buy it. Anybody who is actually engaged in trying to sell a house, a car or a television set isn't the slightest bit interested in statistics – like the number of people who might possibly buy that house, car or television set. All a seller really wants to know about is whether or not there are people willing and able to pay the price he is asking. You don't have to be an Einstein to work out that the more people there are who own houses, and the higher the price of those houses, the fewer people will there be who are willing and able to buy more homes. The 'pent-up demand' idea is no more than the invention of the real estate salesman or property agent. We all love to read about the good, sound reasons why our homes should continue to rise in value way out into the future. This notion, like Mogadon or Valium, helps focus our attention away from the harsh realities of life, of which history keeps reminding us.

In some respects, the choice of housing as a vehicle for a speculative mania is probably one of the most dangerous. In 1958 I bought a share called Oil Recovery. I watched it go up and up and up. I then watched it go down. I sold out as quickly as I could and managed to hold on to a reasonable chunk of the profit. The people who were caught up in Tulipomania probably did the same during the early stage of the decline, if they were clever enough. In other cases, some people were able to scrape together what was left of their profits once they had had enough. But you can't do that with a house.

Just think what happens if houses start to fall in value. All you can do – assuming you decide to sell – is put your house on the market and sit there like a nurd waiting for someone to buy it. Meanwhile, weeks – months – pass, while your house continues to fall in value. Try and tell *that*, however, to someone who has borrowed up to the hilt and has the property bit firmly clenched between his teeth!

I recently read a report in *The Times* which said, 'House prices always move up, step, by step, reaching a plateau, then move higher.' This is a delusion. It is just as fallacious as the assumption that shares in the Mississippi Company would always rise. Not only do residential property prices move up and down quite vigorously. You can see from the past that they have also fallen much faster than they have risen. A collapse in the average price of the family home is certainly not rare. Crashes in residential property values have plundered speculators, property developers and home owners for centuries in every corner of the globe. While the many arguments put forth to justify the preconception that house prices will rise in perpetuity may seem reasonable enough, history shows that residential property has not always protected its owners against inflation or depression. Nor has residential property been able to shelter its owners against political risk. The truth is that, for long periods, residential property has been a very poor form of investment.

Once you put it on the market, the family home is worth only what someone else is willing to pay for it. So long as we believe that other people will be willing to pay more than we paid, and so long as that belief is shared by the whole of the community, house prices will continue to rise. When, as a society, we suddenly reach the conclusion that house prices can rise no further, they will simply cease to rise. A house is merchandise – like a car, or food, or a toothbrush. There is no more reason to believe that

---

The family home is worth only what someone else is willing to pay for it

---

house prices will rise forever than there is to believe that – once falling – they will fall forever. Or that the price of cars, food or toothbrushes will rise forever. After all, we will always need cars, food and toothbrushes! But we shan't need them with the same degree of urgency *all the time*.

The most persuasive evidence revealing the gyrations of the house-price roller-coaster can be seen in America. When it comes to residential property bubbles, Americans look up to no one. Unlike Europe, the Americas, of course, had to be discovered, explored, developed, exploited and plundered. This process naturally led to wild outbursts of real estate mania. There is considerable documentation on calamities, booms and busts in the American housing market over the past 150 years or so. On four distinct occasions, American house prices soared to fantastic heights – during the 1830s, 1880s, 1920s and 1980s. Each upsurge looked much the same as all the others. So far, three out of the four have collapsed. The fourth is yet to do so.

A Land of Promise

The California boom of the late 1880s was a classic example of a speculative mania directed towards residential land and houses. The origins of the boom and collapse go back to the Gold Rush days of 1849 and the spread of irrigation that turned the desert land of California into Hollywood green. In the end, as speculators are ever prone to do, land and house prices were hoisted to inflated levels that could not conceivably be sustained. The California residential property bubble burst in 1889. Land prices plunged to a quarter of their peak value by the time the market stopped falling.

The real connoisseurs of American property crashes regard the Chicago land and house price boom of the late 1830s as the granddaddy of them all. That decade marked the opening up of the American West, and Chicago was the gateway to the Mid-West. It was a time when the entire nation was embued with a spirit of 'get-it-while-the-getting's-good'. Money-making was seen as a virtue – probably more so than ever before. Lying back, or simply living from inherited or unearned income of any type, was considered more than idle: it was plain unpatriotic. Economically, *laissez-faire* was the by-word. It was an anything-goes society, provided the 'anything' meant increasing one's own – and the nation's – wealth and capital! In this truly Horatio Alger age it was the ambition of every poor newsboy and bootblack to rise one day like a phoenix from the ashes and soar high above his humble station. It was bred in the bone of every youngster that he could be President one day – or if not President, at least the head of a bank or a rich cattle man.

Up until this time the attitude of the American people had been hopeful and serious, but from now on it changed to rampant optimism. The nation was growing at a truly staggering rate. Canals were carrying an increasing number of people to all points of the compass. Railroads were building up a head of steam in readiness to span the entire American continent. The invention of labour-saving machinery was enabling goods to be produced more cheaply and in greater abundance, increasing the wealth of the entire nation.

The Monroe Doctrine of 1823 had signalled to the world that America was for the Americans, and it induced a surge of nationalism that continued to sweep the country for over a decade. During the 1830s America opened the gates wide for immigration. Thousands poured into

82

the land of golden opportunity; they too, maybe, could try their hand at rising from new immigrant to Governor of the state, or railroad magnate, or just the owner of a small factory. Factory owners themselves had a ready supply of fresh labour to do their bidding, to churn out more and more goods; to make the business grow – and so increase their wealth.

President Andrew Jackson was boosting the common man, persuading him to hoist himself into the driver's seat. He allowed the state bank printing presses to turn out banknotes in ever-increasing quantities, and soon new banking institutions sprang up like weeds in every city and small town. Corporations in which ordinary people could buy shares also took on a new meaning. The public clamoured to clamber aboard the business bandwagon, forcing the brokerage offices to use strong-arm squads to fight off the angry crowds of would-be investors when there were no more shares for sale. This was no rare occurrence; it happened frequently.

The 1830s were also the time when a buoyant, boastful, bearded, keen-eyed, happy-go-lucky man appeared atop a magnificent piece of horseflesh that would take him from city to city in the Mid-West. He would raise his voice in jovial song – rude and raunchy as the roads, its volume silenced only when there was an opportunity to take a pot shot at a quail or some prairie chickens. When he approached his destination he would dismount and don a clean, stiff-collared starched shirt, affixing a great diamond at the neck in lieu of a cravat. A swallow-tailed coat of the very latest cut would complete his striking ensemble. He would then canter into town with a whoop and a flourish, stopping in front of the post office or hotel. The pop-eyed townsfolk would rush forward to gather round this colourful figure, who would hand out gaudy handbills before embarking on his never-failing spiel. Humour and anecdote were slickly interwoven with statistics and subtle warnings against pimples, black-heads, rashes and sores. In those days cancer was the curse of the countryside, along with other less serious maladies. But the special elixir offered by this imposing spellbinder at 2 dollars a bottle would take care of all that.

William Avery Rockefeller could reel off yarns that would cause bystanders in a bar to roll on the floor with laughter

---

That certainly wasn't the only business enterprise of 'Dr' William A. Rockefeller, as his card styled him. He would trade horses, shoot at marks, run competition races, engage in wrestling matches or offer himself in any competition whatever provided a cash prize was involved. He was a winner, and would usually be seen walking away from the contest with wads of dollar bills clenched in his bear-like fist. A raconteur of the highest order, he could reel off yarns that would cause bystanders in a bar to roll on the floor with laughter. He had no particular weakness for alcohol, but wallowed in every other available vice. Everywhere he went, women loved him. He also loved women.

From this very amiable and likeable sinner John D. Rockefeller was to gain his earliest knowledge of business principles. For this horse-trading, gambling, sport-loving quack doctor was the father of the great John D., oil magnate *extraordinaire*.

America was indeed the land of opportunity in the 1830s. It was the era when Nicholas Biddle was to rise to prominence as the most powerful banker in America. The Second Bank of the United States was authorized in 1817. However, after its first two years in operation it was issuing banknotes by the cartload – and while gold reserves were being drained into the bargain. The United States was supposed to be on the Gold Standard at the time, but the gold backing for the currency was illusory. Between 1817 and 1822 the American monetary system was in a state of wild disorder. The second President of the bank, Langdon Cheeves, was brought in to clean up. By 1823 he had restored the bank's capital and made it ready for the autocratic hand of Nicholas Biddle to create the powerful institution that it became in the 1830s. Biddle ruled the money world with an iron hand, dazzling the men of his time with his abilities and personality.

President Jackson feared the bank, because money is power and that much financial power in the hands of an outsider who was not part of the government and not directly responsible to the President was obviously unnerving. Jackson therefore decided to wage war on it. This was the background to the Chicago land and residential property boom that was beginning to take hold in the early 1830s.

The Chicago Boom

It was in this decade that the great cities of the Mid-West were built, and Chicago became their hub. What made it possible – as so often – was a revolution in transportation. These were still early days in the development of the American railroads, but the canals were already busily transforming life in the north-east. The one that had the greatest impact on Chicago was the Illinois Michigan Canal. By linking Chicago, on the shores of Lake Michigan, with the Illinois River – which joined the great Mississippi at St Louis – it created the greatest waterway network in the world. It joined the Great Lakes to the St Lawrence River, and opened up a great swathe of territory stretching all the way down to New Orleans and the Gulf of Mexico. Chicago was the axis of this colossal network, the depot for the cattle of the prairies, the grain of the Mid-West, the lumber of the great pine forests of Michigan and Wisconsin, and – not least – the minerals of Illinois and Missouri. Here was a real estate man's dream.

84

A well-known journalist of the day, Harriet Martineau, visited Chicago in 1836 and recorded this description: 'Chicago looks raw and bare, standing on the high prairie above the lake shore. . . . A friend of mine who resides there had told me that we would find the inns intolerable, at the period of the great land sales, which bring a concourse of speculators to the place.' She had never seen a busier place than Chicago was at the time of her arrival. The streets were crowded with land speculators, hurrying from one sale to another. A Negro dressed in scarlet, carrying a scarlet flag and riding a white horse caparisoned in scarlet, announced the times of the sales:

> At every street corner where he stopped, the crowd flocked around him; and it seemed as if some prevalent mania infected the whole people. . . . As the gentlemen of our party walked the streets, store-keepers hailed them from their doors, with offers of farms and all manner of land lots, advising them to speculate before the price of land rose higher. . . . [A] friend had realised, in two years, ten times as much money as he had before fixed upon as a competence for life.

Others, she wrote, besides lawyers and speculators were making a fortune: 'A poor man at Chicago had pre-emptions to some land, for which he paid in the morning one hundred and fifty dollars. In the afternoon, he sold it to a friend of mine for five thousand dollars.'

The way even the most cynical observers could be drawn into the fray is illustrated by the case of William B. Ogden, who came to Chicago in the middle of the decade to look after the affairs of a relative who had bought a plot for 100,000 dollars. On seeing the grim site he wrote back archly, 'You have been guilty of the grossest folly.' He then compounded his deceit by selling a third of the plot for the full 100,000 dollars purchase price, which he pocketed. His discomfiture – or was it a trace of remorse –

West of the Alleghenies the banks were printing money just as quickly as it was demanded

---

showed through in his next letter: 'There is no such value in the land, and won't be for a generation.' Little did he know how true his forecast would prove to be. But he was to be hooked all right; and after his blinding light conversion his ardour was as keen as St Paul's. In no time he opened a real estate office, built a block-sized mansion in the centre of town, and was elected Chicago's first mayor in 1837.

In the meantime, the battle between President Johnson and Nicholas Biddle was raging. Jackson declared that the Second Bank of the United States under Biddle's direction had failed to establish a sound currency, since speculation was rife, particularly in Chicago. Between 1829 and

1837 the number of bank loans had jumped fivefold and the number of banks in the United States had increased from 329 to 788. Notes in issue maintained a parallel buoyancy as the printing presses hummed. The value of banknotes in circulation jumped from 60 million dollars to nearly 150 million dollars between 1830 and 1837.

Land sales reached the unheard of pinnacle of 25 million dollars in 1836, driven solely by the availability of easy credit and copious amounts of banknotes. Property in Chicago – whether factories, office buildings, farmland or residential property – ceased to have any investment merit whatever, and became no more than a speculation. People purchased land and houses for no other purpose than to sell them to someone else, at a later date, at a higher price. This meant that the buyers were not at all interested in whether or not they were getting value for money, or if there was an intrinsic potential in what they were buying. All that mattered was their ability to find someone willing to pay them more.

Hunger for property speculation obviously led to hunger for the fuel of property speculation, namely money. Gold- and silver-backed currencies were fairly plentiful in the seaboard cities, but west of the Alleghenies the banks were printing money on their presses just as quickly as it was demanded. The only currencies with a silver or gold backing were Spanish milled dollars and other foreign coins. New money was being churned out daily in the form of currency notes. The only form of control that seemed to operate was demand – the actual demand for currency was the sole factor which determined how much should be printed. There were 634 American banks printing notes; and they had loaned 525 million dollars worth of these notes. The gold backing for all this paper amounted to a mere 35 million dollars – a position which was steadily weakening.

The great financial question of the time was the fight over the Second Bank of the United States – Jackson versus Biddle. It has often been thought that the demise of the Second Bank was the cause of the panic.

The actual demand for currency was the sole factor
which determined how much should be printed

This remains an open question, since no one knows what would have happened had Biddle remained in control of the nation's finances. The country was divided on the subject, and the animosity between the two rivals split the banking gurus of Wall Street into two camps.

By all accounts it would appear that President Jackson wanted to close the Second Bank under any pretext. The notion that Biddle had failed to establish a sound monetary system seems to have been a ruse. Jackson vetoed the renewal of the bank's charter; and Biddle, who was not to be outdone – even by the President of the United States – countered by divorcing the bank from the sponsorship of federal government, subsequently obtaining a charter from the Commonwealth of Pennsylvania. No longer subject to the restraints of federal government or the dictatorial hand of the President, he was now able to expand the activities of the bank quite considerably.

Biddle was particularly interested in property speculation in Chicago. The bank's enormous assets were directed to that area, as were those of many other bankers who were to follow in Biddle's footsteps. The Chicago property boom then took on even more spectacular dimensions. The non-chartering of the Second United States Bank in 1836 led to a renewed banknote orgy involving nearly every bank in the nation. This was coupled with widespread speculation directed towards Chicago, which was held to be the 'best game in town'.

Then came the coup de grâce *endemic to all booms,
delivered by the usual source – the government*

The flames of the property mania were fuelled by the seemingly bottomless pit of bank credit drawn on by the hordes of unregulated banks, which by then were opening by the bucket-shop full. Often these banks operated from ramshackle huts and from the rear of post offices. But to the people of Chicago it just didn't matter. After all, wasn't the future of America – and of Chicago – ensured by the Illinois Michigan Canal and the railroads?

The mania in Chicago was at its height when the earth-moving equipment came rolling down the streets of the Windy City on Independence Day, 4 July 1836, to celebrate the grand opening of the canal. In fact, it was at just about this time that the Chicago property boom reached its peak. If there was any one day that marked the very summit of the mania, that was it! The summer froth was already off the boil in the East. The bull market in shares on Wall Street had been looking tired for the best part of the year. The strain in the financial system was beginning to show throughout the nation. Then came the *coup de grâce* that seems to be endemic to all booms, delivered by the usual source – the government.

In 1836, President Jackson – killjoy that he was! – publicly condemned the rush for land and residential property. On his instructions a circular was issued, demanding that payment for all land and property be made only in fully gold-backed notes. He prohibited the deposit of federal revenues in Biddle's banks and in others in that camp, restricting the distribution of government revenues to those state banks seen to be in line with his edicts.

Jackson's move quickly cooled the ardour of the land and property speculators, while striking a severe blow to confidence in the United States currency, some of which was gold-backed, though most of it wasn't. The situation was further complicated by credit strains in Britain, resulting in the calling-in of loans from those Americans who were borrowing in London to finance their property ventures at home. Several important British mercantile houses in England went bankrupt towards the end of 1836. Britain was also driven to cutting back on her imports of cotton from the United States, thereby depressing the American cotton industry.

The Chicago Crash

The Chicago boom, like the season, turned from summer to fall, and then to winter. In 1837 it finally broke down, precipitating a terrible crash. The inevitable panic erupted with brutal suddenness on Friday, 17 March 1837. The combination of extended credit and cutbacks in order books caused many of the major cotton mercantile houses of New Orleans to fail. Their losses were staggering. Nearly one-fifth of New Orleans bankers instantly became insolvent, and the entire commerce of the city came to a standstill. Its indebtedness, comprising the liabilities of cotton factories and land speculation, reached approximately 200 million dollars – an almost unimaginable level in those days. New Orleans banks were forced to suspend payments. The result was utter, uncontrollable chaos in the money markets.

The bank failures mounted. There was a stampede to buy gold wherever it could be found. Silver also was in demand. Coinage with a silver or gold content disappeared from circulation. All this served to increase the widespread alarm, and financial distress engulfed the whole of America. The entire Southern states were virtually bankrupt. Nine-tenths of the merchants of Mobile, Alabama were forced to close down every one of their operations.

Adding further to the financial maelstrom, there was a collapse of property values in Chicago, where speculation had been more intense than in any other region of the United States. Individuals who at one time could have repaid their debts twenty times over were also failing, largely because gold-backed currency was the order of the day. Credit could not be raised even on residential real estate – the unassailable family home! Chicago bankers were forced to suspend payments. Riots threatened and the state militia was called out.

> The year 1837 will ever be remembered as the era of the protested notes; it was the harvest of the notary and the lawyer – the year of wrath to the mercantile. . . . Misery inscribed itself on many a face but lately radiant with high hopes. . . . Broken fortunes, blasted hopes, aye, and blighted characters; these were the legitimate offspring of those pestilent times. The land resounded with the groans of ruined men, and the sobs of defrauded women, who had entrusted their all to the greedy speculators. . . . It was a scene of woe and desolation.

So wrote Joseph Balestier. The year went down in history as one of the truly great panics – the Panic of 1837. The Chicago Property Crash sent a wave of default rippling throughout the financial system of the East. Wall Street sank into the worst bear market ever experienced up to that time. Over seven dire, lean years the stock market index sank to less than a fifth of its peak value, back to the levels of thirty years before. So much for all the intervening prosperity. The depression of the 1840s was to cast a blight over the middle of the entire century.

As for Chicago property prices, fewer records are kept in hard times than in palmy days! But one individual incident tells the whole tale: a land lot which sold for 11,000 dollars an acre in 1836 would not fetch 100 dollars in 1840. In 1841, Nicholas Biddle revealed that out of pre-crash assets of 74 million dollars – mostly in property – the bank could exhibit no more than 12 million dollars. Accordingly, the bank closed down.

Different Crashes, Same Lesson

The crash of property values in Chicago happened over 150 years ago. The crash of property values in California took place over 100 years ago. As you look at the four walls of your little semi-detached and reflect upon your mortgage payments, you may wish to console yourself by assuming that these are two isolated examples in history, which could have only happened in America during the nineteenth century. If you do that, you're guilty of ignorance or self-delusion – maybe both.

Crashes in property values have happened before and since, and not only in America. In 1773 there was a crash in property values in Britain. In 1838 there was a crash in building land throughout France. In 1870 there was a property crash in Germany. In the 1890s a crash in property values hit Britain again. In his paper 'Urban Land and Building Prices', published in the *Estates Gazette*, E. A. Vallis put the average price of residential land in 1899 at £900 an acre. By 1904 the price had fallen to £130 an acre, a decline of 85% in five years. Presumably the price of the family home bears some relationship to the price of the land it is sitting on.

Besides the crash in property values in Chicago and California in the nineteenth century, one of the most notable of all property crashes happened only sixty years ago. The twenties in the United States were the consumer boom years, the years of the so-called Coolidge Prosperity. A state of mind was developing among Americans not unlike that seen during the 1830s. It was a time when the American Dream began to surface and President Coolidge promised the nation a chicken in every pot. America was a place to live the good life and own your own home – if you were willing to work towards that objective.

From 1919 to 1921 American had been in the grip of a business recession, as were most other countries. After the post-World War I recession had spent its force, and prosperity began to peek over the horizon, subtle changes started to be seen. By 1925 the Roaring Twenties were in full swing. As often during prosperous times, there was a widespread – though only half-acknowledged – revolt against the very urbanization and industrialization responsible for that prosperity. People were yearning to leave the routine standardization and smoky urban congestion upon which the Coolidge Prosperity had been founded.

Living standards were to reap the enormous benefits of the wealth generated by the car industry in America's Mid-West, further enriched by the 'Black Gold' gushing steadily from the Oklahoma oilfields in the south-east. As personal wealth increased, so too did disposable income to be spent on luxuries and to fulfil the desire for endless leisure. An increasing number of Americans who had worked hard during the earlier years of the Roaring Twenties wanted to enjoy the fruits of their labour and submerge themselves in a never-never land that combined baseball and football with comfort and old-world glamour – a Monte Carlo that had bathtubs with stainless steel taps and colonial kitchens; a hacienda on the beach with an eighteen-hole golf course; President Coolidge's voice on the wireless to comfort them; the Ziegfeld Follies to entertain them . . . and a place of investment opportunity which could support them.

Was there such a wondrous place within the continental limits of the United States of America? If not, the inventive genius of the American entrepreneur could be relied on to manufacture it.

A Place in the Sun

There is a dream that assails people in northern climes. Combined with the promise of easy riches, it is sure to stupefy their critical faculties and erode all resistance. That dream is 'the life in the sun'. When Americans marched West in their hundreds of thousands to southern California in the 1880s, it was in quest of that dream. The dream became a pipe-dream – a bubble pipe. When the bubble burst, so did the dream. The people who participated in the boom and bust of the California hiatus were primarily those able to gain ready access to the territory. For many on the Eastern seaboard, California was simply too far away. With memories of both the Chicago property crash and the Californian property crash taking their place in the annals of history, many in the East began to focus on Florida as the place most likely to match the promise of their dreams. Moreover, for Easterners Florida was comparatively close. Its climate was sub-tropical, promising lush vegetation and exotic fruits. Florida was blessed with an immense coastline. At the turn of the decade it was attracting a steady flow of settlers. As the developers proceeded to tame the swamps, the state began to attract a wealthier, more affluent set. These were the well-to-do who sought – and could afford – the pleasure of yachting, big game fishing and the like, along with the delights of an urban civilization that was rapidly taking shape in Miami. As the number of visitors rose, so did the price of residential property.

Like the many speculative epidemics that have occurred in the past, the property boom that ultimately took hold on Florida during the 1920s was slow to start. As with previous property price explosions, a sub-stratum of good sense lay beneath what would eventually become a mania. In the beginning, there were many sound reasons for property investment in Florida. Since 1896 there had been a rail link between Florida and the

---

There is a dream that assails people in northern climes – 'the life in the sun'

---

great northern cities, which made it relatively accessible. The 1920s produced a boom in the number of automobiles on the road. The completion of the Dixie Highway brought the Sunshine State even closer than ever. There also seemed to be a demographic bulge in the number of people reaching retirement age, and deciding to take advantage of the fact, during the 1920s. Florida had an irresistible appeal for those who had spent endless working winters as snowbound residents of New York or Chicago or St Louis.

Prohibition gave Florida added lustre. Only a few miles offshore lay Cuba and the Bahamas, where bootleggers and bathtub gin were unknown. Those so inclined could drink themselves into total oblivion wherever and whenever they liked. Even the Florida-born natives felt the exotic aura attached to these islands just out of reach of the US Customs' patrol boats.'

Rich soil and a good climate made Florida extremely attractive to citrus fruit growers, who were among the first to move in and buy large tracts of land for farming. During the early 1920s farmland was still cheap and could be acquired for just a few dollars an acre. Farmers saw this land as the route to good living at low cost. Developers saw a growing need for vacation residences and retirement homes. They set out to develop the virgin land in the hope of receiving a reasonable return on their investment. Yet others had more modest ambitions: they simply saw Florida as a nice place to live, and moved south to enjoy whatever the Sunshine State had to offer. They bought homes – and the occasional plot of land as an investment. Property prices in Florida started to move up quite sharply until something like a boom began to appear. Suddenly Florida became more than just a nice place to put down roots and earn a reasonable living. Florida became synonymous with the promise of easy riches, a prospect which replaced more basic considerations.

Golconda, now a ruin, was once a famous city in south-east Asia.

There, according to legend, everyone who passed through the city left with great riches. As we shall see, the American genius for promotion ensured that a similar illusion was skilfully created and associated with Florida during the 1920s.

The writer T. H. Weigall had been told while he was in London that a big story was breaking in the state of Florida. By the time his liner reached New York from Southampton on 21 August 1925 he was convinced that what was happening in Florida must be the hottest story of the day. Weigall's New York contacts whisked him off to see the outstanding feature of New York night life in the 1920s – the Ziegfeld Follies. On stage

---

A giant technicolour sky-sign with elegant couples
lolling in gondolas – American-style

---

in the first act was the great comedian Will Rogers. The butt of his slow-speaking, homely wit was the flashly razzamatazz of Florida, and the great fortunes being made there by property speculators. During the second act, an entire sketch was devoted to the delights of the steamy 'Bam-Bam-Bammy Shore' of Biscayne Bay, Florida – 'The Eternal Summer Paradise Where Work Is No More'. Just one well-planned investment was all it would take, the sketch promised. After that, anyone in the audience who decided to take the plunge could escape into a world of sybaritic idleness. They could once and for all turn their backs on the stern Puritan principles of their upbringing, which maintained that leisure had to be earned by a lifetime of toil.

This was the picture of Florida that T. H. Weigall found portrayed in the newspapers, in the theatre, on the wireless – everywhere. On the corner of Fifth Avenue and 42nd Street was a giant technicolour sky-sign depicting every half-educated man's idea of a tropical seashore paradise, with elegant couples lolling in gondolas, drifting gently down invisible canals against a glittering backdrop of Mediterranean castles in the sky – American-style.

Weigall decided the very next day to get himself down to Florida. But it was not that easy: the Clyde Steamship Company could not give him a booking for another month. 'Take the train,' suggested the booking clerk, and Weigall managed to secure a seat on the Southern Express, packed with would-be investors heading for the 'Gold Coast', dreaming their dreams and swopping get-rich-quick stories.

Indirectly, Henry Ford too contributed to the Florida land boom, for the Model T made the state accessible to the average family. They travelled the roads in their thousands, seeking to escape from the foggy north-eastern states and the bone-freezing winters of the Mid-West. An article by Gertrude Shelby in *Harper's Magazine* of January 1926 described the scene as a migration like the pilgrimage of army ants or the seasonal flights of myriads of blackbirds. . . . A broken down truck one day stopped a friend of mine. . . . [He counted] license plates . . . from eighteen different states, from Massachusetts to Oregon. Most of the cars brimmed over with mother, father, several children and the dog, enticed by three years of insidious publicity about the miracles of Florida land values.

Insidious publicity? In a more reserved age, we can only stare in incredulity at some of the grosser examples of 1920s' hype. But apparently they worked. *Only Yesterday*, by Frederick Lewis Allen, must be the best available account of the Florida boom. And it shows that the author had a nice feel for the wilder flings of kitsch:

So to Florida — Where enterprise is enthroned — Where you sit and watch at twilight the fronds of graceful palm, latticed against the fading gold of the sun-kissed sky — Where sun, moon and stars, at eventide, stage a welcome constituting the glorious galaxy of the firmament — Where the whispering breeze springs fresh from the lap of the Caribbean and woos with elusive cadence like unto a mother's lullaby — Where the silver cycle is heaven's Cavalier, and the full orbit its glorious pendant.

That, Allen points out, was written by a bank vice-president. The dream-mongering was necessary in one way, for the well-known disadvantage of Florida is that it mostly comprises unlovely swamp-land — where alligators can be even more rapacious than the real estate salesmen.

Miami Beach was one big mangrove swamp. Then a man named Carl Fisher came along, cleared the trees and covered the place with five feet of sand. Lovingly, Fisher created lagoons and islands; built hotels; and reportedly made 40 million dollars selling plots. Over on the west coast of Florida, Davis Island had been no more than two small outcrops of

---

'So to Florida. . . . Where the silver cycle is heaven's Cavalier, and the full orbit its glorious pendant'

---

mangrove, barely visible at high tide. But that was before C. P. Davis built up an island of sand, complete with paved roads and the customary hotel and villa developments. Of course, the sale of the lots — which raised 3 million dollars on the first day — began before the dredgers had moved a single scoop of sand.

Then there was the city of Coral Gables. George Merrick, son of a retired Congregational minister, had added to the land inherited from his father around the many-gabled house of coral rock near Miami, which gave the place its name. Merrick was busy creating 'America's Most

Beautiful Suburb', with lagoons and yacht marinas fashioned out of the swamps. By 1925 there were two thousand houses along the shady street, all built in what he called a 'modified Mediterranean' style. Coral Gables had a bustling business centre with schools, banks and hotels. The country club sported two eighteen-hole golf courses. The Miami Biltmore Hotel boasted twenty-six storeys. Merrick alone was responsible for the Venetian theme, with canals, real gondolas and gondoliers.

As so often in American business schemes, God was on the side of the Florida pioneers. George Merrick had hired William Jennings Bryan, the famous preacher who used to thunder against the evils of Darwinism. Sitting under his parasol on a raft in a lagoon, Bryan preached the glories of God's sunshine. Afterwards came dancing by the beautiful Gilda Grey.

The financing of both development and sales would be called 'creative' today

---

These developments gave Florida a good name – and more unscrupulous developers the opportunity to spoil it. 'Prospects' is an interesting word used to describe the speculators who came to Florida, found the place of their dreams, and made their fortune in real estate investment. It denotes targets for the real estate agents who were present in stupefying numbers. According to the state census, the population of Miami numbered 75,000 in 1925, as against 30,000 in 1920. And according to contemporary estimates it contained 25,000 real estate agents in that year. The 'prospects', however, were numbered in hundreds of thousands – even millions, by some accounts. There was no shortage of ripe pickings for speculating property dealers.

It required some imagination to see the home of your dreams emerging from a small plot of swamp with the steel skeleton of a skyscraper towering over it. But the new arrivals were soon caught up in the frenzied spirit of speculation that had taken fire in 1924 and was ablaze by mid-1925. The stories of extravagant profits inflated them all. There was the plot near the city bought for 25 dollars by a poor woman back in 1896, which she sold for 150,000 dollars in 1925. Before the boom a New York lawyer turned down a bid of 240,000 dollars for a strip in Palm Beach. In 1923 he accepted 600,000 dollars for it. In 1924 it was broken up and sold for an aggregate of 1.5 million dollars. And in 1925 it was valued at 4 million dollars.

The financing of both development and sales would be called 'creative' today. The trick in the case of large projects was to get the development incorporated as a 'city'. It was then financed by tax-free municipal bonds sold to the public – in New York as like as not. The buyer, meanwhile, could secure a lot with a 10% down payment or 'reservation'. But these lots were not for developing – they were for buying and selling. The big market was in 'binders', which gave the holder the right to purchase the selected property at a future date for only a tiny down payment. The trick was to sell them on before the first payment of principal – 25% of the sale price – became due in thirty days' time. So it didn't matter too much if the land fell a bit short of prime-site status. An increasing measure of 'developers' licence' was allowed in the property prospectuses as time went by, particularly in the matter of location. Sunny 'Melbourne Gardens' was approached – though rarely reached – through prairie muck land, with a few trees and clumps of palmetto, by some hopeful prospects. 'Promoter vision' was fair game also. Manhattan Estates was 'not more than three-fourths of a miles from the prosperous and fast-growing city of Nettie'. Well, Nettie was neither prosperous nor was it a city. It was the name of an abandoned turpentine camp. But with good promotion and a fair wind it might have grown into a prosperous city – some day!

Miami became 'The World's Playground' and 'The Fair White Goddess of Cities'; Fort Lauderdale was 'The Tropical Wonderland'; Orlando 'The City Beautiful'. The timing of Weigall's visit was a fortuitous one, for the boom was at its peak in the high summer of 1925. A dip in railway visitors that autumn, and a pause in the pace of price increases, suggested a slight fading in momentum. The mayors of Miami, Miami Beach and Coral Gables responded nobly with a plan for a pageant whose highlight would be a flower-boat 'depicting in Floral Loveliness the Blessing Bestowed upon us by the Friendly Sun, Gracious Rain, and Soothing Tropic Wind'.

The Florida Property Crash

In the late summer of this year Gertrude Shelby claims to have quizzed over ninety citizens about the durability of the boom. Almost all replied that it would be good for at least another four or five years. The corporate plan of Seaboard Air Line Railway looked even further ahead; its president forecast the population of Miami at one million within ten years. Finally the Governor of Florida, John W. Martin, set the official seal on the boom with his declaration that 'Marvellous as is the wonder-story of Florida's recent achievements, these are but heralds of the dawn.'

The dawn came early in the New Year. At first, the hectic pace of development showed no signs of slowing. In fact, it accelerated. Building materials which had been held up by congestion in the ports and lack of cargo capacity suddenly came through in a rush. The previous summer, a visitor to West Palm Beach had noticed a mound of crated bathtubs on an empty lot. The site, he was told, was to be occupied by 'one of the most magnificent apartment buildings in the South', but only the bathtubs had arrived. Unfortunately, as the number of end game ceremonies increased, the final buyers, who would push prices higher, seemed a bit reluctant to show themselves. For some inexplicable reason, 'America's wealthiest sportsmen, devotees of Yachting and other expensive sports' were not stepping forward. The 'world of large affairs, smart society and leisured ease' seemed content to pursue its affairs and its ease elsewhere, scaling down their purchases of Florida property.

This caused a problem for the speculators who were holding binders in the hope of instant and lucrative resale. As the market evaporated, holders of binders had no option but to pay the next instalment or go into default. A seasonal revival in the spring helped a little, with rail traffic picking up. There was talk of a healthy breathing space. Also Wall Street was booming; clearly a good proportion of the windfall stock market gains

---

Two hurricanes that summer 'showed what a Soothing Tropic Wind could do when it got a running start from the West Indies'

---

would be earmarked for a place in the Florida sun. Mischievous tongues suggested that Wall Street offered a better game for speculators than Florida – now that the gloss was off the boom – but they were dismissed; evidently they were hoping to pick up land bargains if there was a temporary dip in prices. Still, there was no denying that things weren't as busy in the summer of 1926 as in the previous season. Rail passenger traffic – of course, that was the way the riff-raff travelled – was down by nearly half.

It is interesting to speculate what would have happened to the Florida boom without the hurricanes. Yes, that summer providence saw fit to test the mettle of the speculators with two hurricanes which, as Frederick Allen put it, 'showed what a Soothing Tropic Wind could do when it got a running start from the West Indies'. The second of these hurricanes was no joke – it struck the very epicentre of the boom, Miami. Hitting the Gold Coast early in the morning of 18 September 1926, it piled the waters of Biscayne Bay into the lovely Venetian developments, deposited a five-masted steel schooner high in the street of Coral Gables, tossed big steam yachts upon the avenues of Miami, picked up trees, lumber, pipes, tiles, debris and even small cars and sent them crashing into the houses. The terrible wind left 400 dead, some 6300 injured, 50,000 homeless, and thousands of dwellings roofless. On the reluctant admission of an official at Seaboard Air Line, 17–18,000 people were in dire need of assistance. His resistance was due to his worry that the publicity associated with a call for Red Cross funds would do more permanent damage to Florida than could be offset by the benefit derived from the money.

He was right to worry. The subsequent crash in property values was a desolate affair. Immediately after the hurricane Florida property became unsaleable. Defaults then began in earnest, guaranteed by the system of binders and partial down payments. When a speculator failed to get paid for his last sale, he was obliged to default on the original purchase, a situation which often created long strings of default. Sometimes the chain led right back to the original landowner, whose title went back to before the boom. And parallel to the buying chain was a lending chain of banks – with equally disastrous consequences.

In one case a farmer had sold a plot of useless land in 1925 for 12 dollars an acre. Then he had to kick himself as he saw the land sold on and reaching 60 dollars an acre. But after the hurricanes, the entire series of sales ran into a chain default which put the property back in the hands of the farmer. He had never received full payment for his original sale. Just as well, perhaps – he might have bought land with it. Sometimes the property came back to the original owner with exotically named streets and pavements and street lights. The irony was that this rendered it near-useless for the one thing the land was good for – orange groves. Sometimes taxes and assessments easily exceeded the value of the plot, and the property landed in the hands of the hard-pressed municipality.

Yet as late as October 1926, when two hurricanes had battered the state of Florida unmercifully while values were already causing a state-wide panic, the *Wall Street Journal*, among others, stubbornly insisted that the Florida property boom was going to continue. The 'slight hiccough' in the property market was described as only a 'temporary affair'.

The truth was that practically everyone who had any property interest whatever in Florida after the market peak in 1925 was totally wiped out, if that interest was the result of borrowed money. Even those who took out mortgages for as little as 10%, the prevailing purchase price, found that their entire 90% stake had been wiped out and the lenders were clamouring for what remained of the 10% that had been advanced. In some cases, residential property prices fell by more than 90% from their peak values. In certain areas, Florida properties were unwanted and unsaleable at any price.

'Traversing a city in the grip of death'

The collapse in the economy of Florida was remarkably swift. Banks failed throughout the state. The crisis was particularly severe in Miami, where everything had previously been described in the most flowing superlatives. Bank clearings for the city, which had soared to over 1 billion dollars at the time of the peak in property values, slumped to just one quarter of that figure in the two years following the end of the Florida property boom. By 1928 the figures halved again, to 143 million dollars. In 1927 Homer Vanderblue, when visiting Miami, described it as a 'ghost town'. The opulent real estate offices in the city's main thoroughfares were nearly all closed and boarded up, rapidly showing signs of dilapidation. The few hotels that remained were empty. Merchandise sat on the shelves of shops that were also empty. A description of the outskirts of Miami in 1928 in *The Nation* caught the bleakness of the scene: 'Dead sub-divisions line the highway, their pompous names half-obliterated on crumbling stucco gates. Lonely white-way lights stand guard over miles of cement sidewalks, where grass and palmetto take the place of homes that were to be . . . whole sections of the outlying sub-divisions are composed of unoccupied houses, past which one speeds on broad thoroughfares as if traversing a city in the grip of death.'

'A lot of very ordinary toads'

The cruellest cut of all was the way the rest of the nation was still booming. Such had been the public success of George Merrick's Venetian theme at Coral Gables that it was copied on Long Island, in two locations. 'To live in American Venice', gushed the blurb, 'is to quaff the very wine of life.' The other effort, with its 'artistic system of canals and waterways', was called Biltmore Shores, echoing the Miami Biltmore hotel.

With the collapse of the Florida bubble, the Venetian theme, the lagoons and the rest brought painful memories and the hasty modification of marketing plans. The bonds of the city of Coral Gables went into default in July 1930. Its fate points to the despondent reality of the Florida crash: that there was no revival whatever in the fortunes of the tropical paradise before the slump.

The bank failures came thickest and fastest in 1928 and 1929. In those two years, the deficits of the failing Florida banks were higher than those of any other state of America. There were no automatic bail-outs in those days: it was each bank for itself. And by mid-1930 no fewer than twenty-five cities, including Miami, were in default on their bonds. Twenty-six Florida banks had already failed. The Great Depression meant there were more to come.

If you have been mesmerized by the property boom of the last few decades or so, here is a thought that you might wish to consider: if you've been in a poker game for half an hour and you still don't know who the patsy is – you're the patsy! Conventional wisdom has it that residential property values always rise in the long run. So does hot air! But sometimes the run can be so long that most of us are dead. It took Florida property prices forty years to return to the peak values of 1925, the long, steady rise in the rate of inflation notwithstanding. An epitaph applicable to all the property booms in history was furnished by the astute Theodore S. van Dyke, who in *Millionaire for a Day* described the wreckage that followed the Californian property crash of the 1880s: 'We were a lot of very ordinary toads, whirled up by cyclones until we thought we were eagles, sailing with our own wings in the topmost domes of heaven.'

6

The Crash of the German Mark

How investors lost fortunes while the German stock
market rose by 50 billion times in three years, and
millionaires could not afford the price of a loaf of
bread

Double Standards

Sometimes it is difficult to avoid developing a split personality about some
aspects of life. Most of us love to see rising values. What joy when we learn
how our lovely little semi-detached, three up, two down, is now worth
twenty times what we had originally paid for it. On paper, many people
are now worth more than their wildest dreams of avarice a decade or so
ago. The explosive rise in house prices over the past fifteen years has
allowed millions of people to live in better neighbourhoods without
moving.

But there is another side to the coin. Although we like rising values,
none of us is all that keen on seeing the price of our daily newspaper
double, or on finding – no matter how hard we try – that our well-planned
family budget won't stretch far enough. In our schizophrenia, we like to
see the price of oil rise if we're holding shares in an oil company, but we
certainly don't like to pay twice what we paid a few years ago to fill the
tank of the family car. If we're speculating in the futures market we're
delighted to see a big jump in the price of wheat when we learn that a
storm has wiped out a harvest. We're not so enthusiastic when we find
that the rise in the price of wheat has been translated into higher prices for
most food in the shops. There is also a darker side to the massive rise in
house prices. Our delight at the increase in value of our home is often
tarnished when we find that maintenance and repair bills are double or
treble what we paid a few years ago, due to the rising cost of building
materials and labour.

The phenomenon I have been discussing is, of course, our old enemy
inflation. It means rising prices. But the term inflation is somewhat of an
abstraction. The value of an apple and what an apple gives you don't

increase because the price of apples goes up; neither do the value of your home and what your home provides. The *utility* value of your car, your clothes, your jewellery and all your other possessions is virtually the same as it would have been thirty or forty years ago. The increase in the price of these items has not increased their true worth. Essentially, what has happened is that the value of the money you receive for the fruits of your labours has declined.

Money is a loose synonym for wealth, but it is really only one form of wealth. In addition to the money you have in your pocket and in the bank, your wealth also exists in other forms – your car, your house, your

---

People confuse wealth with value

---

furniture, your clothes, the items you may collect as a hobby, the food in your fridge, insurance policies, shares and so on. Anything you own that is of any value, to you or to someone else, constitutes part of your wealth. But people confuse wealth with value. Most of your wealth is actually decreasing in value all of the time (unless of course it acquires 'antique' status). The car you bought eighteen months ago will have a lower value than the identical make and model bought today, because it's had eighteen months' wear and tear on engine, body and so on. If you buy a three-piece suite tomorrow for £1500 and get tired of it a week later, nobody is going to pay you as much for it as you gave in the first place.

Enormous volatility occurs in the value of money – what money will buy. The value of money determines things like the number of shares you can purchase, or the extent to which you may spend on your art collection. If money crashes, then everything you own becomes worthless in monetary terms. A crash in the value of money is one of the worst disasters that can hit a society. Since the prices of goods and services, contracts and obligations of all types are quoted in currency, if that currency becomes valueless the foundation of society itself will disintegrate. Grocers won't sell food, farmers won't grow produce, workers won't work. Why should any of those people perform any of those tasks if the money with which they are paid becomes as valueless as a share certificate in a bankrupt company, even before they can spend it?

If money crashes, pensioners who were counting on their life savings to sustain them in the final years of their lives will face a terminal experience sooner than they had anticipated, having no means to purchase the necessities of life. Imports into a country whose money has crashed will simply stop: no foreign supplier will be willing to hold, or be forced to accept, a currency that has no value or whose value is continually falling. In an advanced economy trade becomes impossible without money, while the engines of production switch off.

Most of us have been programmed to live in fear of stock market crashes, crashes in commodity markets, business failures, bank failures, recessions and depressions. When a currency crashes, the aftermath can be far, far more debilitating than any other financial dislocation imaginable. Simply staying alive and maintaining one's sanity become a monumental task.

If all this sounds like the ravings of a demonic doomster, just read on. What I am describing actually happened several times in history. During the nightmare years in Germany, from 1918 to 1923, money not only crashed – it died. Historical truth is often stranger than fiction. Those six years encompassed one of society's most violent examples of fiscal irresponsibility. It happened as a result of the German government's resistance to the recessionary forces of the post-World War I era, in exactly the same manner as both the United States and Britain have been attempting to thwart the recessionary forces in our society of the 1980s – by printing money.

Prelude to the German Disaster

Just before World War I the German mark, the British shilling, the French franc and the Italian lira were all worth about the same. If you were to cross the border from Italy into Germany you would find that a hotel room, a basket of fruit or an all-night wing-ding would set you back the same number of German marks as a similar escapade would cost in lire. In the USA there was a variation on the theme. To buy one dollar would mean you needed four German marks. Ten years later it would have been possible to exchange one British shilling, one French franc or one Italian lira for up to one trillion German marks – provided you wanted German marks. But by that time most people didn't want German marks and refused to accept them in exchange for anything.

Before 1914 the industrialized world lived under the Gold Standard, enjoying price stability and stable currency rates and in blissful ignorance of the inherent worth of this state of affairs. The mechanism of a Gold Standard means exactly what is implied. The price of gold was fixed by international agreement. Each currency could be exchanged for its gold value if surrendered to the authorities. Since the price of gold was fixed, the exchange rates of the various currencies were also fixed, and were therefore not prone to behaving like an elevator with a lunatic at the controls.

At this time the German mark – issued by the central bank, the Reichsbank – was steady as a rock: Germany was an industrial power with an exceptionally high ranking among the major trading nations. The country was prosperous, and adhered rigidly to the revised banking laws of 1875, which laid down that one-third of the currency issued should

101

have a gold backing. The other two-thirds was to be backed by high-grade commercial paper issued by the government or by individuals and businesses whose credit rating was beyond dispute. The amount of commercial paper taken by the banks and ultimately used to issue more currency was intended to be relative to the level of economic activity. So if the German economy was robust and growing, then more currency could be issued and more notes taken to back the currency in order to meet the demands of business. If the economy started to flag, then the amount of currency being issued would be reduced. This was indeed a sound monetary policy which made a considerable contribution to the strength and stability of Germany. Before World War I, currency was being issued at a relatively high level in the light of Germany's expanding industry and world leadership in optics, chemicals and machinery.

When the Kaiser twirled his moustache and strode into battle in the summer of 1914, he was confident of a quick victory and a relatively short conflict. It didn't work out that way. What had previously been a booming economy was soon under siege. The blockade imposed by the Allies brought Germany's international trade, the backbone of her economy, to a virtual standstill.

Not everyone shared the Kaiser's confidence even at the outset. In July 1914, after Sarajevo but before Germany had officially joined the growing conflict, a substantial exodus from the country was underway. Vast sections of the public began to panic, turning to the Reichsbank in order to convert their paper currency into gold, which they were entitled to do. Within a short time 100 million marks had been redeemed for gold.

Ordinarily, if Germany had continued to abide by the 1875 rules the sharp fall in economic activity, coupled with the loss of 100 million marks' worth of gold, would have resulted in correspondingly vast withdrawals of currency from circulation. But the German authorities panicked, along with the people. In fear of the political consequences of such a move and the manner in which the deflationary impact of reducing

---

From that point onwards, Germany could print money at will

---

the currency in circulation could undermine the morale of the troops, emergency legislation was passed abolishing the convertibility of the currency into gold. In everyday language, Germany went 'off the Gold Standard'. From that point onwards she could print money at will, unrestricted by the amount of gold required to back the currency.

World War I lasted far longer than Germany had anticipated, and its cost was far greater than could ever have been conceived. At the same time, the plunge in economic activity meant that government revenues had declined sharply. The old Imperial German government did not wish to remind its people of the true burden of war by the imposition of heavy taxes to finance it. So in order to acquire the funds needed to manufacture guns and weaponry, Germany began to borrow . . . and borrow . . . and borrow.

The government approved a credit of 5 billion marks for war materials. Then came a further departure from the rules. Treasury bills of three-month maturities were issued by the government in the amount of 5 billion marks, and were substituted for the commercial paper previously used as backing for the currency. Unlike commercial paper, Treasury bills did not represent the underlying security of the issuer of that commercial

---

Germany had not only quit the Gold Standard, she had also quit the commercial paper standard, leaving the currency with no backing at all

---

paper. They were nothing more than promissory notes, sold by the government to the Reichsbank, which permitted the Reichsbank to print more money at will. Germany had not only quit the Gold Standard, she had also quit the commercial paper standard, leaving the currency with no backing at all. In other words, it was worth no more than the paper it was printed on.

As I mentioned when discussing John Law's scheme, the value of money is based on the same laws of supply and demand as anything else you care to name. When the supply of clap-traps is more than people want, the price will fall. The only way clap-trap holders can get rid of them is to reduce the price until it reaches a level at which people will be tempted to go for clap-traps once more. The same principles hold true for currency. The more of a currency there is, the less valuable it becomes if there is no guarantee – such as gold backing – of goods and services for which that currency could be exchanged.

The German currency began to lose value as fast as the amount of paper marks in circulation grew. In just two weeks alone, during 1914, the amount of money in circulation was increased by 2 billion marks. The debt of the Reichsbank soared that year from 0.3 billion marks to 55 billion marks. Between 1914 and 1918 prices in Germany doubled. This may have caused discomfort – even distress – but halving the purchasing power of German money was not yet a catastrophe. After all, during one decade, spanning the mid-1960s to the mid-1970s, US prices doubled. In Britain at about the same time, it took even less than a decade for prices to double.

As World War I continued the Berlin government went on issuing more paper Treasury bills to sell to the Reichsbank, which was then able to issue still more paper marks. By the end of 1918 the currency in circulation had risen to 35 billion marks, which brought about another drop in the value of the mark, this time far more devastating than any fall during the war years. But the worst was yet to come!

The total expenditure of the German nation during World War I came to 174 billion marks, of which a staggering 167 billion had been spent on the conflict. But Germany's total income during those same years came to no more than 121 billion marks. Ergo, Germany was left with a shortfall of 43 billion marks plus expenses. Germany had big problems, but they were only just beginning.

The war had brought about a sharp decline in the value of the mark, along with severe hardship throughout the country. By the time the Armistice was signed, on 11 November 1918, the German economy had been thoroughly gutted and dissected like a laboratory frog. Much of her industry had been levelled to the ground. There had been about 6 million human casualties in the fighting. The mortality rate of the civilian population had taken a quantum leap. Productivity had collapsed. Reserves of food and raw materials were exhausted. War widows and the war-disabled, demobilization of the forces and the unemployment that this would create, all needed vast sums of money.

In addition, the terms of the Armistice were heinous. To those Germans who recalled the manner in which their country had demanded – and had been paid – cripping war reparations of 5 billion francs after the last war with France, in 1871, it must have come as no surprise that the French now showed no mercy to the vanquished German people. Apart from surrendering huge quantities of war materials, the Germans were obliged to deliver 5000 railway engines, 150,000 railway wagons and 5000 trucks. A further condition was the delivery of a certain number of telegraph poles, a detail which was to play a crucial part in the abasement of the nation and the destruction of its currency.

Post-war Mistakes

It has been claimed that the nightmare collapse of the German currency was unavoidable. Opinions vary, but generally it is felt that the path Germany was forced to tread had been laid down from the moment the guns fell silent on the Western Front. Some of the reasons for the direction taken by Germany remain cloudy, however. The Berlin government in theory could have adopted a frugal monetary policy, introducing high taxes and tight fiscal measures in order to pay off the war debt step by step. But further financial pressures applied to a war-ravaged, disenchanted, hungry population might well have led to revolution and another German war – a civil war. So the authorities decided to embrace the softer option. The bulk of government expenditure would continue to be covered by borrowing deficit spending, the issue of Treasury bills and the printing of more and more currency.

While the course adopted by the government may or may not have been inevitable, the consequences of their actions were. Having fallen by 50% between 1914 and 1918, and a further 50% between 1918 and 1919, in 1920 the German mark continued to fall by a further 42%. By February that year, the exchange rate against the American dollar had reached 100 marks to the dollar, twenty-five times the pre-war rate. Germany's overseas markets suffered – what was left of them. Exports fell by 40% during 1920. Between March and July unemployment shot up from 1.9% to 6%. To make Germany's position even more precarious most other industrialized countries remained linked to the Gold Standard, while Germany was juggling a time bomb as she tried to soften the impact of declining business conditions through ever-increasing monetary stimulation. Shades of John Law again!

By mid-1920 conditions had started to stabilize to some degree and the mark began to hold its own in the foreign exchange markets. But business conditions were far from encouraging. Wartime price controls continued long after the fighting ended. Even when those controls were relaxed, firms were still unable to raise their prices to a level which would compensate for rising costs, due to the low level of demand in the economy. During 1920 net profits of 1485 German companies averaged only one-quarter of the level of pre-war earnings. That was allowing for monetary depreciation, but not for the illusory inventory profits that were no more than the product of a rise in price of materials employed in manufacture. In other words, the situation was even worse than it looked on paper.

That year, 1920, was the one that plunged the entire world into deep recession – the worst since the Long Depression of the 1890s. The timing could not have been worse for Germany, currently engaged in a desperate struggle to restore her industry to its former glory – or just a small part of it. Most countries in the industrialized world, still on the Gold Standard, allowed their economies to decline in a disciplined way as observance of the Gold Standard required. But during desperate times politicians become equally desperate. When the recession struck the world's export markets during 1920, Germany again attempted to stave off the full force of global economic contraction by printing more money. From June to November 1921 the mark fell again, losing about three-quarters of its value against the dollar. The dollar rate rose to 270 marks. It was then that things *really* began to get rough!

The Allies' Pound of Flesh

This was the moment when the full weight of the war reparations burden was to make its impact on the German economy – though the Versailles Peace Treaty of 1919 never actually laid down the total reparation payments that would be demanded. Although Germany had left the Gold Standard, the Allies insisted that reparation payments should be linked to the gold mark value of the amount demanded at the time of the Versailles Treaty in 1919. In addition to cash payments the treaty required Germany to surrender all public property in her previously occupied territories and colonies, as well as her principal foreign investments. Her entire navy and complete stock of war materials were also to pass to the victors, as well as a sizeable chunk of her merchant marine. An assortment of livestock, industrial equipment, coal, consumer goods and rolling stock – forgotten at the time of the Armistice demands for railway engines and wagons –

If the terms of the London Ultimatum gave J. M. Keynes vertigo, the German government went into convulsions

---

were also on the list. A further penalty was that Germany had to build 200,000 tonnes of shipping for the Allies every year as a sort of interest payment. As a closing gesture, the Allies insisted that Germany should bear the entire cost of the Allied Occupation, including any further occupations which might be undertaken should Germany fail to meet the requirements of the Versailles Treaty in full and on time. The Allies meanwhile would occupy three German cities – Düsseldorf, Duisburg and Ruhrort – in the Rhine-Ruhr area. But all this was no more than a down payment. The final account was yet to be rendered.

After diligent efforts to determine precisely how much blood could be squeezed out of a stone, the Reparations Committee completed its final account in April 1921. On 5 May Lloyd George, the British Prime Minister, handed the German Ambassador what has since been known as the London Ultimatum. This was the straw that broke the camel's back – as well as its hind legs, forequarters, ears, eyes, nose and throat. It set down that the total sum due from Germany in respect of the damages caused by the war would be 132 billion marks, to be backed by gold for the purposes of any calculation necessary should the mark continue to fall in value. That came to about 33 billion US dollars for starters!

As a gesture of goodwill, the Allies would permit Germany to pay the reparations in convenient quarterly instalments, to the tune of 2–6 billion gold marks per annum. The precise amount to be paid by Germany in any one year would depend on her economic performance during that year. The principal would attract interest at the rate of 6% per annum for the duration of the reparation period, calculated at forty-two years. Payments would be made at fixed intervals on the due date. To the aforementioned sum would be added a further payment, equivalent to 26% of Germany's exports, every year of the obligatory period. Initially, however, one billion gold marks were to be handed over as a down payment before the end of

August 1921. Controls would be set up to ensure the continuity of the payments. Should Germany refuse to accept the terms offered, the Allies would instantly impose trade sanctions and occupy the entire Ruhr valley; this penalty would also be imposed for late payment. The response to those who criticized the extreme severity of the Allies' demands was that the financial burden to be borne by the German people was ludicrously light compared to the hardship and suffering imposed on the Allied populations in the course of a war which Germany herself had instigated in a ruthless bid for power.

By and large, the terms of the Armistice had been considered tough but fair. The additional burden imposed by the Treaty of Versailles was considered to be ruinous, but well within Germany's capacity to pay – though J. M. Keynes thought that it went far beyond anything that the German economy was capable of delivering. Keynes predicted the mark would fall by a point a day for the next two to three years. If that was Keynes's reaction to the Treaty of Versailles, can you imagine the sick feeling he must have experienced when the details of the London Ultimatum became known? And if they gave Keynes vertigo, the German government went into convulsions. Indeed, the government of the day felt it was impossible to accept the Allied terms and instantly resigned. A new government was quickly formed and hastened to accept the Allied terms, though they had no idea at all how they would meet the demands. The Germans had arrived at the point where they could no longer redeem maturing bonds and increase their borrowing power by the now universal expedient of selling more bonds. The humiliation of Germany's unconditional surrender, the heavy payments under the terms of the Armistice and the Versailles Treaty, coupled with the plunge in the value of the currency and the post-war political turmoil, had already undermined the credibility of the new government. The Weimar Republic was a fragile plant from the very first.

Privation in the New Germany

Despite the disillusion and the hardship, bourgeois values, attitudes and habits were deeply ingrained in Germany. Ordinary citizens continued to work at their jobs and worry about their children's exam results; they manoeuvred for a promotion and rejoiced when they won it; and generally speaking they went on expecting life to improve. But the price spiral led to complaints about the high cost of living. Teachers and civil servants protested that they were being squeezed, and factory workers pressed for wage increases. An underground economy developed, reinforced by the not uncommon desire to beat the taxman.

Without a doubt the Weimar government faced some awesome problems, and bore an extremely heavy responsibility for a proud yet defeated country. But it compounded many of its problems by a series of disastrous political and economic blunders. It made no real attempt to deflate – or even to stabilize – the over-burdened and over-extended monetary and financial structure it had inherited. Instead of asking for further sacrifice so that some kind of financial order could be restored, the new social-democratic leadership sought to win over the public and restore confidence by means of promises. They promised increased wages, shorter hours, an expanded educational system, improved pensions and a wide range of social benefits. The government committed itself to the further expenditure of thousands of billions in paper marks. All this, remember, on top of the demands set out in the London Ultimatum. Guess where all that money was going to come from?

The Weimar government faced awesome problems which it compounded by a series of political and economic blunders

---

The London Ultimatum's down payment of one billion gold marks, due in August 1921, was made as stipulated, although the German authorities had great difficulty in raising the foreign currency they needed to convert sufficient marks into dollars. The problem was exacerbated when a Dutch loan of 270 million gold marks contracted by the Reichsbank several years earlier suddenly had to be repaid at short notice. The foreign currency which a country ordinarily earns through its trade transactions, and which comprises a nation's foreign reserves at the central bank, had in Germany's case been depleted as a result of the first down payment to the Allies under the London Ultimatum. The only way the German authorities could possibly get hold of enough foreign currency to pay the Dutch was through the sale of paper marks on the foreign exchange market. The paper marks were duly issued through the creation and discount of Treasury bills!

The flood of paper triggered an immediate burst of speculation against the mark, and it plunged. On 20 October 1921 further fuel was added to the raging inferno of inflation. The Council of the League of Nations decided that Upper Silesia should be partitioned, and one of Germany's richest industrial areas given to Poland. This action was the kind of psychological shock that invariably leads to a flight of capital. In this instance capital quickly scrambled out of marks and out of Germany. By November the mark had fallen to a mere 1.5% of its pre-war value, standing at 300 marks to the US dollar.

On 15 November a further 500 million gold mark payment was due under the London Ultimatum. There was wide speculation that Germany would be unable to make the payment, which would lead to trade sanctions, further occupation and the sequestration of land and goods.

The mark continued to plunge. But somewhere, somehow, the German authorities managed to scrape together enough foreign exchange to meet the deadline.

Following the payment, the mark began to stabilize and actually edged higher on the world's foreign exchanges. Speculation against the mark, on the assumption that Germany would be unable to come up with the payment, had been overdone. 'The German mark has hit bottom!' was the frenzied shout of one foreign exchange dealer when it was announced that Germany had met its obligations in full. Until February 1922 the mark made steady progress on the foreign exchanges, and in early March it was back up to 200 to the US dollar. But from mid-March onwards it began to slide again, though only gently at first. May 1922 saw the first appearance of 10,000 mark notes, of which 19 million marks' worth were issued.

On 24 June that year right-wing fanatics assassinated Walter Rathenau, the moderate, able German Foreign Minister. Rathenau, son of a German-Jewish industrialist, was a charismatic figure in Germany, and the idea that a wealthy dignitary could be shot dead in a law-abiding society shocked the world. It also shattered the faith of the German people, who desperately wanted to believe that everything was going to be all right. Nervous citizens began to switch out of currency and purchase what were considered to be real assets – *Sachwerte* – rather than holding paper money that was shrinking in value. They chose diamonds, works of art, antiques, stamps, coins and property. 'Pianos', wrote the British

---

The League of Nations decided to give one of Germany's richest industrial areas to Poland

---

historian Adam Fergusson in his book *When Money Dies*, 'were bought even by unmusical families.' Sellers held back because the mark was worth less and less every day. As the purchasing power of the currency went down and the number of marks needed to purchase the necessities of life went on climbing, the German Reichsbank responded by simply printing more paper marks and issuing more Treasury bills. Yet the authorities did not see anything wrong in what they were doing. A leading German financial newspaper said that the amounts of money in circulation were 'not excessively high'. Dr Rudolf Havenstein, President of the Reichsbank, told an economics professor that he needed a new suit, but that he wasn't going to buy one until the value of the mark went up and the price of suits came down. Presumably he never did buy his new suit!

By June 1922 the German mark was back down to 270 to the dollar. That meant it had fallen no less than 35% from the level of 200 reached three months earlier. Between February and June 1922 the amount of currency in circulation rose by 50%. During the same five-month period the cost of living index all but doubled.

Yet, for reasons related more to the poor performance of the German economy than to its inflationary potential, the mark continued falling throughout 1922. It was widely noted that the earnings declared by Germany's major industrial companies – although declining – remained quite high, despite the serious deterioration in economic activities. It was further noted, however, that once inflation was taken into account those company earnings were grossly overstated and totally unrealistic. Although the authorities attempted to tighten monetary policy from time to time, the measures were either unproductive or quickly reversed. The mark continued to fall, and prices continued to rise. As a consequence German living standards fell. The rise in price levels meant that any increase in domestic earnings was quickly lost through the rapid decline in the purchasing power of the currency. The dividends paid by German companies to their shareholders represented a steady running down of capital rather than a distribution of real earnings.

By mid-1922, with the memory of the death of Rathenau still fresh, the public had become so totally demoralized that the German authorities abandoned any attempt to support the currency and curb inflation. They gave in to the clamour for easy money, regardless of the inflationary consequences, whenever – and from whomsoever – they came.

The Reichsbank changed tack and began to supply credit in copious amounts direct to industry. It also deliberately encouraged the wider use of commercial paper, which it willingly discounted, issuing new, freshly printed paper marks in exchange, thereby putting even more paper money into circulation. During 1922 the value of the commercial paper discounted by the Reichsbank rose from one billion marks to no less than 422.2 billion. Commercial paper companies – some of which were rapidly becoming less than creditworthy – joined Treasury bills in the role of 'engines' for the creation of more and more paper money. One commentator jocularly referred to the German mark as 'the mini-mark'. But if it was a joke, it wasn't funny.

In June 1922 it was little wonder that the German mark was in free fall on the world's foreign exchange markets. The currency continued to decline at an accelerating rate throughout the year. Between June and December the mark fell from 270 to the dollar to no less than 8000. Remember those telegraph poles? They delivered the *coup de grâce* to the German currency during the autumn of 1922.

The Occupation of the Ruhr

Under the terms of the Armistice Germany had to deliver a consignment of 125,000 telegraph poles to the French; huge quantities of coal, too, had been promised under the Versailles Treaty. Both were due for delivery that autumn. The Germans were genuinely unable to manufacture the

110

telegraph poles or to find enough coal to make the delivery. So French and Belgian troops marched into the Ruhr and occupied it. A public uprising and civil war erupted in Germany. The results were predictable – arrests, bloodshed and loss of life.

The official policy of the Weimar Republic to the occupation of the Ruhr was 'passive resistance'. Civil servants and railwaymen alike were ordered to strike, disrupting the vital administrative and transportation services, and any activities which could make life easier or more convenient for the occupying forces were also ceased. Germany's passive resistance prevented the occupying forces from restoring production to any meaningful degree. But the price paid was a high one. Not only did Germany lose the wealth-generating resources of the Ruhr when she could least afford to do so, but the government had to provide for the unemployed and refugees who had lost their livelihood as a consequence of the passive resistance. On top of that there was the damage caused to the rest of the economy by general unemployment, as well as constant disruptions, dislocations and administrative difficulties. The German railways depended on coal from the Ruhr. Without it – and with the railway workers idle – food and supplies could not be delivered to other regions.

As early as 1921 the German authorities had warned the Allies that the demands of the London Ultimatum were totally unrealistic, and that it would probably be impossible for Germany to meet them. They had also stated categorically that they would probably be unable to make the 1922 payment. Heated discussions had taken place throughout the year, and the Allies had made limited concessions and adjustments. But these had not been enough.

It was now becoming abundantly clear that J. M. Keynes and others who had sympathised with the plight of Germany in the light of the massive reparations bill – and had been criticized as 'soft' for so doing – had been 100% correct in their assessment. But this did not make the Allies any less intractable, or willing either to moderate their demands or to save the German nation from total collapse. As Adam Fergusson noted when he summed up the reasons for the Weimar Republic's failure to solve Germany's main problems at this time: 'What really broke Germany was the constant taking of the soft political option in respect of money.' There was one matter in respect of which Germany had no option. During early 1923, she would be forced to announce her intention to cease all further reparation payments of any kind.

When Money Died in Germany

At the end of 1922 the price of necessary goods and services had increased by more than fourteen times in six months, so the rise in the currency in circulation became explosive – as did the German deficit. Until late 1922 printing money to keep the economy moving had certain beneficial side effects. In April the rate of unemployment had been under 1% and by the summer there was full employment. But by December the unemployment rate was back up to 2.8%. German industries, especially those in the export trade, enjoyed a boom during 1920–2 when most other countries were suffering the ravages of a deep global recession. Because the mark was falling faster than the price of German goods was rising, those goods were extremely competitive in world markets. In the autumn of 1922 the working week of a British coal miner was down to a mere two days, while his German counterpart was on overtime. Of course they *had* to work all

---

'What really broke Germany was the constant tak-ing of the soft political option in respect of money'

---

the hours God sent them, in view of the disastrous fall in the purchasing power of their wages as inflation raced ahead.

As the fateful year of 1923 began, whatever small benefit had resulted from the government's policy of printing money and debasing the currency had disappeared without trace. At the same time, a further plunge in the mark heralded a new phase of rising prices, more terrifying than ever seen before in any country. It was to end in the complete and irreversible collapse of the mark.

At the beginning of the year the mark was trading at 18,000 to the dollar. In the spring a Reichstag committee was convened to examine why it had fallen to 30,000 to the dollar. By the time the committee first met, on 18 June, the mark was down to 152,000 to the dollar, and in July it was trading at one million to the dollar.

Throughout 1923 the mark fell victim to one massive selling wave after another, bringing social misery and political turmoil in its wake. The German currency went over the cliff-edge of sanity, and all semblance of propriety gave way to panic. I have said on many occasions that markets can do anything they like, any time they like, without reason or reservation. The collapse of the German mark proved that to be true beyond all shadow of doubt.

Still the government's financial policy remained unchanged. The only method they could find to cope with the problem was to keep the printing presses going as fast as they could run. Between December 1922 and 15 November 1923, notes in circulation rose from one billion to 92.8 trillion. By the end of 1923, the total stood at a staggering 496.5 trillion. On 15 November 1923 the German floating debt stood at 189 trillion marks. Mere numbers had begun to lose their meaning. Only 3% of public expenditure was covered by taxes and other income. The remaining 97% was covered by nothing more than the output of the printing presses.

The currency was losing value so fast, and prices rising so rapidly, that

112

some employees demanded to be paid their wages two and three times a day. Vast quantities of emergency notes, known as *Notgeld*, were issued by towns and cities throughout Germany. Many of the earlier issues of German currency notes were overprinted, some twice on the same piece of paper. It was just a matter of adding zeros – provided the physical dimensions of the note were such that it would take that number of zeros. The British Embassy in Berlin noted that the number of marks to the pound was equal to the number of years to the sun. More prosaically Dr Hjalmar Schacht, later Germany's National Currency Commissioner, explained that at the end of World War I you could have bought 500 million eggs for the same price as one egg five years later. Such lunatic comparisons suited the spirit of the times.

It had now become clear, even to the most casual observer, that Germany was rolling downhill into a bottomless, black hole. Over the years, German industrialists had gradually acquired experience in dealing with a falling currency and rising inflation. Whenever industry antici-pated a rise in costs due to the fall in the exchange rate, they would ruthlessly hike their prices to compensate – adding just a little more as an 'insurance'. But the 'insurance' was never quite enough, and the currency always seemed to fall further and faster than most businessmen were able to anticipate.

By the end of 1923 confidence in the mark had completely evaporated. Economic conditions were dire. Rather than raise prices in anticipation of a further fall in the currency, industrialists started to divert funds away from the manufacturing of goods and the provision of services and use them for speculation. Business was of secondary importance, and gamb-ling on the fall of the mark became the best game in town in late 1923. Of course, this encouraged further and more pronounced falls in the value of the currency. Wild spending sprees were financed by the ill-gotten gains to be won by exploiting a dying currency. But the terminal stage of the game was to be far less rewarding than most had expected.

Wild spending sprees were financed by the ill-gotten
gains to be won by exploiting a dying currency

For those living through such an era, the main question was: 'How do we survive when the price of a newspaper is 200 billion marks?' The Berlin correspondent of the *Daily Mail* mentioned that he was 'amazed when I found today that one had to pay 24,000 marks for a ham sandwich whereas yesterday in the same café a ham sandwich cost only 14,000 marks.' As a footnote to his dispatch he did say that, fortunately, wages were being adjusted to suit the circumstances: 'The salary of a Cabinet Minister has been raised from 23,000,000 marks ten days ago to 32,000,000 marks today.' Germans no longer used purses or wallets;

daily monetary requirements were transported in a suitcase or a wheel-barrow or a baby's pram. The *Daily Mail* man described this absurd situation:

> The cashier of my bank handed me 4,000,000 marks in 1000 mark notes, each worth less than half a farthing . . . he obligingly did them up for me in a newspaper parcel which I afterwards put on the table of the restaurant where I lunched and unpacked when the waiter brought the bill. But this difficulty will soon disappear for we expect to have 4,000,000 marks notes by the end of next week.

Germans no longer used purses or wallets, but a suitcase or a wheelbarrow or a baby's pram

---

In Berlin the price of potatoes, eggs and butter was changed six times a day. Grocers refused to part with their goods in exchange for paper money, so barter was used instead. By late 1923, prices were rising so fast that wages were paid at two-hourly intervals. Even before this time, one factory worker wrote:

> At eleven o'clock in the morning a siren sounded and everybody gathered in the factory forecourt where a five-ton lorry was drawn up loaded brimful with paper money. The chief cashier and his assistants climbed up on top. They read out names and just threw out bundles of notes. As soon as you had caught one you made a dash for the nearest shop and bought just anything that was going.

Each morning those same workers would read in the newspaper – if they could afford one – the price of public services, to discover whether they could still afford the fare to work – or to the money distribution centre if they were out of a job.

In *The Great Inflation* William Guttman and Patricia Meehan recount the story of a doctor who set out to take a tram to visit a sick patient. The doctor was forced to return home because he found he didn't have enough money to pay for his tram ticket. The patient died of malnutrition the following day. Another poignant tale told to them concerned a young widowed mother:

> A friend of mine was in charge of the office that had to deal with the giving of salaries, pensions and special grants to the police of the whole district around Frankfurt. . . . One case which came her way was the widow of a policeman who died leaving four children. She had been awarded three months of her late husband's salary. My friend worked out the sum with great care, checked it and double-checked it and sent the papers on as required to Wiesbaden. There, they were checked

again, rubber stamped and sent back to Frankfurt. By the time all this was done and the money was finally paid out to the widow, the amount she received would only have paid for three boxes of matches.

While the jobless, the homeless, the relief lines and the soup kitchens may appear symbolic of depression, it is actually difficult to grasp the extent of the problems the German people were experiencing as the reverse of the phenomenon known as depression – hyperinflation – gripped the nation. It was noted by Lloyd George, who in 1932 attempted to describe the situation: 'Words such as "disaster", "ruin", and "catastrophe" had ceased to rouse genuine apprehension any more – so widespread was the use of these terms. During the German hyperinflation, the meaning of disaster was devalued along with the mark.'

Some anecdotes, with hindsight, now seem quite amusing. A student ordered a cup of coffee, priced on the menu at 5000 marks. He then decided to have a second cup, but in the meantime the mark had taken a further tumble. The café proprietor quickly adjusted the price to 9000 marks, which was what the student had to pay for his second cup. 'If you want to save money,' he was told, 'and you want two cups of coffee, you should order both at the same time.'

There were many such tales, some of them from a different currency viewpoint. The *New York Times* tells of a visitor to one of the 'lesser restaurants' in Berlin. He flourished a dollar bill and asked for all the dinner it would buy. He was served with a sumptuous meal. As he was about to leave the waiter arrived with yet another plate of soup and another entree. The waiter bowed politely: 'The dollar, sir, has gone up again.' Leopold Ullstein, the publisher, tells how one German family wanted to give their old cook a single US dollar to mark ten years of faithful service. But objections were raised in the family: 'She was . . . too simple and unsophisticated to handle such a fortune. The only way would be to set up a trust fund at the bank to administer the dollar for her.'

'The meaning of disaster was devalued along with the mark'

The year 1923 brought catastrophe to the German bourgeoisie, as well as hunger, disease, destitution and sometimes death to a far wider public. Once the gold and jewels had gone, people were forced to offer their furniture and even personal belongings to obtain their daily crust. After a time, many had nothing left to offer. Those who had loaned money to others found themselves repaid in worthless paper marks. The principle that a mark was a mark was firmly adhered to, so debtors walked off scot-free. Mortgages were repaid in full at one-ten thousandth of their original value. The German government, the German states and the

German municipalities found their funded indebtedness melting deliciously away; while those solid citizens who had faithfully and patriotically invested in the 'gilt-edged' securities issued by the government found their investments translated into worthless paper. All the fundamental canons of bourgeois society were turned upside down. Those who had saved money saw those savings vanish in the night.

The desperate masses, at least as badly off as the middle classes, became angry and unruly. Militant strikers gathered outside factory gates and rioting broke out in the streets. On 22 July 1923 *The Times* noted:

> There was an outbreak of Bolshevism in Breslau. A large mob raided the commercial centre of the town and broke into, and looted, fifty or sixty of the large shops, causing enormous losses to the owners. A 'state of siege' was eventually declared and the police used firearms to restore order. Six rioters were killed and a score or more wounded.

The German states and cities were desperately in need of funds. The state of Oldenburg came up with the device of rye-backed paper, and began issuing the first of several 'rye debentures', as they were called. Each of these debentures had written across its face the state's promise to repay enough paper marks to exchange for 150 kg of rye, whatever its market price that day. There is a parallel here with John Law's pledge that his bank's notes could be exchanged for coin of the same quality and value as on the day the notes were taken up. The purchaser of the debentures – in other words, the lender – paid over a sufficient number of paper marks to buy 125 kg of rye at the time of the transaction. The difference – equivalent to 25 kg of rye – represented the interest for the use of the marks over the period of the loan, which was a fixed four years. This was the first kind of investment that seemed feasible at the time, but it pointed the way to the ultimate solution which came with the introduction of the Rentenmark. But that's anticipating events. . . .

It's an Ill Wind

Amidst this unbridled and unprecedented chaos, there were, unbelievably, a small number of opportunists who figured out a way to capitalize on the situation. Speculators, and those with access to overseas earnings or a foreign bank account, enjoyed what must have been a bonanza. Farms, mineral rights, urban property, factories, service companies – you name it – were up for grabs, within the grasp of anyone who had even a small amount of 'real money'. Guttmann and Meehan quote the tale of a junior bank clerk whose duties involved the handling of foreign currency. All he had to do to earn a sizeable illicit profit for himself and his employers was to delay making the book entries for the money that regularly passed through his hands: 'At the beginning I would be bold enough to keep the money for a day or two without telling my boss. Afterwards, I would show him what a wonderful profit I had made. Later on I became bolder and kept it even for a week. That gave you a colossal profit and that went on and on.'

Foreigners swarmed into the country to buy for a song anything and everything they could lay their hands on, from castles on the Rhine through town property in Berlin to the very goods on the shelves in the shops. They revelled in a strange sort of communism, a world in which things of value had become unbelievably cheap. Prices were frantically marked down in the stores, provided you could pay in foreign currency – such was the anxiety of the shopkeepers to convert their merchandise into sound foreign currency. People called it the 'sack of Germany'.

But all good things come to an end. The German government intervened and forebade the export of goods from the country except under special licence. Departing tourists were stopped at the frontier and searched. Unlicensed goods were confiscated.

The Age of Bedlam

The agony experienced by the German people as the currency collapsed was described by the chroniclers of the period as 'an age of bedlam of unprecedented dimensions ... a kind of lunacy gripping the people'. Bosch or Bruegel would have delighted to portray the macabre scenes.

'Zero stroke' or 'Cipher stroke' was the name given by German doctors to a prevalent nervous malady that was caused by the weird numbers that people were forced to cope with when trying to think and calculate in millions, billions and trillions. William Guttman's brother worked at the University Psychiatric Clinic in Munich, and he described how the borderline between madness and reality was blurred by this condition:

When a new patient was brought in, the doctors started their investigation with a simple test to find out whether, at least on the face of it, he was normal. They would ask him a few elementary questions such as, how old are you, how many children have you got, what is the height of the Zugspitze [mountain]? And the answers might be, 'I'm 25 million years old, I have 1000 or 15,000 children etc.'

Inflation and the suffering it brought reinforced the decline in the nation's health – particularly among children and the elderly – which had begun with the Allied blockade. Infant mortality rose sharply. Despite the issue of fresh milk being limited to families with babies, small children continued to show signs of malnutrition. Frequently underweight, they were prone to rickets and tuberculosis. Their parents were exposed to scurvy and stomach disorders due to their extremely poor diet and the falling standards of food hygiene. Unable to afford the necessary fuel or warm bedding – probably because their blankets and warm clothing had already been traded for a meal – many older Germans fell prey to hypothermia, pneumonia and acute rheumatic complaints.

Medical attention was difficult to come by. Dentists and doctors demanded butter and eggs, not currency, in payment. But the farmers were holding back their produce. They too refused to accept paper currency. 'We don't want any Jew-confetti from Berlin,' a chronicler quoted a Bavarian farmer saying. Disorientation, paranoia, dementia, schizophrenia, psychosis, acute depression and mental breakdowns were piled on top of the wide variety of physical infirmities the German people were already suffering.

Drugs and Depravity

Another sort of decline was also rife – moral decadence. The German people displayed a diminishing ability to distinguish between right and wrong. In a society where materialism had reached its most horrifying extremity there was a callous disregard for the rights of one's fellow men.

During the sequence of depressions that have dotted the landscape of history, hardship, hunger and poverty on a massive scale have often tended to unite people. In America during the 1890s brotherly love was rediscovered. As town after town witnessed the closure of factories and businesses workers would head for other towns where they might find work. Newcomers were welcomed. Those who were already established in jobs would help the new arrivals, sharing their food and whatever else they had in a community spirit. People knew they needed each other. They helped each other. But this was certainly not the case in Germany during the 1920s. A sick joke in a German magazine epitomized the now cynical attitude of the bourgeoisie: 'Think of a friend in need at Christmas and you can be absolutely certain your friend will think of you the very first time he is in need again.'

A young mother trying to obtain milk for her baby, but lacking the necessary papers due to a bureaucratic oversight, was told she could have none. 'Drown it!' was a stone-faced civil servant's response to her anguished plea. Pets too were at risk, as the amount of dog meat offered for human consumption grew. In 1923, at the height of inflation, 6430 dogs found their way to the dining tables of the German people.

A story reminiscent of the demon barber, Sweeney Todd, is that of a landlady who was particularly noted for her ability to keep her boarders regularly supplied with meat. She claimed a relationship with a secret and mysterious supplier in Munsterberg. Every Thursday she would travel to the town carrying a large empty leather bag, which on her return would be

118

full. During an investigation she refused to divulge the name of her supplier because then, she said, everyone would go there. . . . Munsterberg was where the mass-murderer Denke conducted his operations during his 1923 rampage of terror!

Selfishness, licentiousness and avarice reigned supreme among those few Germans who had in some way managed to escape the ravages of inflation. These were the individuals who offered pennies for the belongings of the well-to-do, which they would then sell for foreign currency. A pittance would be paid for jewellery, clocks, clothing, furs, antiques, china and any other possessions offered to the profiteers. The 'haves' seemed to gain enormous pleasure from the constant humiliation of the 'have nots'.

Another nightclub act involved a donkey engaged in sexual intercourse with a twelve-year-old child

---

In his memoirs, *The World of Yesterday*, the writer Stefan Zweig recalls that palaces of vulgar and coarse amusement mushroomed in the centre of Berlin. Male prostitutes would parade along the Kurfürstendamm. Berlin had a 'witches' Sabbath' atmosphere, said Zweig. He likened the dances of homosexuals and lesbians to orgies transcending those of decadent Rome or what might be expected at a party given in Dante's *Inferno*. Prostitutes followed anyone whom they believed to be a tourist, chanting, 'Fucky sucky one American dollar!'

The average sixteen-year-old girl in Berlin would have been insulted by the suggestion that she might be a virgin. In the city's parks trying to avoid stumbling over the fornicating bodies was like running an obstacle course. A 'threepenny upright' was the invitation often extended to British male tourists strolling through them.

One nightclub featured a female who would insert a large, freshly lit cigar into her vagina in full view of a gaping audience. She would then proceed to generate huge puffs of smoke from the cigar by manipulating her pelvic region. Any man – or woman – who agreed to smoke the remainder of the cigar after it had served its initial purpose would then be invited to partake of the other favours she had to offer.

Another den of iniquity that was popular at the time borrowed a leaf from the last days of the Roman Empire, when the 'ladies' of the court adopted the practice of bathing in sperm, supposedly for the purpose of prolonging life. In this particular Berlin nightclub a dozen or so males, hired for the purpose, would masturbate into a huge vessel in which lay a woman writhing and wriggling to express her delight. Another act involved a donkey engaged in sexual intercourse with a twelve-year-old child, and yet another starred a beautiful young woman in her early twenties satisfying six penes at the same time. Two of the penes were the subject of ambidextrous masturbation; two were being fellated simul-taneously; the manner in which the act was performed with the other two is best left to the imagination. Obviously the beautiful young woman was not lying on her back!

Life for those Germans who had not been decimated by poverty was one of sordid, animal degradation and decadence. The objective for those who could afford it was to escape the realities of day-to-day existence by whatever means were available. The money you spent on a bottle of cham-pagne in the evening might only buy a match in the morning. Berlin was dancing like a smouldering fuse, attached to a load of explosives.

Gambling became excessive and widespread. The number of illegal gambling dens spread like an epidemic, their smoky rooms packed with sensation-seekers, wedged close together around the green baize tables. Gambling offered one last chance to forget – if only for the time it took to deal a half-dozen hands of cards. Why not stake the whole bundle – and it *was* a bundle – on the turn of a single card or one spin of the wheel? After all, every minute of every day represented the biggest gamble of all.

People offered their blood by the bucketful in ex-change for a bowl of soup

When all the possibilities of erotic pleasure had been exhausted, when the roulette wheels stopped spinning and the champagne had gone flat, there was still one more game to play. Drug-taking became widely prevalent in Germany in the early 1920s. With the demand for drugs there came also a vast army of peddlers and pushers.

Tiny spoon-like objects with that little screw of paper containing a pinch of the fashionable white powder became the symbol of the age for a delinquent population desperate for a means of escape. Cocaine became the alpha and omega of life itself. The local pusher – or 'candyman' as he was called in the vernacular – could also offer a variety of uppers and downers. For others who had acquired a taste for mind-altering subst-ances in a military hospital there was that precious phial bought for a stack of paper from a taxi driver who slept with a nurse, or from a whore who coerced the hospital administrator into making another 'wastage entry' in the hospital records. The needle might be painfully blunt or swarming with hepatitis or jaundice bacilli. But the user would have his or her reward – several hours' journey to blissful oblivion, floating on a morphine cloud.

One section of the population, and one only, took a more positive escape route. The utter hopelessness of the material outlook for the intelligentsia of Germany drove them into an almost feverish search for intellectual satisfaction during the Weimar Republic. One description spoke of those years . . .

when a frenzied juggling with the materials of existence represented life in a world of cultural and social relations, [and] the power of thought, of abstract speculation, of artistic literary creation came vividly, at moments, to expression. In the cafés, the art centres, theory was passionately discussed and wordy conflicts were staged round aesthetic and philosophical doctrines.

The majority of the German people, however, lacked both the intellectual capacity to seek such philosophical escape routes and the wherewithal for the less savoury ventures into mindlessness. For them, the only way out was to 'liberate' whatever they needed to stay alive. Crime rates – particularly against property – rose in inverse proportion to the fall in the value of money. In 1913 the number of persons convicted of theft stood at 113,000. The figure for 1923 was 365,000. Apart from the comparatively excusable motives of desperation and poverty, a new lack of inhibition made stealing a normal, acceptable way of life. No copper pipe, or brass armature, or sheet of lead on a roof was safe. Any car might have the petrol siphoned from its tank or the wheels removed from its chassis. Railway carriages were a constant target for passengers, who would strip them of their curtains and leather window straps. It was easier to buy food with a piece of metal that could be melted down into scrap or a strip of leather that could be used to repair a shoe, than it was with an offering of paper money. An old army expression runs: 'If you can't move it, paint it!' The corresponding credo for the German people during the 1920s was: 'If you can move it, steal it!' And to augment what they stole people offered their blood to hospitals by the bucketful in exchange for a bowl of soup and the price of a tram-ticket.

A Return to Sanity?

On 20 November 1923 the issue of mark notes was at last suspended. The newly appointed Chancellor, Stresemann, decided to abandon the policy of resistance in the Ruhr and to reopen negotiations with the Allies on the reparations question. A new President, Hjalmar Schacht, took over the Reichsbank.

Though the currency was worthless, Germany was still a rich country – with mines, farms, factories and forests. The time seemed propitious to attempt a reorganization of the monetary system. A temporary, emergency currency, the Rentenmark, was introduced in strictly limited quantities, to get the country through this tricky period.

The Rentenmark was not actually Schacht's idea, but since he was instrumental in the execution of the scheme he received the credit for it. As a result, for decades afterwards he had a reputation for financial wizardry. The backing for the Rentenmark was neither gold – which the country

121

didn't have – nor those Treasury bills that had been printed and issued at will. Under the new regime the currency was to be solidly underpinned by mortgages on the land and bonds on the factories. Nine zeros were struck from the currency – one Rentenmark was equal to one billion marks.

All money is a matter of belief; the word 'credit' derives from the Latin *credere*, to believe. The backing for the Rentenmark was indeed a fiction. Factories and land in Germany could not conceivably be turned into hard cash and gold or used in foreign countries. But the Germans wanted desperately to believe in the Rentenmark, and so they did. The factories functioned again and the farmers began delivering their produce. The central bank kept the belief alive when it totally refused to allow the government to make further borrowings of any kind. Spending in the shops became less frenetic. In his book *Paper Money* Adam Smith quotes a woman from East Prussia: 'I remember the feeling of having just one Rentenmark to spend. I bought a small tin bread bin. Just to buy something that had a price tag for one mark was so exciting.'

But many of the lifetime plans of the average German citizen had vanished into thin air. Since it was still traditional for a bride's family to offer a dowry, many weddings were cancelled. Elderly people whose remaining years were dependent on the proceeds of life insurance policies, pensions and annuities found themselves destitute. The Rentenmark was incapable of offering a solution to such problems; nor was it capable of resuscitating the fortunes of those people who had worked a lifetime to find their savings would not buy a crust of bread or a cup of coffee.

Pearl S. Buck, the American writer, was in Germany during 1923. Later she described the lingering effects of those terrible years on the German psyche: '. . . they had not lost their self-assurance [but] lost . . . were the

---

'The market woman . . . lost the capacity for surprise. And nothing that has happened since has been insane enough or cruel enough to surprise her'

---

old values of morals, of ethics, of decency'. Thomas Mann perceived the same degeneracy, whose legacy would last for decades: 'The market woman who without batting an eyelash demanded a hundred million for an egg lost the capacity for surprise. And nothing that has happened since has been insane enough or cruel enough to surprise her.'

Unlike the lessons of several other crashes, those of the Great Inflation of Weimar Germany may be rather elusive. The monetarists tell us that if governments are not allowed to print money at their whim, we won't have the kind of nightmare experienced by Germany during the 1920s. That lesson is obvious. But the German insanity provides a far more important lesson – to do with confidence, belief and instinct. When people begin stampeding into markets of which they have little understanding, propelling price levels to margins that bear no relationship to known values – as they have done in recent years – they are losing belief in their currency and bank deposits as a store of value.

As we look back through history at the records of financial manias and panics, it appears that they typically end in a great burst of lunacy. Some inherent madness comes to the surface, and the mob appears to be invaded by witches and demons as it celebrates the mechanics of its own destruction. If this is indeed the sign, then surely we must now be approaching a similar time. Who can say that flagpole sitting, marathon dancing or Tulipomania are any more lunatic or socially destructive than bingo, marathon running and the mindless stampede by the financially unwashed into Stock Exchange investments, along with the completely unquantifiable level of off-balance sheet risks assumed by the world's leading banking institutions?

7

The Great Wall Street Crash

How the crash in share prices on the New York
Stock Exchange in 1929 caused personal bankrupt-
cies, poverty and suicides, acting as the precursor to
the worst depression in history

The Economic Boom . . .

'The sound went on all through trading hours, and reached its peak
around noon. It wasn't an angry or hysterical sound. This was the most
ominous thing about it. It was a kind of hopeless drone, a Greek dirge
kind of thing. It was damned distracting, I must say.' So goes an
old-timer's memory of Wall Street in late 1929, quoted by John Brooks in
Once in Golconda. By then contemporary accounts were describing a
kind of dumb-struck despair, as share prices were whittled away day after
day and it dawned on investors that there was to be no quick recovery
from the October crash. It was not just a bad dream. The reality was the
ruin of thousands of lives; and it was the paper riches, which had seemed
to offer an endless vista in the summer, that had been the cruel illusion.

The mystery of the Crash of 1929 and the Depression of the 1930s is
that they hit so much harder in America than elsewhere. Why should the
most powerful economy in the world have suffered so disproportionate-
ly? J. K. Galbraith had it right when he said of the Great Crash that 'the
causes of the crash were all in the speculative orgy that preceded it'. But
the history of earlier depressions suggests – and the events of the 1920s
corroborate this – that the causes of the Depression, as opposed to the
Crash, were all in the economic boom that preceded it.

In the late 1980s the USA was the world's biggest debtor. So it was in
1914, on the eve of World War I. That conflict transformed the scene.
America became the supplier of the Allies' war effort, a role she continued
to play after she joined them in 1917. The USA ended the war as the
world's greatest creditor nation, and as the saviour of the forces of
freedom. In short, World War I established America as the number one
world power, her economy enormously strengthened by the demands of
war while those of most of the other participants had been debilitated.

The war boom carried on into peacetime. Commodity prices carried on rising in the scramble to replace resources depleted by war; the stock market had never seemed healthier. And then followed the crisis that characterises the aftermath of every major war – deflation and slump.

... That Always Precedes the Slump

The slump of 1920–2 was sharp and painful everywhere, but what was notable about it was the swiftness with which America emerged from the dive, to power forward to a peak of prosperity which has passed into legend. From the summit of the post-war boom in May 1920 wholesale prices in America plunged 42% in the succeeding twelve months, while the Dow Jones Industrial Index slid 33% between April and December. That industrial recession has been called the most precipitous in American history. Steel output plunged from 42 million tons in 1920 to 20 million tons in 1921. Business failures doubled, with bad debts soaring to an easy record. Exports slumped 3.7 billion dollars – also a record.

It was the same story, only worse and more prolonged, in Europe. In France wholesale prices sank 47% in the eighteen months from May 1920. In Britain the fall was 49%, and the slump struck with frightening ferocity. Within a year, unemployment had hit 1.5 million. By December 1922 it was 2 million, or 18% of the workforce – a level not seen in a hundred years of records. That winter, the sight of unemployed ex-servicemen rattling collection boxes in the West End was to leave theatre-goers with unnerving memories which would not go away – as the 1920s' slump would not go away. For Britons in the 1930s, 'the slump' meant the depression of the 1920s.

The recovery that began in America in 1922, and resumed after a slight pause in mid-decade to reach boom proportions in the late twenties, passed Britain by. UK unemployment stayed high throughout the decade, particularly after the General Strike of 1926. In 1925 sterling had moved back on to the Gold Standard at its pre-war level, which proved to be too high, exacerbating the depression in the coal, steel, shipbuilding and textile industries. Real income per head was lower in 1929 than in 1919, according to a League of Nations study. The reason why Britain was to suffer less in the 1930s was that it had had no boom in the 1920s.

Germany, in turn, was slow to recover from its hyperinflationary depression. Japan suffered relatively subdued conditions in the 1920s, including a major banking crisis in 1927. Only Canada shared fully in the boom times of America, while France and Italy did so to a lesser degree.

The long and the short of it is that Americans, as they looked at their country and at the world around them, got the inescapable impression that God truly did bless America. And this impression was probably shared, somewhat ruefully, by many observers in Britain.

The Fun and the Fantasy

Meanwhile, something remarkable was happening to the citizens of the USA – a change in their morals, values and behaviour. It's almost as if America grew up in the 1920s. The special *timbre* of the decade that was to be called the Roaring Twenties has been burned into the collective consciousness of subsequent generations, to whom the jerky films of the period live nostalgically on. We still remember the early movies of Gloria Swanson, and Rudolf Valentino in *The Sheik*; we are still haunted by the atmosphere of Scott Fitzgerald's *Tender Is the Night*. This America was light years removed from the puritanism of the early pioneers, who, in one of the most astonishing paradoxes in history, were to leave their imprint on the whole decade in the form of Prohibition.

What happened to America was the return from 1918 onwards of 2 million soldiers. On being demobbed it was inevitable that these servicemen, who had been exposed to death and life and love with the *mesdemoiselles* from Armentières, would be restless. They found themselves rejecting the narrow values they found back in Iowa or California or even Manhattan, and the result was an instant upheaval in American morals.

The technological drive of the twenties came from the motor car, radio and electricity. There were 6.7 million motor cars in America in 1919 and 23 million in 1929, when car sales alone amounted to about one-tenth of the Gross National Product – in other words, some 10% of the total goods and services produced in the USA. Mass production was America's genius, the great size of the domestic market permitting production figures which were impossible elsewhere. But what struck foreign observers was the spirit of American business enterprise.

'Moses was one of the greatest salesmen and real estate promoters that ever lived'

The decade began with condemnations by the religious establishment of 'excessive nudity' (when skirts rose ten inches above the ankle) and 'improper dancing' (the charleston). But by the mid-twenties business had turned the tables and was actually using the religion of the founding fathers in its own cause. According to Frederic Lewis Allen's *Only Yesterday*, a pamphlet from the Metropolitan Casualty Insurance Company declared that 'Moses was one of the greatest salesmen and real estate promoters that ever lived.' The best-selling non-fiction book in both 1925 and 1926 was *The Man Nobody Knows*, in which hundreds of thousands of Americans learned that Jesus was 'the founder of modern business'. He 'picked up twelve men from the bottom ranks of business and forged them into an organization which conquered the world'. His parables 'were the most powerful advertisements of all time'.

126

Indeed, America in the 1920s was the birthplace of modern advertising: this and the newly invented hire purchase were the two key dynamos behind the consumer spending explosion of the 1920s. By the end of the decade, advertising amounted to 1.5% of national income and hire purchase sales to over 5%. Whole new markets – like cosmetics, vitamins and even cigarettes – were created by advertising. Perhaps it even gave the decade its two hallmarks, which were fun and fantasy – the hallmarks, too of the stock market boom.

Visions of Riches

Economists point out that the period 1922–9 was not one of uninterrupted expansion. House-building peaked in 1925 and did not reach that level again in the decade. There was a downturn in production in 1927, thought to be largely accounted for by a six-month shutdown at Ford, to switch from the Model T to the Model A.

Much the same could be said for the long US expansion between 1982 and 1987, the longest in post-war history. This latter expansion showed many of the characteristics of the 1920s' boom in America. It, too, was born out of an exceptionally deep economic trough – and a disinflationary one, if not a deflationary one. It, too, was much more of an American phenomenon than a worldwide one. And it, too, was accompanied by a similar crescendo of speculation and debt build-up.

The spirit of 'God Bless America' was plain to see in President Coolidge's State of the Union message in January 1928. No Congress had ever surveyed 'a more pleasing prospect [of] tranquillity and contentment . . . and the highest record of years of prosperity'. Astonishingly, the credit was attributed not to the excellence of the administration: 'The main source of these unexampled blessings lies in the integrity and character of the American people.' To this, J. K. Galbraith added trenchantly in *The Great Crash 1929*: 'One thing in the twenties should have been visible even to Coolidge. It concerned the American people of whose character he had spoken so well. Along with the sterling qualities he praised, they were also displaying an inordinate desire to get rich quickly with the minimum of effort.'

The 'inordinate desire' first became apparent in the Florida land boom of 1925–6 (see Chapter 5). Palm trees, sandy beaches, a subtropical climate: Florida was irresistible to the hearts of those weary of grim northern winters. It was in 1925, in sympathy with the Florida boom, that share prices got away in Wall Street. Until 1924 they had been held down to a ceiling in the low 100s on the Dow Jones Industrial Index, which had been set to a base of 100 back in 1915 – just as in the 1960s and 1970s the Dow stuck around 1000. In 1926 they paused, as the disaster of the Florida property crash was digested. And in 1927 they flew again to take

127

the Dow above 200. During the rest of 1927 the advance was steady and comfortable; and that was the year in which the seeds of the ensuing euphoria took root.

The New Era

Shares had taken twenty-five years to double since the turn of the century, and they had doubled again in just two years. In 1928 the pace accelerated. In March, sales of Cadillacs – the yuppies' Porsche of the 1920s – in New York hit an all-time high. The talk was not of earnings or dividends, but of 'pools' (syndicates who blatantly manipulated shares for profit – the equivalent of the arbitrageurs of the 1980s) and the next round hundred that Radio (RCA) or Otis or Allegheny would be boomed to. As the year wore on, money grew too valuable to be wasted on Cadillacs – it was needed for margin.

Margin was the formula for disaster in the 1920s' share mania. You could put down as little as 10% of the value of a share and get the rest on tick from your broker. During 1927, these broker loans had risen an extraordinary one billion dollars to 3.5 billion dollars. In the course of 1928, they were to rise a further 2.2 billion dollars – and about the same again in 1929. At that point the borrowing amounted to maybe 5000 dollars per shareholder, which was nearly one-tenth of the total value of shares quoted on the Stock Exchange – including those belonging to the institutions and to inactive holders, neither of whom traded and who would not dream of borrowing to buy stocks. And that was not the end of the story by any means.

Many knew in their hearts that the growth in broker loans was a bad thing. But the bull market itself, with its eagerness to buy shares, was the best thing that ever happened to anybody – wasn't it? And anyone who berated it was on a consistent hiding to nothing – not least because they were always crying 'Wolf'. It was in November 1927 that Coolidge had innocently coined the phrase 'new era'. In no time the phrase had acquired capital letters and become a creed of the crowd – rather like 'Reaganomics' or 'Thatchers's Britain'. The New Era was an 'ever-rising plateau of prosperity', as the economist Irving Fisher was unfortunately to describe the conditions in late 1929. Very few were willing to be bearish and bad-mouth the market in these circumstances – the most remarkable exception being the editor of the *New York Times*, Alexander Dana Noyes.

The first crack in the 'Coolidge' market came on 12 June 1928, when for the first time the volume of shares traded passed 5 million. Said the *New York Times*: 'Wall Street's bull market collapsed with a detonation heard around the world.' Of course that proved to be nonsense. By August the Dow was 20% up on the June lows. The punters were reassured; the confidence of the bulls was reinforced. So shares powered ahead through the summer and autumn to a peak in November, during which share volume twice exceeded 6.5 million and the Dow neared the magic 300 mark.

In succession to Coolidge, Hoover had been elected President in a landslide in November. The market rallied after a nasty break on 8 December when Radio slumped 72 points: presumably a bull pool had pulled the plug, for Radio was perhaps their favourite counter. The basic technique consisted of zigzagging a share upwards in such a way as to attract maximum attention and hence maximum public following – which in turn would allow the operators to exit with huge profits, whereupon the share would fall away with nothing but sellers around. Thus ended the most exuberantly profitable year Wall Street would see to this day.

As America entered 1929, a million or two of the 120 million population, mostly on the East Coast and embracing much of the wealth of America, were whirled up in a cyclone they could not possibly understand. Could they have been in some way responsible for the economic horror that was to follow? Not just the Crash that was their personal ruin – that goes without saying – but the Depression that was the misery of millions in America and beyond?

In *The Great Depression* Lord Robbins wrote: 'It is agreed that to prevent the depression, the only method is to prevent the boom.' Clearly the broker loan borrowing that pushed shares up far higher than they would otherwise have gone in 1929 was responsible for pushing them lower than they would otherwise have fallen in 1932. But this form of 'leverage' was only part of a web of borrowing that was to destroy the economy as well as the stock market.

The hallmark of the great bull market is participation by the mass public

---

The hypnotic commitment to the fantasy of great and quick riches, shared by almost all those in charge of the financial institutions of the day, shaped the weapons of its suicide. The arch-promoter of the cult of stocks for everybody was actually a high street bank, National City. Its President, Charles E. Mitchell, employed an army of salesmen to hawk shares around the country like brushes. Naturally the clients were encouraged to borrow for the purpose. In 1929 John J. Rascob, chairman of the Democratic National Committee as well as a director of General Motors, published in the *Ladies' Home Journal* an article entitled 'Everybody Ought to Be Rich'. All you had to do was invest 15 dollars a month in shares and you would collect 80,000 dollars (well over a million dollars in today's money) in twenty years' time. Clearly he sensed that that was too long to wait for the promised land. So out came the Rascob plan for the enrichment of the common man. It was no more nor less than a highly geared investment trust: you put in 200 dollars; the trust added a further 300 dollars of borrowings, so it could buy 500 dollars' worth of shares for you. If the shares doubled, you would make 3.5 times your money. And if the shares dropped 40%. . . . Admittedly then the trust would be wiped out, but Rascob found it inconceivable that shares could fall 40%. The party chairman's brain was addled, it seems.

Doubtless his plan was to invest in the highly geared investment trusts – Shenandoah, Allegheny, Blue Ridge and others with more prosaic names like the Goldman Sachs Trading Corporation – which, from small beginnings in 1927, had mushroomed. That way the gearing and the rewards could be doubled and trebled. Unfortunately so would the risks. At the height of the market the investment trusts were valued at 8 billion dollars – a tenth of the value of the entire market. By 1933, nearly all had been wiped out. Their names have vanished from history.

Blow-off

Shares spent the first five months of 1929 fluctuating – rather as they did in late 1986. Then in June the market took off again. The boom was led by investment trusts and electricals. General Electric and AT & T both rose 50% between May and the end of August. Westinghouse was up 75%. It is at this point in the story that we hit the clichés about the barber, lift operator, bootblack – you name them – offering share tips to one and all. Perhaps one of the bootblacks was Aristotle Onassis, who passed through that humble trade on his way to becoming a multi-millionaire shipowner.

By their nature, great bull markets end in 'distribution' by investors who sell shares that have risen way beyond their expectations to others who are drawn to buying shares 'because they are rising' – i.e. have risen. (The hallmark of the great bull market is the arrival of newcomers: participation by the mass public. There was an awesome instance of the bull market in gold in the winter of 1980–1, which saw an amazing stampede into coins by the public, particularly in France.) Distribution in Wall Street began in earnest in that consolidation period early in 1929.

Another phenomenon of bull market tops is the so-called 'final speculative blow-off'. With hindsight, the blow-off can be very precisely sited on 3 September – the day after the Labor Day recess and the hottest day of the year – when the Dow hit that famous peak of 381 that it wasn't to see again for over two decades. Between 30 June and 4 October, according to Federal Reserve figures cited by Professor Kindleberger in *The World in Depression*, total brokers' loans exploded from 7 billion dollars to 8.5 billion dollars.

Finally, great speculative peaks invariably coincide with tight money conditions. On 9 August, the New York Fed raised its interest rate from 5 to 6%. That was very high for those days – though nowhere near as high as the rate for brokers' loans, which were up to 12–18% in late summer.

With the experience of October 1987 fresh in the mind, there is something clammily familiar in the way the Great Crash stole up on Wall Street in October 1929. There was nothing exceptional in the nine-point break in the market on 5 September – except for the eerie rationalization of the event by observers of the day. It came to be called 'the Babson break', in honour of 'a frail, goateed, pixyish-looking man in Wellesley, Massachusetts' – in John Brooks's words – who for the past several years had been forecasting like clockwork a crash in late summer. All was quiet until mid-October, apart from a 'mystery decline' – a sharp break on 24 September from which the market recovered with aplomb – that discomfited the bears like Noyes of the *New York Times*.

But the bearish case was not based on observations from the business background. The data showed industrial activity peaking in June. Certain industries, like construction and automobiles, had topped out in March. But it must have looked like a temporary recession – 'the runner catching his breath', as the Boston News Bureau put it on 19 October – similar to that of 1927, which had left the stock market unscathed.

Also on 19 October the Harvard Economic Society, the leading business analysts of the day, noted that business was facing 'another period of adjustment' but added that 'if recession should threaten . . . (as is not indicated at present) there is little doubt that the [Federal] Reserve System would take steps to ease the money market and so check the movement'. The Society was absolutely right about the Fed taking steps, but the movement proved to be uncheckable. The theory that a collapsing economy was the cause of the Crash doesn't hold up.

The Coming of Fear

Against this background the market action on Saturday, 19 October was rather spooky, coming, as it did, after a six-point fall in the Dow the day before. Sunday's *New York Times* announced: 'Stocks driven down as wave of selling engulfs market.' The omens were not good for Monday, and sure enough stocks were down again at the start of the new week.

Then on Wednesday something sinister happened. Quite often during the busy days of 1929 the stock ticker which recorded all share transactions on the New York Stock Exchange had run behind. It was one thing for that to happen on good days: the punters just didn't know exactly how rich they were. But of course on a bad day what they didn't know was how much poorer they were. People had had some nasty shocks on Saturday and Monday on account of delays in the ticker. This was particularly alarming in the case of shares bought on margin. For if the speculator was unable to find cash to make up the collateral that had been eroded by falling shares, they were sold out willy-nilly. That Wednesday, the stock index tumbled 7% with an unprecedented 2.6 million shares traded in the final hour, leaving the ticker way behind. If New Yorkers were in the dark, it was worse for stockholders elsewhere, for a blizzard had blown down telephone wires in the Mid-West, leaving millions incommunicado.

The next day, 24 October, later came to be called Black Thursday – though for blackness it wasn't a candidate compared with Black Tuesday, 29 October. But then in terms of the plunge in values neither of them was in the same league as Black Monday, 19 October 1987. The lessons of 1929 no longer lie in the horror of free-falling share prices, for we have seen worse. The lessons lie in the pattern of inevitability that unfolded as the Crash developed; in the constantly recurring hopes that each leg in the Crash was the last one; in the fools' rally that followed it in early 1930; in the interplay between sliding share values and the collapsing economy; in the spread of the slump from America to the rest of the world; in the depth, darkness and despair of the Depression for the people who lived through it; in the attitudes of those who survived and even prospered in it; and finally in the ground that the Depression laid for the great post-war expansion.

Actually, Meltdown Thursday would have been an appropriate monicker for 24 October. The danger was forced selling from the mass of margin calls that had gone out the night before, and the possibility that this would develop into a self-feeding avalanche. It was clear from the opening weight of trading that 24 October would be special: the day was to tally a total volume of 12.9 million shares – nearly twice as much as had ever been seen before. The direction of prices was never in much doubt, but it quickly became apparent that the violence of the fall was out of the ordinary. However, this was at first only apparent to the specialists on the floor, since the ticker tape was soon lagging. Next came a new nightmare.

Something sinister happened – the ticker which
recorded all share transactions had run behind

The lighted screen, on which the latest (outdated) trades were flashed, showed only the last digit of the price. So sellers found to their horror that '3' for Radio meant not 63 (down 5¾ from the opening) but 53 – and when the fill for an order 'at market' came back, it was at, say, 48, five points lower than the latest ticker. At the end of the day, the ticker was four hours eight minutes behind.

John Pierpont Morgan, founder of the bank named after him, had won fame by single-handedly stopping the Panic in 1907 dead in its tracks. Now the bank's floor broker Richard Witney, soon to be President of the Stock Exchange and later to be jailed for fraud, was about to become a national hero for the same reason. At about 1.30, when the Exchange had already got wind of a long-awaited support operation, Witney walked in and issued the most famous bid in history: '205 for 10,000 steel.' He carried on with more huge orders and the day was saved – a day that might otherwise have been worse than the famous one five days short of fifty-eight years later.

Wipe-out

But that was nothing but a Pyrrhic victory. The following Monday the Dow opened at 298 – already it was off 22% from the peak. By the close of Black Tuesday, 29 October, following complete pandemonium on the Stock Exchange and after 16.4 million shares had been traded, it was down to 230.

Did anyone commit suicide in October 1987? A murder or two were recorded, but no suicides. The stories recounted by J. K. Galbraith, 'of pedestrians picking their way delicately between the bodies of fallen financiers' on the pavements of Wall Street and Broad Street in 1929, are picturesque but exaggerated. Sidney Weinberg, senior partner of Goldman Sachs, said later, 'I don't know anybody who jumped out of a window.' But as the days went by grim reports of suicides were to appear in the papers – including that of two men who had jumped hand in hand from the Ritz (they had a joint account). 'Goodness gracious what for. We used to say to each other: Are they nuts? What is money?' So said jazz trumpeter Jimmy Portland while reminiscing to Studs Terkel, whose masterpiece *Hard Times* is one of the great original documents of the Depression.

Had they not borrowed to buy shares, no one would have committed suicide. As it is, those who did lost more than everything. In addition to the money, they had speculated with their ego, and, it must be supposed, could not bear to live having lost. They had been soaring gods, and could not abide being crawling mortals.

Share prices zigzagged down to hit their lows for the year on 13 November – ten weeks after the peak – with the Dow at 198, down 48% from the high in the fastest fall in history. Brokers' loans at year-end had more than halved to 4.1 billion dollars. Unfortunately they still amounted to 10% of the total value of shares. Hard-hit punters had to find over 4 billion dollars to save their credit.

The annihilation of confidence cannot be so easily measured; but the economy went into a nose-dive immediately after the Crash. The impulse did not come from any credit crisis. Heroically, the New York banks absorbed the massive redemptions of call money on the brokers' loan accounts (and others) from regional and foreign banks. The call money rate stayed at a lowly 6%, as the Federal Reserve System lowered interest rates immediately to 5%, and in steps to 2½% by June 1930 – along with large injections of liquidity.

Imports actually hit their all-time peak in October at 396 billion dollars; by December they had dived to 307 billion dollars; and by July 1930 they were down to 218 billion dollars. Car production plummeted from 416,000 in September to 92,000 in December. Commodity prices in September were mostly above their June levels. By December they were sliding across the board: copper down from 75 dollars a ton to 8.30, coffee from 22.5 cents a pound to 15.5, cotton from 17.6 cents to 16.6, tin from 45.4 cents to 37.9. By September 1930 the figures were respectively

---

Two men jumped hand in hand from the Ritz (they had a joint account)

46.3 dollars, 12 cents, 10.1 cents and 25.3 cents. And as if any further proof were needed that the stock market was calling the tune of the economy, business actually began a tentative recovery in early 1930 – when the famous fools' rally in the stock market was underway. The uninitiated bought shares at this time, not realizing that such upturns after a crash are very short-lived and there is no profit to be made. In the five months from 13 November, the Dow recovered 99 points or exactly 50% from the 198 low. US employment 'actually picked up from the December level', according to Kindleberger. Industrial production levelled out. Imports rose in March and April, held steady through June, but collapsed in July.

The stock market, they say, does whatever it needs to do to prove most of the people wrong most of the time. Surprisingly, most of the victims of the Crash – and of the following Depression – blamed themselves. As the rally developed so did the feeling that the Crash had all been a ghastly mistake – an aberration. Had not the President and all his men, and the leaders of industry, assured one and all that business was 'fundamentally sound'?

But fate was just preparing its unkindest cut. The rally in stocks, the stabilization of business, the told-you-so's from all the New Era men were nothing but a vicious trap. In May the dreaded bear market was underway again, and those caught in the fools' rally knew they had been had. By the end of the year, the market had cascaded down 60% from the recovery top. Another false dawn came in early 1931, and there were two more that year. Each painful recovery raised the hope that the low had been seen; each ensuing sickening crash was like October 1929 in its violence. There were five of these downdraughts in the course of 1930 and 1931. And then, in 1932, a hellish final slaughter wave, a virtually uninterrupted avalanche worth any two of the earlier air pockets, dumped shares down into the dark depths visited half a century earlier.

Hard Times

Bonds are usually a safe investment because the return is in some way guaranteed. Were bond investors spared in 1929? Only those holding the very best paper, the kind issued by the government and AAA corporations. Many lower-grade bonds and risk-laden 'junk' bonds became worthless as innumerable businesses went bankrupt. Hundreds of banks failed, though oddly enough there was nothing that could have been called a banking collapse until 1933. National income during the Depression was cut by 55%. Unemployment rose to 13.7 million or 25%.

But the stories in *Hard Times* say much more about the human distress than any statistics could. A farmer from Iowa recalled:

First they'd take your farm, then they took your livestock, then your farm machinery. Even your household goods. ... Grain was being burned. It was cheaper than coal. ... In South Dakota, the county elevator listed corn at minus three cents. *Minus* three cents a bushel. If you wanted to sell 'em a bushel of corn you had to bring in three cents.

One woman told of having her first pair of boots in 1940, when she got married. There were thousands in similar conditions.

It is generally agreed that in America the Depression ended in early 1933 with the accession of Roosevelt and the proclamation of his New Deal, though some claim it lingered on until 1939. Almost his first act in office was to close all the banks and insurance companies so that they could sort themselves out, for the financial system had utterly collapsed.

The Contagion Spreads

The way the slump spread elsewhere, all over the globe, leaves little room for doubt that it was by contagion from America – and hence from the Crash of '29. The Crash itself was instantly echoed in Canada, Britain, the Netherlands and Belgium. The slide in stock markets elsewhere began in earnest on the failure of New York's fools' rally in May 1930.

Compared with the decline of 89% in the Dow from the September 1929 peak to the mid-1932 trough, declines elsewhere ranged from 85% in Canada to just over 50% in Britain and France. Germany was near the bottom of the scale, while the Netherlands (80%) and Belgium were nearer the top. However, shares everywhere other than Canada had peaked before September 1929 – starting with Germany in early 1927, and following with Belgium, Switzerland, Sweden, France, Britain (January 1929) and the Netherlands. Finally, in France and Belgium the bear market was to go straight on through 1934, while in Britain alone equities were to regain their 1929 highs by 1935.

135

Until mid-1931, the global slump was the worst recession in memory. After the failure of Austria's Credit-Anstalt in May 1931, the implosion of Europe's financial system proceeded like a black hole. There were runs on the banks of Hungary, Czechoslovakia, Romania, Poland and finally Germany; a run on gold at the Reichsbank; the failure of the Danatbank; and the closure of the German banking system. German unemployment stood at over 4.5 million. World trade had collapsed from 35 billion dollars in 1929 to 12 billion by 1933, and took with it the economies of Canada, Australia and most of Latin America. Sterling abandoned the Gold Standard in September 1931 and plunged from 4.86 dollars to the pound to hit 3.25 dollars in December. The pound took twenty-five countries with it. The round of competitive devaluations continued, taking the yen with it in December. The only exception was Germany, which under 'Hunger Chancellor' Brüning pursued deliberate deflation in preference to anything that had the faintest whiff of Weimar. The final spectre to rise from the Depression was Nazism.

Why Did It All Happen?

For all great historical events there is an immediate cause, which seems readily apparent to all, and also an underlying cause whose origins are less readily detectable. On the surface it appeared as if the Great Depression and worldwide slump were due to the crash of the stock market that led to the collapse of the banking system and evaporation of personal savings. But this theory does not answer the question of why the shares on the Stock Exchange crashed to begin with. If we delve deeper into the origins of the Crash, what we really find is an 'exhaustion of excess'.

One of the harbingers of the great boom in share prices that preceded the Great Crash was the growth of the motor industry. When we consider that the number of cars produced in America during March 1929 was actually higher than the number produced in December 1987, it can be readily appreciated that demand in 1929 could not possibly absorb supply. When the crunch came in the motor industry it was catastrophic. The level of car production fell from 660,000 in March 1929 to 92,000 by December that year. Those employed in that and related industries were immediately put out of work. A depression was the inevitable outcome. The long period of expansion fuelled by the growth of the car industry had reached the end of its tether.

In the post-mortems that followed the Great Crash, many voices were heard to say that the Crash had been caused by the rising wave of international protectionism and the instigation of the Smoot-Hawley Tariff Act. But this conclusion fails to differentiate cause from effect. The Smoot-Hawley Tariff Act did not come into effect until June 1930, long after the collapse in the stock market was underway. US protectionism

136

during the 1930s was a major problem for foreign countries, but less so for Americans. At the time, US imports amounted to only 4% of Gross National Product, while world trade was only one-third of global Gross National Product. It certainly wasn't the failure of world markets, due to protectionism, to absorb the production of American goods that caused the stock market to crash. The real reason was the blind overproduction of American goods by entrepreneurs who failed to realize there were limits to the ability of the domestic market to absorb them. The true culprit was greed undeflected by reality.

Government is a favourite scapegoat at such moments in history. Many people held the view that the US government was responsible for the Great Crash because of its failure to execute the necessary bail-outs and to boost money supply enough to prevent the collapse of the economy. This argument may seem acceptable to those ignorant of what actually took place, but as a percentage of Gross National Product, money supply in the USA rose steadily from the time of the Great Crash until shares hit bottom in 1932. The suggestion that the US authorities did not expand the money supply during and after the Crash is therefore totally false.

It may be argued, by those who exercise genius with hindsight, that the authorities did not expand the money supply fast enough. This argument, too, is shallow. It is true that the money supply was contracting in nominal terms because the economy, too, was contracting. Yet the degree of economic contraction was attributable to far more than an inability to finance requirements. For example, against a fall in money supply of only 13%, Gross National Product in Canada fell by 33%. The fall in the US money supply may have seemed horrendous at 33% in nominal terms, yet Gross National Product in the USA only contracted by 4% more than Gross National Product in Canada.

Indirectly the authorities were responsible for the Great Crash by allowing the explosive rise in the level of debt

---

Indirectly – and only indirectly – the authorities were responsible for the Great Crash by allowing the explosive rise in the level of debt. I say 'indirectly' because it must be remembered that it is people themselves who decide to incur debt. The authorities do not force individuals to borrow. The only guilt shared by the authorities is in allowing the credit to become available through lenient monetary and fiscal policy, which is usually demanded by the people.

As America entered the slump, farm debt was estimated at 12 billion dollars, hire purchase debt at 6 billion dollars, and stockbrokers' loans at 8.5 billion dollars. Overall, debt represented no less than 150% of US Gross National Product, the highest level ever recorded in the United

States, challenged only by the fiat economy of John Law's Mississippi Bubble. When share prices on the Stock Exchange began to collapse, the debt that was secured by shares had to be liquidated. The liquidation of debt became a self-feeding chain reaction that riddled the entire economy. The resulting economic implosion in dollar terms saw the US economy reduced to half its size by the end of 1932, meaning that debt in relation to income had soared to the crippling level of three times Gross National Product.

The cause of the Great Crash is no mystery. The culmination of speculative excesses combined with excesses in production, founded on the kind of manic build-up in debt that has preceded every mega-slump in history, simply represented the seeds of its own self-destruction. In its inimitable wisdom, the New York Stock Exchange began to anticipate the inevitable outcome when the Crash began in the summer of 1929.

8

The Crash of the Banks

How the banking moratorium during 1933 reduced
America to a barter system while a large number of
banks never opened their doors again

The Gorilla at the End of the Tunnel

By the summer of 1932 the Crash of '29 seemed only a fading echo, a
tragedy that had spent its force. By most accounts, a world economic
recovery and a return to prosperity were underway, much to the relief of
the many who had suffered the long years of depression. As it turned out,
the light at the end of the tunnel was analogous to a gorilla with a
flashlight waiting to maul the complacent who actually believed they had
seen the worst of the financial crisis. In March 1933 the United States
experienced one of the most violent financial debacles in modern history.
Yet this was a purely American phenomenon – the downward plunge of
US business activity between January and March 1932 was in stark
contrast to the steady improvement experienced in most other major
countries.

How did it come about that the bastion of twentieth-century capitalism
burst into flame again so quickly? What forces turned the first gentle
zephyrs of social restoration into a typhoon of fear and panic during forty
days of political paralysis?

The World of Rock and Roll Banking

What I am going to talk about is so important – and so are the lessons that
could be learned for the future – that it is worth taking a little time to fill in
the background and describe the nature of the fractional reserve banking
system, which represents the foundation of modern banking. I apologise if
you think you're going to be bored, but this is where the key to the
banking crisis of the 1930s lies. The likelihood of a recurrence of such a
crisis can be directly traced to the heart of the system that governments
have perpetuated in their own interests.

139

Despite the enormous effect it has on economic activity, the true nature of bank credit is not very well understood outside the limited circle of bankers and professional economists. Bank or deposit credit may be defined simply as an obligation on the part of a bank to pay a certain sum of money on demand, and this obligation is identified only by an entry in the books of a bank, without any currency or other transferable documents being involved. Although bank credit was originally established as the result of a specific deposit (or specie), the extension of such credit on the basis of external collateral (property, shares, insurance policies and so on), or simply on the presumed good faith of the borrower, has been practised since the fifteenth century. In modern times, such externally secured and non-secured bank credit has become by far the dominant instrument of finance. As a result, the reliability of modern bank credit as money today rests heavily on the prudence and discretion of the bankers.

So long as the borrower does not draw his 'deposit' in cash, but simply transfers this credit to others by means of a cheque, very little actual money or 'reserve' is needed by a bank to support the credit. The bank's credit can be multiplied endlessly as cheques drawn on 'created' bank credit can be deposited in other banks and become assets used to create new loans and more credit. John Law tried to quantify the commercial wealth of France through the use of banknotes, and his successors tried to monetize the very soil of France through the device of the *assignats* (see Chapter 3). But these futile efforts have been magnificently eclipsed by the modern banker, who has turned debt itself into money by the magic of bank credit and the chequebook. The use of bank credit as money is so much a part of the modern financial structure that most people are dumbfounded to learn that the actual amount of currency available, both in circulation and held by banks as reserves, would redeem only a small fraction of the so-called deposits of banking and financial institutions.

From the standpoint of the depositor in a bank, the entire affair is a matter of confidence. If people believe their money is safe sitting in the bank they'll leave it in the bank, fortifying the safety of the bank. If people lose confidence in their banks or in the banking system as a whole, and all rush to take out their money and stuff it in their mattresses, their money in

---

The modern banker has turned debt itself into money through the magic of bank credit and the chequebook

---

the whole banking system becomes unsafe. The situation is beautifully illustrated by the story of the Irishman in America who, after climbing out of the quarry where he was working, strode into his local bank in dust-covered overalls and shouted: 'It's me – O'Flaherty. If me money's here, oy don't want it. If it ain't here, oy want it now!'

The fractional reserve banking system is exactly what it sounds like. Only a fraction of the money that a bank deals in need be held in reserve at the bank. Banks can be illiquid, or insolvent, or both. If a bank is illiquid, this is not a major problem so long as the call on the bank's liquidity does not exceed the cash on hand. Solvency can be restored through the central bank, which is usually the lender of last resort. If the bank becomes illiquid and insolvent simultaneously as a result of droves of customers demanding their money – this *is* a problem! The bank closes, often never to reopen.

The Domino Effect

The major banks don't simply use the world's monetary system – they *are* the world's monetary system. However, the true conditions of a nation's banking system can never be fully ascertained at any given moment. Unlike companies, banks do not have to disclose very much about their operations but are able to hide their affairs behind a cloak of mystery. Governments feel that public confidence in bank deposits is far more important than the principle of public disclosure. Information that might lead to an inquiry into a bank might also lead to a situation where frightened investors would pull their money out, not only from the bank under investigation but from other banks also. Anything that might lead to a crisis in confidence and a banking panic must be avoided at all costs.

The dreaded fear of every banker is the domino effect. It's a relatively simple concept. Let's say there are fifty thousand John Q. Publics who have their money deposited in the Tremendous Growth Savings Bank of Lower Slobovia, Wisconsin (in the USA banks are run on a state-by-state basis, not nationally, which means there is a proliferation of small banks). Now, let's suppose a clerk at the Tremendous Growth Savings Bank discovers that the bank has loaned 99% of its available capital to an oil drilling syndicate which has sunk 100% of its capital into drilling a dry hole. In no time at all that syndicate is going to go under and take the bank with it. So the well-informed clerk tells his neighbours. His neighbours tell their friends. Like greased lightning, the entire population of Lower Slobovia, Wisconsin is going to appear at the doors of the Tremendous Growth Savings Bank demanding their money. The bank, which was insolvent, will then become illiquid, and be forced to close. That's the fall of the first domino.

Presumably a number of John Q. Publics who had their money deposited in the Tremendous Growth Savings Bank and were unable to get it out in time will have money in other banks in Lower Slobovia. It is also probable that the insolvent Tremendous Growth Savings Bank will have borrowed from other banks in town. Those who are concerned over the failure of the Tremendous Growth Savings Bank – even though they may

141

not have any money there – will join those who were unable to get their money out and run to the other banks in Lower Slobovia, if only to get some ready cash while the getting is good. It is more than likely that some of the other banks will topple under the demands from their depositors and be forced to close their doors. That's the fall of the second domino.

A prudent move by the local authorities at this time would be to close all the banks in Lower Slobovia, pending a relaxation of the panic and an attempted restructuring of the system. Of course, if this happened all the John Q. Publics who had money in banks outside the town would turn there for ready cash. Once again there would be a build-up of pressure, leading to more bank closures. The state authorities might have no alternative but to close all the banks in Wisconsin. I don't need to tell you what comes next. . . . Eventually no bank in the country is safe – which is precisely what happened in the USA between January and March 1933.

The Seeds of Calamity

The structural deficiencies in the banking system had been apparent for several years before the disaster. Sowing the seeds of calamity were those with a traditional penchant for sowing seeds, the farmers. During the early 1920s the banks were falling over themselves to lend to farmers, encouraging them to increase their yields. The cash accumulated in the banking system at that time was the result of years of lending at usurious interest rates, aided and abetted by expansionist government policy.

When the price of farm products fell during the late 1920s, farmers were forced to increase their borrowing at the banks just to survive. In some states, at one point during the 1920s, up to 85% of farms were mortgaged. Compounding the inherent weakness of the banking system in the United States were the large numbers of independent businessmen who were acting as bankers and whose lending policies were less than prudent.

In 1929, world over-production of wheat caused a precipitous drop in its price, and sharp sympathetic falls in the prices of other farm produce. Thousands of farmers were bankrupted and took their small local bankers into the abyss with them. In areas devoted to arable farming the strain on small regional banks was intolerable. Throughout the late 1920s, the failure of several hundred banks each year in the United States was commonplace. When one failed, the assets of others were frozen while depositors elsewhere received a pregnant warning to the effect that they must not ask for their money back.

Yet throughout the Roaring Twenties confidence was high and people were apathetic about possible banking problems. The stock market was reaching new all-time highs nearly every day. When 346 banks failed during the first six months of 1929, no one took much notice. It wasn't until the Crash of '29 – a crash that shifted sentiment decisively and dramatically – that people began to listen to the alarm bells that had been sounding in the banking system for many years. During early 1930 the public began running scared of the banks, and finally they began to pay close attention to the rise in the number of bank failures.

There were 1352 of them in the fiscal year 1930. During fiscal 1931 the number of failures leaped again, reaching 2294. The situation was becoming alarming and there were repeated calls for the government to step in. Following the release of the 1931 figures, President Hoover set up the National Credit Corporation in an effort to enlist the co-operation of the bankers. The object was to enable the strong banks to help the weaker ones, who from time to time might find themselves with liquidity or solvency problems. Capitalized at 500 million dollars, subscribed by the principal US bankers, the Corporation helped save hundreds of banking institutions that autumn.

For a while, the wave of bank failures abated. But when they began to erupt again, the new scheme collapsed in a shambles. More funds were required, but the amount forthcoming was not sufficient. The 'strong measures' promised by the government were too little, too late.

Congress then created, as a 'bankers' bank', the Reconstruction Finance Corporation (RFC), which was more generously capitalized than the National Credit Corporation had been. It was to start off with 2 billion dollars, later raised to 3 billion and then to 3.5 billion in yet another desperate effort to rescue the rapidly collapsing American banking system.

In the 1932 fiscal year the number of bank failures was down to 1456 from the record level of 2294 the previous year. The US banking system was not going to suffer the domino collapse so many had feared. But the tide that had been set in motion was genuinely unstoppable. The excesses had by no means been wrung out of the bloated credit system. Farmers, businessmen and others were still being forced into bankruptcy in ever-increasing numbers. The bad loans on the books of the bankers were escalating rapidly.

Banks are able to hide their affairs under a cloak of mystery

---

During March and April 1932, two events sent shock waves through the US financial system. The first was the suicide in Paris of a man named Ivor Kruger, exposing an unimaginable web of fantastic speculative pyramiding – the financially risky abuse of the holding company system. The second was the collapse of the Insull utility empire in the American Mid-West. By annihilating the savings of tens of thousands of small investors, and by further assaulting public confidence in banks and investments in general, these two crashes carried the nation once again to the brink of a general money panic. They couldn't have come at a less opportune time, since those directing the battle for financial survival in Washington firmly believed that every weapon and every available resource of the US economy had already been mobilized.

Many people believe that the collapse in the banking system was triggered by the figures regularly published in the RFC lending lists. The sums allocated were intended to provide the substructure for America's entire financial system. In September 1932 it was revealed that 1.5 million dollars of the 3.5 billion allocated had already been loaned by the RSC in its first six months of operation – yet there was still no evidence of any appreciable improvement in financial conditions, and banks and corporations continued to topple. As bankers and investors became progressively aware of the total inadequacy of the measures that had been taken they were horrified. In the weeks following the RFC report runs on banks were intensified.

The publicity that the RFC lending figures were to attract was electric. One Congressman claimed that they resulted in the closure of several hundreds of banks which could have weathered the storm if it had not been for the added pressure of 'publicity runs' – when one bank in a small community had borrowed from the RFC, depositors tended gradually to shift their money into a bank that had not borrowed. At the same time, fear of the consequences of publication restrained many hundreds of other needy banks from seeking RFC assistance.

The immediate effect was to focus increasing pressure upon those very areas which the RFC arrangements had been designed to protect. The ultimate consequence was to tighten credit generally, at a time when public confidence and fluid credit offered the only hope for resuscitation of the economy.

Hundreds of anxious depositors began lining the streets of Des Moines, Iowa, to draw out their money

It is not known whether the cause of the crisis was the publication of RFC loan figures; the bankruptcy of an increasing number of major companies and financial institutions; the plight of the farmers; the turmoil occurring in gold and currency markets that emanated from Europe at the time; or merely the uncertainties of the election in November 1932 of a President with a totally different style and set of values from Herbert Hoover. What does seem clear is that the banking crash of the 1930s was building to a crescendo during the winter of 1932. The bread lines and soup kitchens, the shanty towns on the outskirts of the major cities, the long, disconsolate queues in front of the banks that might soon close their doors – those scenes of distress, despondency and desolation have been printed thousands of times in words and pictures. But while it may not have seemed that conditions could get any worse, they could and they did, as America headed down the road towards a bankrupt society.

The State Moratoriums

Until October 1932, the bank failures were confined to small and medium-sized townships. Decisions to close the banks were usually made by the local mayor, whom the community knew and trusted. But in October the crisis took on a new and more menacing phase as people throughout Nevada began a stampede on the state's banks.

Many of those who rushed to draw their money out were shocked to find that the banks had already closed. On 22 October the Governor of Nevada ordered the closure of all banks in the state in an effort to preserve whatever was left of the state banking system. It was clear to him that very few of the banks could possibly meet the demands of the thousands of depositors who were requesting their cash.

Because the difficulties were principally of local origin and character, the bank moratorium in Nevada didn't excite any general alarm much beyond San Francisco. It wasn't until December that the truly abnormal strains began to appear on a national scale. Runs on country banks and loan associations occurred successively in Arkansas, Illinois, Iowa, Minnesota, Missouri, Tennessee, Pennsylvania, Washington and Wisconsin. In these widely scattered local crises appeared the first signs that fear was turning into panic.

In January 1933 a landslide of local panic spread to an increasing number of secondary cities, and runs developed on the banks of Little Rock, Chattanooga, Mobile, Memphis, St Louis and Cleveland. In the state of Iowa, the panic seemed to be taking on even greater proportions than elsewhere, and hundreds of anxious depositors began lining the streets of Des Moines to draw out their money. When the mayor decided to close all the banks, a state-wide crisis ensued. Acting on the Nevada precedent, the Governor of Iowa closed all the banks in the state in the hope that calm would eventually be restored.

New Orleans, San Francisco, Kansas City, Nashville and Baltimore were the next victims. But, miraculously, each outbreak was quieted by effective emergency action from the authorities, thus averting nationwide attention. Aside from the moratoriums in Nevada and Iowa, in only two major cities was banking suspended for more than a day. The quick mobilization of resources, the transfer of adequate protective funds from city to city and the prompt enlistment of an emergency currency from industry for the purpose of helping banks during a run seemed to contain the epidemic. But suddenly the emergency support operations seemed to stop working, and warnings of a money panic began to appear in the daily reports of the Comptroller of the Currency.

In Detroit the situation was already bad because the Depression had hit automobile manufacturers harder than any other US industry. Detroit was almost totally dependent on the automobile, and unemployment there was on a scale unparalleled in any other major city in the United States. The city had piled up a staggering volume of delinquent taxes while facing a local welfare burden that had swelled enormously during the previous three years. With the city's municipal bonds in default, its finances were being borne almost entirely upon the shoulders of local bankers and industrialists. In February 1933 Detroit was also faced with the weight of a gathering national banking crisis.

Officers of the RFC were informed that Detroit was in an extremely precarious state. President Hoover immediately took the lead in the battle to prevent another state banking moratorium, particularly since Michigan was one of the more powerful and influential states. But during the course of the attempted rescue operation a feud broke out between Henry Ford and Senator James Couzens over the two rival banking groups in the city. Ford had threatened to withdraw an unusually large deposit from one of the banks, which would have led to an immediate chain reaction of banking closures throughout Detroit and the rest of the state. In order to prevent this the Governor of Michigan closed all the banks in the state, and President Hoover's plans to rescue Michigan were brought to an end. On 14 February the Governor's proclamation was released, without consultation of the Treasury or the White House. Next morning, the news was blazoned on headlines from coast to coast.

America Goes Bankrupt

Tremendous pressure was at once thrown upon the Federal Reserve banks in Cleveland and Chicago, as well as upon larger member banks in Ohio, Indiana and Illinois. At the White House, it became apparent that a larger-scale plan of defence was needed. No longer would it suffice simply to buttress a weak spot in Detroit or to defend local pressures elsewhere. The new objective was to devise a means of protecting every bank in the country against the consequences of runs from frightened depositors. This was indeed a Herculean task, beyond the powers of mere mortals.

As this mammoth operation was being planned in Washington, an attempt on the life of President-elect Franklin D. Roosevelt set another wave of terror careering across the nation. Even during times of economic stability and relative normality, any shock or civil excitement tends to induce extreme caution in depositors and investors. People have a way of being highly protective of their savings. In times of great stress, such as prevailed during February 1933, the perceived effect of violent incidents

146

can be magnified out of all reason. That assassination attempt was indeed the death-knell for the banking system of the United States of America.

Early in the afternoon of 21 February Cleveland bankers telephoned the Federal Reserve Board reporting that they were under renewed pressure. The escalation of the panic was attributable to the sudden move by bankers in New York and Chicago, who had begun calling in loans made to corresponding banks in the Mid-Western states. At the same time, large industrial concerns were busily transferring heavy balances from banks in Mid-West cities to New York, hoping that the New York State banking system might hold – at least for a while. A further spread of panic was signalled by the state of New Jersey, where the Governor passed a law authorizing state banks to limit the amount of funds depositors could withdraw. During the evening of 22 February, a national holiday, Cleveland banks formally requested Governor White to declare a state-wide banking holiday. He refused on the grounds that such a proclamation would do more harm than good. Cleveland was saved for a few days because the RFC made money available.

A measure of the times was that serious street rioting was hardly noted in the national press

---

In the background, panic suddenly began to rage in Indiana. When the banks were due to reopen on the morning of the 23rd, following the national holiday, Indiana moved towards a bank holiday; as did Arkansas on the 24th and Maryland on the 25th. On the 26th, cities in Ohio and Indiana made desperate moves to protect depositors. On the 27th Pennsylvania authorized its banks to restrict withdrawals. The state of Delaware made a similar move on the 28th. A measure of the times was that serious street rioting was hardly noted in the national press. As the rip-tide of disaster swept over an increasing number of major cities, beleaguered bankers turned frantically to Washington – some of them demanding cash by aeroplane.

Also on the 28th, new state bank holidays were proclaimed in Nevada, Alabama, Kentucky and Tennessee. The most menacing news of all was the suspension of two banks in the District of Columbia, one of which was within five hundred yards of the US Treasury. In terms of the size of potential losses this was far less important than any suspension that had occurred during the previous ten days. But the psychological impact was potent. From New York to San Francisco newspaper headlines shouted: 'Washington Bank Suspends!' For many people, the only glimmer of hope was sustained by their faith in the federal government. But if banks could fail in the very shadow of the Treasury – what then?

During the first three days of March no fewer than sixteen states declared bank moratoriums. On the eve of President Roosevelt's

147

inauguration Governor Lehman closed all the banks in New York State. Only ten states had banks which were functioning and maintaining normal operations. There was insufficient gold left in the coffers of the Treasury to back the currency, and not enough cash left to meet the government payroll. The United States was technically bankrupt.

On the morning of 4 March, as control of government changed hands, Roosevelt knew he had to act – and act quickly. Within hours he took three major decisions. The first was to declare a national bank holiday for four days, which was subsequently extended to eight days. The second was to call Congress so that it could decide how best to reconstruct the US banking system. The third was to summon the nation's leading bankers to Washington to advise him how to deal with the crisis.

At 10.30 a.m. on Sunday, 5 March 1933, President Roosevelt released from the White House his historic proclamation closing every bank in the land. At the time there was no plan for the resumption of banking activities. The financial heartbeat of the greatest capitalist nation in the world had virtually come to a stop.

Life in a Cashless Society

Imagine what it would be like if you were to wake up one morning and suddenly discover that every bank in the country was closed indefinitely. You would have to plan your survival on the basis of the loose change in your pockets and whatever money was in your child's piggy bank. Suddenly, in the USA in 1933, the agony of apprehension was over. Something that everyone could understand had finally happened, something as clear and unequivocal as a clap of thunder. There was a sense of relief, that kind of mild euphoria that comes with the sudden release from pain. Grim, even tragic, though the closure of the banks may have been, people often laughed and made jokes of their common dilemma.

Human reactions revealed amazing resourcefulness and adaptability to the strange new conditions. In California, a hanging was delayed because it was illegal to excute anyone on a bank holiday. IOUs appeared on collection plates in churches. Salesmen stranded in cities away from their homes were reduced to hawking the contents of their sample cases in hotel lobbies. Businessmen met their payrolls with post-dated cheques, promissory notes, their own merchandise, or company-backed 'scrip'. The city of Cleveland circulated thousands of scrip 'dollar bills' signed by the mayor and treasurer. A three cent stamp had to be affixed each time a scrip changed hands. When a bill had acquired thirty-six stamps, the city promised to redeem it for 1.08 dollars in 'real' money. Telephone slugs, postage stamps, bus and subway tokens, foreign coins and even cigarette coupons all played a vital role in this 'funny money' situation. However, many businesses, such as hotels, restaurants, grocers and drugstores, preferred to deal on credit – though it was only available for their regular customers.

As the days of cashlessness continued, one of the most critical shortages was of coins. With only a 50 dollar bill in your pocket you were as bad as broke if you wanted to buy cigarettes – unless, of course, you were willing to pay 50 dollars for a ten cent pack. Shopkeepers would cruise the streets looking for newsboys who might be willing to sell them some small change – the going rate was 80 cents for a dollar bill, but the larger the bill the worse the rate of exchange for the bill owner.

The promoters of a boxing tournament at New York's Madison Square Garden announced their willingness to accept any usable barter in exchange for tickets: included in the items offered was said to be a pair of ladies' silk panties. When the Irish Players were scheduled to perform in Chicago, people took sacks of potatoes in exchange for admission.

For the majority of the American people the novelty and black humour of a cashless existence were a veneer that quickly wore thin. Those who were still wage earners could not afford to miss a single pay cheque by even a day without acute distress. Yet raising the fare to get to and from their place of work, or school, or the local welfare office, was often a continual family problem. Applications for public assistance soared beyond the immediate resources of government. Thousands began to suffer from hunger, cold and exposure. Some local authority workers with uncashable pay cheques in their pockets fainted on the job due to lack of food.

A Bruised and Battered Banking System Appears

During the bank holiday, squads of Federal Bank examiners worked round the clock going over the books of every bank in the nation to determine which could be safely reopened, which would have to be reorganized before opening, and which would have to be liquidated. The most feared imponderable was whether, when the banks did open their doors again, still panicky depositors might withdraw their money and thus cause the lethal process to begin all over again.

On the evening of Sunday, 12 March President Roosevelt spoke over a specially installed radio microphone at the White House, delivering one of his now famous Fireside Chats, in an effort to assuage the fears of the nation before the banks reopened the next day: 'Confidence and courage are the essentials in our plan. You must have faith; you must not be stampeded by rumours. We have provided the machinery to restore our financial system; it is up to you to support and make it. Together we cannot fail.'

The President's emotive speech should serve as an object lesson to all public speakers on what to do with a big vocabulary – leave it at home in the dictionary. 'Some people spend a lifetime juggling with words, with not even an idea in a car load,' mused the great philosophical humorist Will Rogers. 'Our President took such a dry subject as banking (and when I say "dry" I mean dry, for if it had been liquid, he wouldn't have had to speak on it at all) and made everybody understand it, even the bankers.'

At 9 a.m. on 13 March most of New York City's 140 banks reopened for business as usual. There were similar reopenings in cities throughout the country, characterized by uncomfortably long queues and agitated crowds. As the doors opened the anticipated rush descended upon the wary bankers. Another onslaught of withdrawals appeared inevitable. The Federal Reserve banking network was the key to the system. Each Federal Reserve bank had a direct wire to the White House where officials gathered to monitor the level of withdrawals from each of the member banks, standing ready to announce a further bank holiday at the first sign of crisis.

By noon on that critical Monday the first returns began appearing on the Federal Reserve wire. New York announced that during the first three hours of business the member Federal Reserve banks in the city had taken in 10 million dollars more than had been withdrawn. The Cleveland banks reported deposits exceeding withdrawals by just under 2 million dollars. Similar reports began coming in from the major banking centres across the nation. To the amazement and relief of all concerned, people were putting more money into their accounts than they were taking out. The panic was over.

But it wasn't all sweetness and light. By the end of the first hundred days of the Roosevelt administration some two thousand banks had disappeared, in addition to the several thousand that had failed prior to the national bank closures. As a result of either mergers or permanent closure,

---

When the promoters of a boxing tournament announced they would accept barter in exchange for tickets, a pair of ladies' silk panties was offered

---

9106 banks ceased to exist while 5 billion dollars in depositors' funds remained frozen. In less than three years America had lost more than one-third of its entire banking system. Many who had had funds deposited in the banks that failed had lost their entire life savings.

Could it happen again? There is a universally shared view that a banking calamity on the scale seen during the 1930s in America is not even a remote possibility. Governments have supposedly become far more knowledgeable and far more sophisticated. Most people are happy to accept the idea that mechanisms now exist which would preclude any major banking crisis. As politicians are fully aware, it's a very simple task to convince people of the notions they are willing to accept to start with.

For close to four decades there has been little mention of banking problems in the USA. In recent years these problems have suddenly come to the surface again. Not that long ago Continental Illinois – at one time the ninth largest bank in the United States – was the subject of a massive rescue operation by the Federal Reserve. The collapse of ESM Government Securities in 1985 led to the traditional domino effect, involving the closure of the Home State Savings Bank of Ohio which had invested heavily in them. That in turn led to the closure of seventy-one non-member banks in the state of Ohio.

Not since the Great Depression have ordinary citizens in America experienced the type of financial panic that gripped the ordinary conservative citizens of Cincinnati. Radio station chat shows and newspapers throughout the state were deluged with queries from anxious depositors aware of the problems facing Ohio's banks. Some had camped out for hours on the pavements in front of their savings banks when at 7.30 a.m. on 15 March the Governor of Ohio ordered a three-day bank holiday for the seventy-one local savings banks which were insured by Ohio Deposit Guarantee Fund.

'We have provided the machinery to restore our financial system; it is up to you to support and make it'

During 1985 there were 138 bank failures among federally insured banking institutions in the United States. During the first half of 1986 there were ninety-six bank failures in the USA compared with sixty-six during the corresponding period the previous year. During early 1988 the Federal Home Loan Board in the United States produced a document referred to as a 'supervisory briefing'. Its 1200 pages examined the affairs of 383 savings banks whose conditions range from 'brain dead', or hopelessly insolvent, to 'critical', with problems threatening survival. Banking institutions on the list are reeling from a combination of bad loans, inept management, fraud and hyper-speculation, along with a host of other problems. It is estimated that approximately 10 million dollars per day is being lost by allowing these insolvent savings banks to continue to function.

So far, the escalation in bank failures in America has failed to arouse major national concern – it took some time for the bank closures in the USA during the early 1930s to shake the complacency of the populace. There is nothing more than a thin and fragile thread of confidence holding the entire world banking system together. That thread could break at any time in the future, as it has done in the past. No one can state with any useful or meaningful degree of certainty – given the evidence – that a crisis of confidence sufficient to close all the banks in America could not occur at any time.

9

The Crash of the Silver Bubble

How the silver cartel bankrupted those who
believed they could control it

The Greatest Wildcatter of Them All

Wall Street once ran from a graveyard to a river. It now runs from an
ocean to an ocean. During the seventeenth century, when Tulipomania
mesmerized the Dutch, the aftermath of the panic was basically confined
to the Netherlands. Panics and crashes during the eighteenth and nineteenth centuries had their repercussions on a much larger scale, spanning
continents. Now any crash, anywhere, becomes a global incident.

As markets have changed over the centuries, so too have the men who
attempt to master them. Giants of a new breed are in control today – or
should I say, are permitted to take the helm for as long as their nerve and
capital can hold out. The new breed operate in markets on a scale never
dreamed of before. They speak casually of hundreds of millions and
billions as the men of the old markets spoke of hundreds of thousands and
millions. The new men influence governments, penetrate multi-national
industries and affect the lives of people the world over. The Crash of the
Silver Bubble reflects the exploits of one man, Nelson Bunker Hunt, along
with the fate of those who shared his mania.

Nelson Bunker Hunt's was certainly not a rags-to-riches story. In fact,
at several stages in his illustrious career it seemed that the trend could
easily be in the other direction. Unlike a large number who found their
calling in speculative markets, Nelson Bunker Hunt had inherited a vast
sum of money. His father, H. L. Hunt, was at one time reputed to be the
richest man in the world. Nelson Bunker Hunt was born with the
proverbial silver spoon in his mouth, which remained there until adult-
hood. He was 'an arrogant, spoiled, filthy-rich kid', according to the
comments of his contemporaries.

Bunker's father was certainly *not* born with a silver spoon in his mouth
– it is doubtful if he ever had a spoon at all. The story of Haroldson
Lafayette Hunt is in the true Horatio Alger tradition. Born in Vandalia,

Illinois in 1890, he could read at the age of three and displayed a phenomenal memory which he retained throughout his life. From near infancy he displayed the signs of genius and also its antithesis. Like Henry Ford he was basically an extremely intelligent but only partially informed man. He left school at eleven and became a drifter at the age of thirteen, wandering through the West as a barber, cowhand and lumberjack. In his memoirs John Paul Getty, the mega-millionaire oil magnate, said: 'H. L. Hunt is the best poker player I ever met.' It was but a short step to running a gambling saloon of his own in Arkansas, and the proceeds were ploughed into the cotton industry.

Early in his life H. L. Hunt became a moderately prosperous cotton farmer, but the deep recession of 1920–1 brought an abrupt end to these activities. For lack of anything better, he turned to oil and was almost literally swept off his feet towards riches. According to the Hunt legend, he struck oil on his first attempt with a drilling rig he had purchased with a 50 dollar loan. Another version is that he won the rig in a poker game. Whichever was the case, after much successful drilling in Arkansas Hunt shifted to East Texas, not then considered a likely territory for oil wildcatting. But it was in East Texas that H. L. Hunt dealt himself the biggest and most rewarding hand he ever held.

The big killing for H. L. Hunt – and many others – came in the early 1930s. An old man called Columbus M. Joiner – known as 'Dad' to his companion wildcatters – was drilling on the Widow Daisy Bradford's farm in Rusk County, East Texas. The first two wells that Dad drilled turned out to be dry. But he persevered, raising money for his third venture by selling shares to the neighbouring farmers, with the help of Mrs Bradford and a local bank manager who also agreed to work on the rig in his spare time to help save on costs.

John Paul Getty said: 'H. L. Hunt is the best poker player I ever met'

As a young man Dad had made and lost two fortunes as an independent wildcatter, and his success at finding new oilfields in unexpected places had earned him the title 'King of the Wildcatters'. Now over seventy, he wanted one final success so that he could retire in luxury. In early October 1930 the shaft went into the ground, the drill bit turned and at last struck oil. With a tremendous roar a vast black plume raced through the top of the rig. Dad, his crew and the shareholders danced and rolled as the spray of black gold rained down on their heads and bodies, and the scenario was established for countless Hollywood films.

But in real life, unlike the movies, those stories don't always have a happy ending. Dad had created a glut of oil that was unleashed on a market shrinking in the darkness of the Depression. The price of oil collapsed. Adding to his problems, most of the oil was coming from areas outside his control and could not be capped and preserved for better times – as the Middle East oil sheikhs have done throughout the 1970s and 1980s. His own lease covered only a few square miles. It wasn't until H. L. Hunt arrived on the scene, after building a reputation as a notable wildcatter, that Dad was offered any glimmer of hope. Hunt agreed to purchase all Dad's oil interests, even those where title appeared questionable. In the circumstances, Hunt's price of 30,000 dollars in cash, 45,000 dollars in short-term notes and a guarantee of 1.2 million dollars out of future profits looked very generous.

Most oilmen appeared to regard H. L. Hunt as 'more than a little kooky'

When Hunt agreed the deal he knew the field had already produced 3500 million barrels of oil and was yet to show the slightest signs of drying up. It was the strike of the century! By the end of the episode Hunt had cleared an estimated profit in excess of 100 million dollars and had become one of the wealthiest men in America. Dad fell back on hard times and retired to a street with the appropriate name of Mockingbird Lane, where he died in 1947.

H. L. Hunt, described by Ferdinand Lundberg in *The Rich and the Super Rich* as a 'small town cracker-barrel philosopher', was of the Andrew Carnegie and Henry Ford ilk. By 1957 he had wildcatted himself into an empire beyond his wildest dreams. His holdings sprawled over the American south-west and the Middle East, and included a network of newspapers and radio stations. The violence of the diatribes in his personally subsidized radio programmes – carried to 331 cracker-barrel stations – led many observers to the conclusion that they may have helped nurture the assassination of President Kennedy. According to Ferdinand Lundberg: 'The programmes, seeming overtures to *Schrecklichkeit*, are prepared and taped by a stable of about twenty-five henchmen Hunt maintains in Washington DC. In general, views blandishing Ku Klux Klan mentality are broadcast.'

On the very morning of Kennedy's assassination – in Texas – the Hunt radio programme in Dallas and other areas predicted pessimistically that the day was soon coming when American citizens would not be allowed to own firearms with which to oppose dictatorial leaders. From the cracker-barrel point of view, the right to bear arms against an adversary was important to red-blooded free citizens.

Hunt staged his alarmist programmes through a series of incestuous foundations – Facts Forum Inc., the Life Line Foundation and Bright Star Foundation. It was believed that Hunt had mysterious and powerful friends in, or behind, the Internal Revenue Service. Although none of these foundations was listed in the exhaustive Foundation Directory, and despite strongly sponsored protests, the IRS granted these propaganda foundations of H. L. Hunt complete tax exemption. The Life Line Foundation originally received tax exemption as a religious organization!

In 1957 H. L. Hunt was listed as the second richest man in the world, his wealth exceeded only by the fortunes of John Paul Getty. He was No.2 on *Fortune* magazine's list of the rich, and his net worth was estimated at between 250 million and 3 billion dollars. While an ebullient orator of his cracker-barrel philosophies, he was quite secretive so far as his personal finances were concerned. A more accurate assessment of H. L. Hunt's personal worth was not possible to come by. However John Paul Getty, who had a penchant for accuracy, stated categorically: 'In terms of independent wealth, there was only one H. L. Hunt.' Despite his reticence about the extent of his wealth, Hunt had been overheard introducing himself to strangers by chirping: 'Hello, I am H. L. Hunt, the world's richest man . . .' Behind the immense wealth, many suspect there were certain flaws in the character of H. L. Hunt which would not be considered wholly rational. He has been suspected of being the financial angel for various far-out, right-wing agitational groups. H. L. Hunt was also regarded as being dangerous. The last US President of whom Hunt is said to have approved was Calvin Coolidge in the twenties, and he maintained that stance until the day he died in 1974. One of his immortal sayings was: 'Everything I do, I do for profit.'

Not unlike the role played by playboy John Paul Getty, Hunt maintained the public image of being a penny-pincher rather than a big spender. He was far from popular among his fellow industrialists. According to Ferdinand Lundberg: 'Most oilmen appear to regard him as more than a little kooky.' Suspicions regarding his mental stability were further aroused when he took his biggest and saddest personal gamble ever, involving the life and sanity of his eldest and favourite son, Haroldson Lafayette Hunt III. Sadly, the young H.L.H. III was a manic depressive. For several years he had been undergoing treatment without any visible signs of success. At the age of twenty-six, a frontal lobotomy was suggested as a final solution. H.L. Senior decided to take the risk and agreed to let his son undergo the operation – after all, he was a gambling man for high stakes with high rewards. But H.L. Senior lost the bet, and Haroldson Lafayette Hunt III lost a great deal more – he lost his mind along with his depression.

The Life and Times of a Now Defunct Billionaire

Looking back at Nelson Bunker Hunt's financial escapades, it can be seen that he exposed himself to enormous financial risk, a great deal of which was totally unnecessary. Since he had acquired so much wealth the easy way, it would not be unreasonable to question why he invited so many hazardous undertakings which led to disaster on more than one occasion. The answer probably lies somewhere in the misty realm of Freud's Oedipus Complex. Certainly Bunker had great admiration for his father and wanted to be worthy of the Hunt tradition. His father had found wealth in the ground. Bunker, being the good son that he was and wishing to follow in his father's footsteps, wanted to use his talents to the fullest. In the process he was prepared to assume immense risks to prove he was the man his father wanted him to be and hopefully to become the favourite son, a role his poor insane brother had acquired.

It was clear from the start that as a risk-taker Bunker was no slouch. In fact, he is the only gambler I know who has ever gone double-or-quits on a billion dollars! But that was to come later. While Bunker was still in his thirties, the heir apparent took the gamble that was to make him the man with the largest oil reserves in the world. This he achieved within H.L.'s own lifetime – in Libya, then still ruled by King Idris.

It was a play that only a very rich man could afford. Already Bunker had gambled in Pakistan and lost – managing to waste 30 million dollars in drilling dry holes. Here in Libya Bunker had to compete with the major oil companies, and his search for oil was to take no less than five years. In the event it was BP, perhaps the world's most successful exploration company, that struck it rich for him during 1961 in an unpromising stretch of desert. The Sarir field proved to be one of the dozen richest in the world. Probable reserves were estimated to be close to 10,000 million barrels. What's more to the point, Nelson Bunker Hunt had acquired half of it!

Unhappily, a group of young officers headed by the comparatively obscure Colonel Ghadaffi seized control of the country. Bunker was pressed to agree to a 51% handover, but refused to negotiate. So his share in the Sarir field was nationalized. The compensation he received was 17

Nelson Bunker Hunt would always travel tourist class – but he'd happily hire a private jet to clinch a deal

---

million dollars – around one half of 1% of the nominal value of the crude in the ground. (This, remember, was a comparatively short time before the Middle East war, which was followed by OPEC's oil price hike on Christmas Eve 1973.) Bunker never quite got over that incident – though he must have made at least 100 million dollars from his Libyan gamble.

The Hunt clan were different from the nouveau riche, the merely rich and the super-rich. They never at any time gave the impression that they regarded the acquisition of great wealth as an imposing dynastic imperative – a responsibility that had to be nurtured and handed on. When Bunker said neither he nor his father was motivated by money, I'm sure he was being truthful, in his own way. The Hunts were primarily interested in playing that winning hand in a game that involved the highest possible stakes. They would never count their winnings, or be greatly concerned about what happened to them.

Bunker was described as possessing 'as much finesse as a stampeding bull elephant'. His favourite beverage was Coca-Cola, and he was known to drown the most exquisite Napoleon brandies in the stuff. His favourite food was hamburgers, hot dogs and flapjacks. He would always travel tourist class – not to save money, but simply because first-class accommodation had no value to him. But he'd happily hire a private jet or buy a dozen racehorses – to clinch a deal or win a race.

The existence of so many Hunts from so many
families diluted and mocked any sense of dynasty

Perhaps the primary influence behind the Hunts' refusal to think in dynastic terms lay in a peculiarity of Hunt Senior – he was a family man, but not in the normal sense. H.L. believed in very, very large families, and harboured the strange notion that he was gifted with a 'genius gene' which he believed it was his God-given duty to spread as widely as possible. The Hunt 'genius gene' gave rise to three families which produced a total of fourteen *known* children. The existence of so many Hunts from so many families diluted and mocked any sense of dynasty.

During the early 1970s Bunker and his brother Herbert suddenly began to focus less attention on oil and turned their hand to silver. The switch was not based on economic perceptions or detailed analysis. They were in it for the oldest reason in the world – to make another fortune. For Bunker, that meant one thing and one thing only – he was determined to become the richest man in the world, just like Papa!

What was in Bunker's mind in the summer of 1973? His share of the Sarir field had been nationalized on 11 June – a losing poker hand. But Bunker was a big rancher and was watching the price of cattle soar to levels beyond the wildest dreams of avarice. Back in the sixties, cattle prices had been good for a while. They had fluctuated between 25 and 30 cents a pound for live animals. But at the turn of the decade prices began to move up sharply. Thirty-five cents a pound or better was the reasonable expectation for a lean and frisky steer. The spring of 1973 presented a wholly different picture. Prices were jumping by leaps and bounds. At one point late in the year live cattle prices touched 60 cents a pound. This was at least a modest compensation to Bunker, owner of forty thousand head of cattle.

It was the same picture for commodities during the summer of 1973. Soya beans, in which Bunker had a flutter from time to time, also careered upwards. Wherever Bunker looked, he saw the same pattern emerging.

157

There was one exception – oil, whose price was controlled by the cartels and the major oil companies. In oil, a totally different scenario was being written.

The explosive rise in commodity prices did not go unnoticed by the oil sheikhs of the Gulf and the members of OPEC. Under the direction of Saudi Arabia's brilliant and cultured oil minister, Sheikh Yamani, since early 1973 OPEC had been negotiating with the major oil companies for a substantial increase in the price of oil. Sheikh Yamani's negotiating theme was that oil was rapidly running out. If the world carried on consuming at the rate it was going, there would be no oil left in the ground and his people would become destitute. But it was a year of world recession, and manufacturing industries were having a tough time. The suggestion of a hefty increase in oil prices would probably have been a non-starter had it not been for the jump in commodity prices. This encouraged OPEC to look for much bigger rises and to be far more adamant in their demands. When it became clear that the negotiations were not going to bring the desired results, OPEC was emboldened to go solo. In two steps, the cartel quadrupled the price of oil in late 1973.

It didn't take long for Bunker to work out that OPEC was able to engineer a four-fold increase in the price of oil – and get it – because they were in control of a large portion of the world supply. It was probably then that Bunker was struck with his vision, an idea that could only have been envisaged by the sons of the richest man in the world. What was the idea? This is just supposition. But, as I see it, Bunker looked at Herbert and Herbert looked at Bunker . . . then in unison they yelled: 'Eureka! Why can't we do for silver what the Arabs did for oil?'

The Choice of Silver

What made silver so attractive to the Hunt brothers? Why not gold? After all, gold has been the subject of manipulation by individuals and governments throughout the ages.

To start with, Americans could not buy gold. This in itself would limit speculative potential for the physical market. Secondly, the largest single hoard of the metal was in the hands of private individuals in India – 7000 tonnes of it, which would be difficult to control. By custom, an Indian bride is supposed to be accompanied by a dowry of at least 100 grams of gold ornaments. The trend of the gold price is always a source of concern to Indian parents. If the price moves too high, there is a cutback in the number of marriages which deflates the price. Thirdly, America had abandoned gold convertibility, effectively freeing its price, which had stood at 35 dollars an ounce since 1944. As a result of the move away from gold convertibility gold had begun moving upwards with other commodities, breaking upwards of 50 dollars. By spring 1973 the price had nearly trebled, to 100 dollars. No, for Bunker gold had moved too far, too fast.

There were also soya beans, wheat, hogs, pork bellies, canary seed, peppercorns and the like, but these were scarcely worthy vehicles for Bunker's bid to become the richest man in the world. Silver was a noble metal; as noble in some ways as gold. And for Americans in particular there was something reassuring about silver. There were links with the old silver dollar, for which Alexander Hamilton had recommended a mint be set up in Philadelphia. Americans could also buy silver in any quantities they wanted, and in any form.

'Eureka! Why can't we do for silver what the Arabs did for oil?'

Silver could also respond to some of the factors that were attributable to the sharp rise in the gold price. The Silver Purchase Act of 1934 placed a cap on the price of silver. If the price fell below 1.29 dollars, the US Treasury had to keep on buying the metal until it reached 1.29 dollars or better. In the deflationary 1930s the price had fallen below that level on several occasions. By 1939, when the United States Treasury had accumulated a huge hoard of 3 billion ounces, the price fell to a mere 35 cents an ounce. By 1963 the price was back up to 1.29 dollars again, thanks to costly intervention. It was then that the US Treasury decided to discontinue purchasing silver. The price remained at 1.29 dollars until 1967, when the Treasury banned the redemption of dollar bills for silver and discontinued its use in coinage. In 1970 it ended sales of silver. That was the time that public interest in silver was just starting to bubble. When Bunker cast his gaze on silver, the upward movement in the price level was still in its early stages. Surely, he reasoned, the same lift-off that had happened to gold and other commodities must come to silver.

By 1971 the price was still only 1.60 dollars and had begun to weaken, due to the Treasury's decision to abandon gold convertibility. It was perceived that such a decision would increase the demand for gold and reduce that for silver. This was true, but only for a short time. The price of silver began rising again in 1972. By early 1973 it topped 2 dollars, and by the summer of that year the price was 3 dollars.

By December 1973 it is reputed that Bunker and his brother Herbert – who was as much of a 'silver bug' as Bunker, maybe more – had accumulated 35 million ounces of silver in the form of futures contracts, along with several million ounces of the actual metal. This purchase of bullion proved, from the outset, that the Hunts intended to be long-term holders of silver for reasons best known to themselves. By late 1974 their interest in silver was up to 50 million ounces, worth 22 million dollars. In early 1975 interest in the metal began to wane. Inflation began to subside a little in places. Economic recovery inspired speculative interest in share markets and other forms of investment, detracting from the investment prospects of precious metals. The silver market went to sleep. Most ordinary humans would have refused to sit out those four long years while silver stagnated. They would probably have sold out. But not the Hunt brothers. It has been estimated that by the end of 1976 Bunker and Herbert Hunt controlled more than 100 million ounces of silver, worth maybe 500 million dollars in the money of the day. That would be the equivalent of well over a billion dollars today.

Enter the Saudis

In September 1977 Bunker and Herbert appeared before the Supreme Court on charges of criminal conspiracy. Along with other members of the Hunt clan they were accused of accumulating a futures position in soya beans which was eight times the limit laid down by the regulatory body, the Commodity Futures Trading Commission (CFTC). They had purchased futures contracts for 24 million bushels of soya beans, no less than 37% of the 1976 US crop. With that kind of hold on the market, the Hunt family could have created bedlam in the soya bean price were they ever to call for physical delivery of the soya beans against their purchase contracts. As it happened, the price had advanced from below 5 dollars a bushel in early 1976 to over 7 dollars by January 1977, and over 10 dollars by April of that year. Shortly after that, the CFTC ordered Bunker to cut back his positions. Then, to Bunker's fury, they published full details of the affair for all to see.

A move of that kind is sudden death for a big player in commodity markets. It's like letting all the other players in a poker game look at your Royal Straight Flush while you're trying to up the ante. As a result of this unprecedented and vicous move every soya bean trader in the world knew precisely what Bunker was holding and what would subsequently be coming on to the market. Bunker claimed he lost money – though there is evidence to suggest this was not the case. In any event, the soya bean incident seemed to be a warm-up for what the Hunt brothers had in mind for silver. . . .

The scenario shifts to Longchamp racecourse, the setting for the most fashionable event of the French racing calendar, the Prix de l'Arc de Triomphe. At Longchamps in October 1978 Bunker Hunt, himself a famous racehorse owner, joined a clique of Arabs who shared his passion and his depth of pocket. A meeting took place with a Palestinian called Mahmoud Fustok and a friend of his, Naji Robert Nahas, a middleman from Beirut. Fustok, who held a Saudi Arabian passport, was brother-in-law to Prince Abdullah ibn Abdul-Aziz, head of the Saudi National Guard and next in line to the throne after his half-brother King Fahd.

160

Nahas was, like Bunker, a gambler on a rare scale. The upshot of the meeting was that Bunker fired him with his dream of cornering the silver market. In late summer the price of gold had broken through the 200 dollar level, and at the time of the Longchamp meeting it was racing towards 250 dollars. Silver had perked up too – topping 6 dollars in October. Everything was beginning to fall into place for Bunker. During 1979 inflation was accelerating around the globe; the US dollar was under critical pressure; and OPEC was manoeuvring for its last great throw – the second mammoth oil price hike.

Bunker's silver dream was getting daily more credible to the princes of Arabia (yes, by now it was princes in the plural). Through the good offices of John Connaly, former Governor of Texas (down on Bunker's payroll as ambassador extraordinary), the Hunts had been introduced to two key insiders at the Saudi court. They were Ghaith Pharaon, son of the royal physician, and Khalid bin Mahfouz, head of the National Commercial Bank in Jeddah and effectively royal banker. There had been speculation that those contacts led to Crown Prince Fahd himself, who in his youth had been perhaps the most prodigious casino gambler in the world. Now there was a new twist to Bunker's dream. As he had done once with oil, Nelson Bunker Hunt would emerge as the man with the largest holding of silver in the world – with the help of Saudi money.

Here's how the game is played in barest outline. First accumulate very quietly. Allow the price to rise gently. Then start releasing a few rumours, while adding to holdings – not necessarily all that heavily, but certainly a little less discreetly. Then start your selling in complete secrecy as public enthusiasm mounts and the price rise gains momentum. A touch of price volatility does no harm at this stage. Finally, before the public following has reached its peak, distribute everything that remains. This was the strategy followed by the very successful pool operators on Wall Street in the 1920s (see Chapter 7).

Through the good offices of the former Governor of Texas the Hunts were introduced to two key insiders at the Saudi court

---

The details can vary enormously and may be crucial. For example, appropriate use of the futures market will greatly increase the chances of success – particularly when used in conjunction with dealing in the cash market for actual physical silver. The futures market was used extensively during the rage of Tulipomania (see pages 6–7). The principle is always the same. The great bulk of contracts are never settled by delivery – although the buyer retains the right to delivery. That right to delivery was the key to the game the Hunts and their Arab allies planned to play with silver – or it would have been had the plan not gone horribly wrong.

It was the Beirut middleman, Nahas, who set up the dealing apparatus for his Arab friends. Nahas settled on one Norton Waltuch, head of the New York office of Conti Commodity Services, as broker. Conti dealt for Nahas personally. Conti also dealt for the Banque Populaire Suisse of Geneva and an affiliate by the name of Advicorp, which were the vehicles used by the former Palestinian Mahmoud Fustok – Prince Abdullah's trusted adviser. Waltuch was also the broker for a Bahamas-registered commodity fund, Conti Capital Ltd, in which Naji Nahas was a shareholder. So too were members of the Kaki family of Jeddah (proprietors of the National Commercial Bank), into which Khalid bin Mahfouz, head

---

The web was completed by a company incorporated in Bermuda

---

of NCB and banker to the royal court, had married. The web was completed by a company called IMIC, incorporated in Bermuda in July 1979, a joint venture involving the Hunt brothers and their other Saudi partners. It is clear from the names of the directors that IMIC represented the interests of Khalid bin Mahfouz and sundry other Jeddah bankers and merchants. There was also a plan, to be launched before June 1979, which would have provided a breathtaking solution to the problem of disposing of the vast stocks of silver the conspirators would accumulate.

It must be obvious that if deep, deep pockets go into the silver market, it is relatively easy to drive the price up. The catch is that, if all else remains equal, the sale of all those positions will drive the price back down again as far and as fast as it was forced up in the first place – unless, that is, the silver can be disposed of in ways which don't affect the price. The wholesale way of ensuring that is to find an outside taker for the lot; and the plan, leaked in June by the chief trader for IMIC, was to use the Saudi Arabian Monetary Agency. SAMA, the Saudi central bank, had reserves of 60 billion dollars, and it could be argued that silver bullion would not be an inappropriate holding for an entity that would normally be a holder of gold.

In the late 1970s David Hargreaves, now an independent consultant to a firm of metal brokers, was actively dealing metal in London. He recalls a feeling – but no more – that something was going on in the background: 'I believe it started at the beginning of 1978, when Bunker and Herbert Hunt and their cronies were active in the States. They had certainly become quite active here in Britain. I had one or two of them aboard that began very, very quietly indeed.' Much more was taking place in the United States, 'particularly in New York and Chicago. There was quite a bit going on in South America too. They infiltrated very easily into a lot of areas. A whole lot of money was being put into place. A lot of people were corrupted. They didn't show their hands until late '79. As I recall it, we saw the price of silver beginning to move in London around August and September.'

Naturally enough, the Hunt brothers had not waited for the formation of IMIC to bolster their underlying silver holding, which was 75 million ounces in futures positions and an unknown quantity of bullion. The way they now proceeded to operate gives a clue to Bunker's solution to the selling problem. It was evident that for the climax of the pool operation he and Herbert had fixed on February-March 1980 – the maturity dates for their fifteen thousand contracts.

The next move was to buy a little over ten thousand further contracts for February and March, simultaneously selling the same number for May and June. The reason for employing such tactics (it is called a straddle) in that particular context was that the Hunts were looking beyond the climax of the squeeze to the effect of 'pulling the plug'. They might wish to call for delivery on 50 million ounces of silver or more. After that happened, the price would surely plummet. But the brothers would be protected by their sales of the May and June contracts.

Operation Silver Pool swung into action on 1 August 1979. The timing was immaculate. In July the price of gold had topped 300 dollars, and platinum was soaring. The public was coming in. The cognoscenti in Britain were buying their Krugerrands. In France elegant ladies were buying *louis d'or* or *lingots* over the bank counter in Paris's smart 16th *arondissement*. Soon they were to be copied by little ladies in black all over France. The public saw increased inflation and an escalating gold price running hand in hand. Surely, what went for gold must go for silver! But there was still time for the conspirators.

In Paris elegant ladies were buying louis d'or *over
the bank counter in the smart 16th* arondissement

At the start of August the silver price was around 9 dollars. That month IMIC bought eight thousand silver contracts – 40 million ounces – through bankers Merrill Lynch. The Banque Populaire bought about 7 million ounces worth, and Naji Nahas, reputed to be rather short on cash at the beginning of the story, had accumulated nearly 9 million ounces. The price of silver had risen, but at 10.60 dollars it had by no means run away.

The new buyers were sitting on over half a billion dollars' worth of silver contracts. The required down payment, or margin, was under 30 million. But the pool's paper profit would have easily covered that – leaving them free to accumulate the same amount again had they so wished. Meanwhile Bunker's and Herbert's 75 million ounces was worth nearly 800 million dollars. Their main broker, Bache, held a further 13 million ounces for other members of the family. And at a conservative estimate the Hunts' silver bullion holdings were over 17 million ounces, maybe way over.

Then, in September, the silver price took off. This was not the result of further massive buying by the pool. It was rather that the initial purchases in August had been met by professional short sellers – people who sell what they don't own in the hope that prices will fall and they can buy it back more cheaply – who had taken a risk that the blip in prices would be only temporary. But when the price stayed firm – and not one contract came back on the market from the pool – they had to cover. The move to cover became a scramble. Silver almost hit 18 dollars, ending September at 16.50. This made the pool's holdings worth over 2.8 billion dollars.

Beyond the edge of the pool, hundreds of smaller players were preparing to follow the Hunt brothers and take the plunge – in some cases eager to dive for pennies. As David Hargreaves remembers:

[The Hunts] relied upon these others to keep the whole thing going; a lot of them were second and third line people, the kind of people who came to me to deal. But they were close to Hunt . . . and they thought what was going on in the market was too good to miss. So whereas Bunker and Herbert and the others were dealing in billions, those that kept coming to us in London were dealing in the millions and thousands. They built up their own momentum which carried them along.

October and November saw a pause in the run on the silver price, although it was still outperforming gold. By now the regulatory authorities, notably the CFTC, were growing concerned. They had established that the Hunts were in cahoots with Saudi Arabian interests, but there was

If all the Hunts' silver futures had been delivered, they would have needed two thousand Boeing 707 cargo flights

nothing illegal about that. There were no position limits – limits to the number of contracts any trader or group could hold – on the silver exchanges in Chicago and New York; and there was absolutely no evidence of manipulation. The pool had bought in huge volume, rolled over their position from one month to the next as appropriate to investors, and had even exchanged contracts for metal. Not only was this not manipulation, it was the opposite! Of course, it did smack of a 'corner': the pool's huge position undoubtedly gave it a degree of control over the silver market. The rumour was that the Hunts planned to take physical delivery of part or all of their futures position. That might cause chaos because of the sheer amount involved – up to 80,000 tons. (Just to carry that lot would call for two thousand Boeing 707 cargo flights.) But that was the unassailable right of anyone holding a futures contract. Without that right, futures markets would be a sham. A further consideration was that the great bulk of the pool's futures position was due to mature in February and March, and that was some way off.

In late October the Chicago Board of Trade felt it had to act. It imposed a limit of six hundred contracts – 3 million ounces. Since that would not take effect until 1 April 1980, it would not avoid a squeeze in March. The largest New York exchange, Comex, did not move, even though the

People pushed their way through Hatton Garden
bearing plastic carriers crammed with forks, ladles
and sporting trophies

commercial interests were pushing. The producers, bullion users and metals refiners, like Engelhard, Johnson Matthey and Mocatta, naturally hold large physical stocks. They chiefly use futures markets as sellers. The commercials wanted limits on purchases, not sales. Anyone could see the one-sidedness of that position. But they were the establishment; and they would be the ones to win in the end.

But what about those who were equally certain to end up as losers? Quite a few market men experienced something of a tug-of-war with their conscience. So many of the wrong people were being drawn in. If you were trying to give out logical research and market information then, as one metals analyst told me, once silver had risen to over 12 dollars an ounce he had to say quite frankly: 'I've been watching this market, and there's no rhyme or reason for silver to be at this level. Sorry – but you're on your own. But by the time it was 24 dollars, and people were still pouring in, there was nothing for it but to start dealing again.'

In December 1979, the Hunts' great gamble was hitting paydirt. OPEC had raised the oil price yet again – to about triple its 1978 levels. The American embassy in Teheran was besieged. The USSR was preparing its invasion of Afghanistan. Inflation was heading for double figures in the USA and Britain. The price of gold had bounded to over 500 dollars, then over 600. Under these circumstances the price of silver also had to take off, corner or no corner. And it did. The pool's timing really has to be admired. Silver left the teens behind and galloped up through 25 dollars. This was where Bunker Hunt and his allies turned their back on reason, giving themselves up to fantasies of power and greed.

There were incredible scenes in London's silver quarter, reminiscent of the days of the South Sea Bubble. This time the lines of men and women of all classes, jostling each other to gain a place on the pavement in Hatton Garden, were sellers. They'd come because they believed, with the price of silver this high, that there must be profits for everyone – even if it meant selling the family silver! As one City worker who was an eyewitness described it: 'Part of the scrap taken down to Hatton Garden went to three melters, where there were some unbelievable scenes. People pushing their way through with brown paper parcels and plastic carrier bags crammed with forks and ladles, electro-plated sporting trophies and even Sheffield Plate that could never be replaced! All because silver was 20, 30, 50 dollars an ounce.'

In the crazed atmosphere that prevailed as the year drew to a close – with silver up to around the 30 dollar level – Naji Nahas was making claims to his friends in Paris that he had cleared a profit of 1.2 billion dollars. By then Bunker and his cohorts were disregarding every rule in the book, particularly that most important of all that says, 'You ain't got no profit 'til you cash in them there chips.' In other words, the fruits of their machinations would not be seen until they were able to sell the copious amounts of silver that had been accumulated.

The first alarm bells began ringing in earnest when an article appeared in a privately circulated Lebanese English-language newsletter on 10 December. That article was sheer dynamite for the Hunts. In glaring print there appeared the litany of Bunker's relationship with Prince Abdullah, grounded in 'their mutual passion for fine horses'. All was revealed about how the pair had agreed to form a common fund with the specific purpose of buying and holding silver, for sale only after the price reached 25 dollars an ounce at the end of 1979 or early 1980. In the event, the price of silver never even hesitated at 25 dollars. During December it powered on through 30 dollars to close the month over 34 dollars. The Hunts had weeks and weeks to sell above 25 dollars. But they did not move. In fact they bought silver, in the sense that they traded futures for the actual metal.

In Bunker's case, the only possible answer to Bernie Cornfeld's question: 'Do you sincerely want to be rich?' was that he did not

---

Could it be that the great silver gambler just didn't care about money? In Bunker's case, the only possible answer to the question posed earlier by the swindler of IOS fame, Bernie Cornfeld, 'Do you *sincerely* want to be rich?', is that Bunker did not. He just wanted to own a lot of silver – preferably all of it. Yet there are signs that he sensed that, the way things were going, it would not be possible for him to own as much silver as he sought and still stay rich. In a newspaper interview in mid-1980 he claimed he would have preferred the price not to have risen over 20 dollars in 1979. Yet in January 1980 he constantly forecast that it would rise to 85 dollars. In his dream world that is what the price of silver would have done over five or ten years, not in as many months. In the real world he knew the silver boom was a bubble. But he never made the slightest effort to pull out. Possibly the underlying reason was that he knew deep down that if he were able to liquidate his entire holdings (which were daily growing more and more impossible) and face the question of where to put the resulting pile of cash, he would only have wanted to do one thing with it – buy silver.

The Cardboard Dynasty

Even while the market was still strong and climbing, some London dealers who had the advantage of being on the sidelines – David Hargreaves among them – realized that what they were witnessing was not a battle of the giants. It was rather a giant, superbly staged battle of lesser mortals. It was as grotesque as anything Walt Disney could have thought up, but it was patently not the kind of operation that would have been launched by the early Rockefellers, the Carnegies or the Guggenheims. Unlike them, the Hunts appeared to be under some strong compulsion to allow the family treasure to slip through their fingers. Had the Hunt brothers genuinely been looking to consolidate old H.L.'s empire, some expert opinions reckoned, they wouldn't have been drawn into anything so trivial as trying to corner the world's silver market. Because, as they discovered, any such attempt which involved New York would be bound to fail.

Meanwhile, the button on the destruct mechanism had been pressed and the countdown had started. The regulatory bodies were mobilized and deployed, jolted into action by the ever-rising price of silver. There could be no doubt at all according to the evidence: the aggregate positions in silver held by the Hunts and their foreign collaborators, were not being cut back – by all accounts the holdings were getting bigger all the time.

There was no financial futures market in London. That was important. It meant that the mounting pressure and conflicting stresses were bound to be concentrated on commodities. For the money which might have been invested in other areas had nowhere to go but in that direction. That was why market men expected intense volatility.

By mid-January the CFTC had identified some 280 million ounces held by the pool, mostly in the form of bullion. According to one knowledgeable source, the pool held title to the equivalent of 77% of all the privately held silver bullion in the world. Silver had reached the ionospheric price of 40 dollars; the pool's hoard was worth a not so cool 10 billion dollars. During the third week of January the price gyrations in silver became 'nothing less than phenomenal', as one CFTC official put it. The CFTC finally intervened, introducing position limits of five hundred contracts (2.5 million ounces), valid February.

When Bunker and his brother first became attracted to the lure of silver the down payment margin for silver was 2000 dollars per contract. On 9 January 1980 that margin – which had been subject to a series of increases over the years – was advanced to 40,000 dollars for major accounts. On 18 January silver pushed above 50 dollars. Then came the stroke that has become endemic to crashes – the final blow that ends all the suffering. Except that for poor Bunker the suffering hadn't even begun!

The Coup de Grâce

On 1 January 1980, Comex pulled a ruthless trick on the Texan brothers and the 'foreign investors'. It declared all trading on the Silver Exchange 'for liquidation only'. That meant that no new positions could be opened in any silver contract; only closing of existing positions was allowed. In effect, there would be sellers but no buyers.

The general feeling is that the London authorities would never have pulled the rug out from under the feet of speculators the way it was done in New York. In over a hundred years of existence, the London Metal Exchange has called upon its members to stop trading when a disorderly market has seemed to be developing – on no more than two or three occasions. The behaviour of whose who preside over Comex is not quite as gentle. Most of the operators on the London silver markets are unanimous in their agreement that Bunker's 'corner' was a well-organized programme that required considerable skill. But poor Bunker did not take into account the ability – or wilful desire – of the authorities at Comex to step in and call a halt to the game in mid-play.

Could the Hunt brothers have succeeded if they had not been so rash? David Hargreaves believes they could have pulled off their coup: 'If they had just taken the supply off the market, they would have caught the consumers who desperately had to have silver to keep their businesses running; and they'd have caught the people in the futures market who needed to buy physical metal to match future delivery dates. But they didn't. They went into the futures market themselves; and this is where they tripped up.'

The fatal flaw which Bunker Hunt could not see was that by taking the position that he did in futures he became as vulnerable as the wildest speculator. That was because he then had a bigger position than all the known and identifiable physical stocks in the world could possibly have satisfied. He did have a fall-back position in that he had bought a lot of coinage; and it was always felt – wrongly – that the scrap in the coinage could have been melted down and recast into an acceptable form because, says Hargreaves: 'You can't deliver coinage to Comex. It has to be ingots or hallmarked bars. But there wasn't the available remelting capacity. So, if against his short position in Comex he decided to draw on his hoard of

coinage, he could not have had it smelted and put into the system in time.'
Clearly there were certain areas in which Bunker Hunt hadn't quite
thought things through.

Gold crashed in the slipstream of the crash in silver where there was a
market only for sellers – no buyers, thanks to the efforts of Comex. Few
people are fully aware that the initial collapse in the gold price, that began
in unison with the crash of the silver price, was due to the Hunt brothers
and the act of retribution carried out against them by Comex.

But the crash in silver was far more momentous than the crash in gold.
In fact, the silver crash was perhaps the fiercest in the history of any major
commodity. On 21 January silver slid 13% to 44 dollars. The bears
smelled blood. The big shorts in silver, the professional hedgers who sell
to insure against a fall in the value of physical stocks in their warehouses,
had been near their wits' end. In overall terms they had not lost money, for
the rise in the price of silver futures merely equalled the rise in the price of
their physical stocks. But with each leap in the futures price the hedgers
had to make margin payments to make up their losses with the exchange.
For individual companies these margin payments were running into
hundreds of millions of dollars. Here was their chance to turn the tables.
There was but one exception to the 'liquidation only' rule, and it applied
to the hedgers. Now they really could get their own back on the Hunts.

The next day silver bombed: it cascaded 10 dollars, or 23%, to 34
dollars. Such moments are difficult to recapture. In a few hours the
marketplace had sliced 2.8 billion dollars off the value of the pool's total
silver hoard. It's a cliché to point out that sums of this size become
meaningless: Bunker Hunt was later to quip, 'A billion's not what it used
to be.' But those two days' losses amounted to 0.5% of the value of all the
stocks on the New York Stock Exchange. It was now the turn of the Hunts
to find margin to cover the losses on their futures contracts. The borrowing began.

---

*Bunker was later to quip: 'A billion's not what it
used to be'*

A quick tally in February 1980 saw the Hunts still sitting on about 200
million ounces of silver bullion and some 80 million ounces in futures
contracts. All along, the profits on the futures had been used up to buy
more and more silver. The plunge in silver very quickly led to enormous
debit balances in the silver bulls' accounts with their brokers. By the end
of February the Hunts found they owed Bache, their main broker, 233
million dollars. In March silver slid lower, day after day. Naturally, the
plight of the pool was well known to the professionals. And they operated
in the near certainty that every further decline must cause forced selling of
silver metal by the bulls. They could sell with impunity.

The Hunts and their friends turned next to the banks with whom they had agreements. The Swiss Bank Corporation lent no less than 420 million dollars to the pool. So it was that in mid-March the Hunt brothers were in hock for a total of 1.25 billion dollars on their silver gamble – the largest personal debt in history. All the time the silver price went on falling, so their collateral was being whittled away. Yet, something much worse was to hit Bunker and Herbert when they were struggling for survival. It was the deal struck in January with Engelhard to buy a total of 30 million ounces of silver at the price of 35 dollars – a liability of over 1 billion dollars in cash, mostly due at the end of March.

Silver Thursday

On 25 March the Hunts failed to meet a margin call from Bache for 135 million dollars. It was then that the house of cards came tumbling down. Bache had been very patient – in their own interest, of course. But now they saw no other course than to start closing the Hunts' silver futures positions. It was the signal to the professional silver bears that the great debacle in silver was at hand. With their short selling added to Bache's liquidations the price of silver plunged sickeningly from 20.20 dollars to 15.80.

Wednesday, 26 March was the real killer. Bache saw that their sales of silver were having the effect they feared. They were depressing the price to the point where the value of the silver they held as collateral was being dangerously eroded. This was counter-productive. So Bache turned to the other assets they held on the Hunts' behalf and began liquidating huge lines of shares. The result was panic on the Stock Exchange. Rumour fed rumour. The Hunts were in real trouble. The Dow Jones lunged down by 32 points at one moment – one of the largest falls to that date – earning 27 March the name of Silver Thursday. As for silver, the value of the Hunt pool's hoard was struck down to under 3 billion dollars.

Bache's move into the open had a cathartic effect. Not only did stock prices recover to close almost unchanged on Silver Thursday, but the silver price too had seen its lows that day. On Friday it rebounded to over 14 dollars. It was time for the professional bears to close their excess short positions and run for cover.

For the Hunts and their friends the worst still lay ahead. For Monday was 31 March, the day on which the Hunts had to complete on their purchase of 19 million ounces of the 30 million they had contracted to buy from Engelhard at what had then seemed a bargain price of 35 dollars. By Monday they had to find a cool 665 million dollars in cash.

That weekend, huddled in negotiations involving the major US banks and Paul Volcker of the Federal Reserve Board, Engelhard exacted from the Hunt brothers not cash but the jewel in the family crown – their 20%

170

interest in the oil concessions of the Beaufort Sea, then valued at anything up to 17 billion dollars. In May, the Hunts' silver debts were all consolidated in a massive consortium bank loan of 1.1 billion dollars – secured on the assets of the family flagship company, Placid Oil. The three Hunt brothers were in turn called up to mortgage all their assets to Placid Oil. The Fed's anti-inflationary money squeeze was at its height, with interest rates over 20%. This meant that the annual cost of the bank loan was a nightmarish 220 billion dollars.

Like the characters in a Greek tragedy whom the gods would destroy, the Hunts had been made mad

The price of silver recovered over the summer, reaching 25 dollars in August. The Hunts could have extricated themselves from this Doomsday machine, but they would not sell. Like the characters in a Greek tragedy whom the gods would destroy, they had been made mad. In due course their remaining silver hoard, which amounted to over 600 million dollars in the inventory of security for the Placid loan, would have to be sold when the price dribbled back down towards 10 dollars an ounce in 1981.

Then, as early as 1982, oil started to go wrong. The Texas boom busted. Even then bankers and other observers in Texas were anticipating the bust in oil prices that came at the end of 1985. When the oil bubble burst coal prices were torpedoed, undermining another major asset in the Hunt brothers' collection. As for the silver price, by 1986 it was down to 5 dollars an ounce. At every turn, the brothers were being killed softly by high interest rates.

In December 1987 the three Hunt brothers filed for bankruptcy. And the same month hearings began in a criminal suit against them for conspiring to create a false market in silver. The work of the Avenging Furies of the marketplace appeared complete.

171

10

The Crash of the British Second-line Banks

How property speculation in Britain during the 1970s nearly led to the collapse of the entire British banking system

Innocence Abroad

It was Bernie Cornfeld of IOS fame and the Fund of Funds who told the world, 'If you want to make money, deal in money not in light bulbs.' As a not too prosperous youth who was born during the Depression of the 1930s and who had been reading about the great capitalists of Wall Street throughout the 1940s and 1950s, I wasn't all that interested in light bulbs. I did have a burning desire to enter the world of high finance from as far back as I can remember. It seemed my burning ambition was about to be realized when the door was opened for me during the 1950s, when I secured a position with a New York stockbroking firm as a trainee account executive. I soon discovered that, while the bankers and brokers on Wall Street give the appearance of offering you a prayer rug at the temple of investment, all that is actually available is the equivalent of a set of knee pads at the world's biggest floating crap game. Nothing changes. Behind today's glamorous façade of shiny glass skyscrapers and flashing screens is still a seedy world where nothing is ever really quite what it seems to be.

Upon joining the firm, I immediately assumed my role as a gopher – 'Go for the coffee! Go for the sandwiches! Go for the cigarettes!' – which is the Wall Street version of every young stockbroker's 'training programme' in preparation for the New York Stock Exchange examination. My first assignment after passing that examination was the 'institutional desk'. That meant I had to peddle the firm's 'product' to the various fund managers on Wall Street rather than deal with private individuals. The firm's 'product' was any new underwritings or lines of shares they wanted to get rid of. This was not at all what I had expected!

Those were the days of Gerry Tsai, who managed the high-flying

Manhattan Trust, and Jimmy Ling of Ling-Temco-Voigt who taught corporate America about asset stripping. These were the type of people I would be dealing with. If I said my performance as a salesman was less than brilliant during the first few months, that would be an understatement. Then, one day, one particular fund manager taught me the facts of fund management life and launched me on the road to success.

I arrived at his office bright and early on a Monday morning, armed with all the statistics needed for the stunningly lifeless presentation of the securities I hoped this fund manager would buy. He seemed to be listening while I was delivering my dissertation about the benefits of the shares I was trying to sell. At least, he knew when I had finished!

'Who else bought it?' came his somewhat nonchalant response. I was astonished. How could a fund manager of his stature ask me such a question! The nature of the securities my clients bought and sold was strictly confidential. I was an idealist, you see! I never expected to be confronted with this type of situation. What would he think of me if I ever breached the confidentiality of my role?

'Oh, I couldn't possibly give you that kind of information,' was my reply, assuming he would understand. Perhaps I was being put to some kind of test. In my naivety what transpired was even more amazing than the initial query.

'C'mon, kid – have you sold any of that stock to anybody?'

'No, I haven't,' I whispered sheepishly.

'Well, coochy-coo, let me tell you the facts of life on the Street. I'm no hero, get it? I've got a 6 million dollar fund. Across the Street you've got Amalgamated. They have a 12 million dollar fund. Their fund is twice the size of mine. If they bought two thousand of those things you're pushing, I'd have a thousand. Around the corner you've got Pioneer. They're a minnow. Their fund is only 3 million dollars. If they bought a thousand of those things, I'd buy two thousand. If nobody's bought any, I'm not going to be the first in line. Get the picture?'

It was a picture that no one had ever shown me at business school or during my training – but it sure made a lot of sense

---

I got the rose-coloured-sky-blue-pink-technicolour-vista-vision picture with the utmost clarity. It was a picture that no one had ever shown me at business school or during my training – but it sure made a lot of sense. So this was the way the game was played! I figured I'd best learn the rules – and quick – if I was going to survive. I gave a few minutes' thought to what had just taken place and came back to my prospective client with a suggestion.

'Suppose I go over to Amalgamated and give them my presentation . . .

173

and at the end of the presentation, mention that you promised to buy a thousand first. Will you back me up? Will you buy a thousand if they buy two?'

'Sure, kid! Go ahead!' was the encouraging reply from my new mentor.

I quickly ran across the Street to the office of Amalgamated, where I met the person in charge of making investment decisions. I then proceeded to give my normal presentation, but at the end I added the punchline: 'Oh, by the way, I just came from another fund across the Street. Their fund is half the size of yours. They bought a thousand. I guess you want two?'

'Yes, put us down for two,' was the music that echoed around the room.

I couldn't believe what I was hearing. I'd been out on the Street for six months. It was the quickest and easiest sale I had ever made. I didn't really tell a lie. The first fund manager did promise to buy a thousand. I simply didn't mention that the purchase of a thousand was contingent upon Amalgamated buying two thousand. Now there were no contingencies. I was going to have two fund managers who bought what I was selling.

I quickly scrambled together the documentation involved in the transaction and hurried back across the Street to my first contact. I was bubbling over with enthusiasm when I burst into his office. 'Look, look!' I shouted. 'Amalgamated bought two thousand! You said if they bought two you'd buy one!'

'Right, kid!' he said. I watched him pick up his fountain pen with a smile on his face as joy filled my heart. Once again I scrambled together the documentation and hurried out of the door and down the Street to see my next prospect.

From that point onwards, I completely changed my modus operandi. I would deliver my presentation in the usual manner, but always with a tag ending. The tag ending would be something like: 'Oh, by the way, I just came from the Atlas Fund. They're half the size of your fund. They just bought ten, so I guess you'll want twenty?'

Then on to the next firm with my usual presentation and the tag ending: 'Oh, by the way, I just came from the Accumulator Fund. They bought three thousand. Their fund is the same size as yours. I guess you'll want three thousand too?'

I received the Share Pusher of the Month award

That's the way it went, day after day, week after week. I was rapidly gaining a reputation for selling some of the most popular investments on the Street. I soon stopped giving presentations, finding I no longer needed the 'Oh, by the way . . .' tag. I was able to walk into an office and the response would be: 'Hi, Bob! What have you got and how much should we have?'

'I've got a balloon payment debenture on the Happy Mousing Cat Food

Company.' At least they should know a bit about what they were buying, I thought to myself. 'On my book you should have three thousand.'

'OK,' would be the reply on most occasions. 'Put me down for three.'

During the first six months my sales with the broking firm which employed me were at the bottom of the league. Before the end of the year I was given an incentive bonus and invited to join the principal of the firm on his yacht. I received the Share Pusher of the Month award – of course, they called it Account Executive of the Month!

What Security Really Means to a Fund Manager

The story certainly doesn't end there. The moral of the story concerns the fund manager who taught me the ropes to begin with. He subsequently sold his fund and used the proceeds to buy a stockbroking firm. He established the firm on the basis that it would have only one specialization. The specialization was – wait for it! – lunches. That's right! Lunches! No investment advice! No reports! No in-depth research! No commission discounts! Just lunches!

Here's how it worked. Every day a lunch would be organized to which all the local fund managers would be invited. During the course of lunch a presenter would encourage the fund managers to discuss what they were buying and what they were selling, allowing all who attended to take copious notes. If a minimum of 2000 dollars' commission business was transacted with the firm during that week, the attending representative of the fund which had transacted the business would remain on the lunch list. If the amount of commission fell below the suggested minimum or was non-existent, the representative of that particular fund would be dropped from the lunch list and replaced by someone else.

Back in the early 1960s, most of the fund managers on the Street were on a waiting list to get in on those lunches, so they could find out what the other fund managers were up to. So far as I am aware, there is still a very long waiting list for those stockbroker lunches.

Understanding the motives of those to whom your funds are entrusted is vital if you are going to get any indication of how well you're going to do. Most people harbour the illusion that a fund manager will do his very best to achieve the best possible results for his clients. This is not the motivation of the average fund manager at all. That's not how Wall Street works. It's not how the City of London operates. What every fund manager wants more than anything else is just to keep his job. If he invests in a string of securities that no other fund manager holds and it all goes wrong, he'll lose his job. If all the fund managers sink in the same boat with the same securities, no individual fund manager can be criticized or have his job threatened. They don't teach you that at Harvard Business School, but that's what it's all about in the real world. The welfare of those who give their savings to these institutional fund managers has never been anything more than a minor consideration, in the majority of cases.

After spending a few years in London, and becoming familiar with the differences between the London stock market and the New York stock market, I wrote my first book, which was published in 1968 and called *Share Price Analysis*. Shortly after publication I made the acquaintance of a strong supporter of my work, who was employed as a manager with one of Britain's largest funds. Unlike most fund managers I have known, this particular individual was highly scrupulous and only motivated by achieving the best possible results for the funds under his stewardship. If he felt that shares were too high, he would sell some and sit with large amounts of cash until he felt it was the right time to buy again. This is what most individuals expect of a fund manager. It is a fact that fund managers of this calibre are few and far between. Remember, the name of the game for a fund manager is first and foremost to keep his job.

Never Mind the Investors – Sell the Fund

It would be pointless for me to say that this particular fund manager was correct in his strategy on every single occasion. No one would expect him to be. In early 1972 I had a telephone call from my staunch supporter, who told me he had just resigned and was out of a job. It seems a board meeting had been called and a new policy decision governing the management of the fund had been made.

'We are completely dissatisfied with the strategy our fund managers have adopted,' was the opening statement from the chairman. 'People do not give us their money to see us sitting with large amounts of cash, even though the correct strategy might be to sell shares. Our people will forgive us if we lose their money in a falling market. They will not buy our fund if it appears we may not make money in a rising market. We, the board, have therefore decided we would prefer to have all of our money invested even though the market may be falling, rather than have large sums of cash when the market is going up.'

In other words, my colleague was being told that the sale of the fund to the public was to take priority over any investment strategy which might be considered. If the investment strategy served to sell the fund – whether it was right or wrong – that was the strategy to employ. If the investment strategy did not help sell the fund – even though the strategy might be in the very best interests of those who were holding the fund – such a strategy was to be discouraged.

As it happens, investors as a group are mostly wrong most of the time, investing their money in funds when they should have it in the bank, and keeping it in the bank when the time is ripe for investment. The statistics to prove this phenomenon are overwhelming. The policy that will attract new money into a fund is often the worst possible policy for existing holders of the fund, which is why my colleague resigned. He was being asked to perform a task that had absolutely nothing to do with the principles of sound investment management.

Ancient Wisdom

It is important to understand this aspect of the investment business in order to grasp what took place in London during the mid-1970s. By that time I had been fully schooled in the popular delusions shared and promulgated by the investment community on both sides of the Atlantic. When in early 1972 I met a man whom I shall call J.M., I had learned that the basic psychology of the British stock market was a carbon copy of Wall Street; and also that the markets of Tulipomania, the South Sea Bubble, the Mississippi Bubble and others all came to a similar ending.

My good friend J.M. had seen it all. He was one of the old-timers, who had operated in the Chicago grain 'pits' with the famous Jesse Livermore. A 'pit' was the nickname given to that area on the commodity exchanges where wheat, rye, barley, soya beans and other grains are traded. In his breast pocket J.M. always carried a small book called *Reminiscences of a Stock Market Operator*. The author was Jesse LeFevere, who became a close friend of Jesse Livermore's, and the book was a tribute to Livermore and his biography. Inside J.M.'s copy was the inscription: 'To John, the best trader I have ever known.' It was signed 'Jesse L. Livermore'.

J.M. was indeed proud of that piece of memorabilia from the greatest stock market tactician who ever lived. But, as a strategist, Jesse Lauristin Livermore had certain flaws. His downfall was the introduction of the Securities and Exchange Commission in the United States during the late 1940s. When the SEC changed all the rules, Livermore could no longer function. The flaws which made Jesse a poor strategist were the same character flaws exemplified by the manner in which he chose to cope with the vast changes in Stock Exchange procedure, instigated by the newly appointed SEC. During the early 1940s Livermore was sitting at the bar of the Sherry Netherland Hotel in New York. He picked up a paper napkin and quickly scribbled a few words with his well-worn fountain pen: 'My life has been a total waste.' Leaving the note on the bar, Jesse slid from his bar stool and went to the men's room, where he placed a revolver to his temple and pulled the trigger. J.M. was proud of the inscription in that little book, just the same. The distinction between tactics and strategy – pragmatism and intuition – may be relevant, for it perhaps applied to J.M. to some degree.

It takes a long time to learn to operate in markets, I can tell you; and an even longer time to understand how markets operate. There are many who claim years of experience. In most cases those years of experience represent little more than a few months' experience repeated again and again over the years. Twenty years' experience equal to one year's experience repeated twenty times is par for the course.

I met J.M. through John Percival, who was then, back in the early 1970s, senior writer of the Lex column in the *Financial Times*. John, who was an exceptionally keen and astute truth-seeker of markets, was nearly ecstatic when he told me about J.M. and the manner in which market wisdom seemed to pour from the man. I was indeed anxious for John to arrange a meeting. When I finally did encounter J.M. for the first time, he had by then spent over half a century as a professional market operator, and had become the principal of a London stockbroking firm. I shared the enthusiasm of my friend John in no small way. J.M. and I were certainly kindred spirits. Our friendship was electric and spontaneous. From then on we would meet every few weeks for lunch or dinner to discuss what had been happening in markets during the interim.

Of course, the exploits of Livermore would invariably come into the conversation. J.M. would talk about Jesse's 'corners', his pool operations, his access to secret information, the way Jesse's brokers would always get him out of a tight spot because they needed his commission business so desperately. According to J.M., it was the high level of commission on trades that ruined Jesse. We would also talk about Jesse's love for the ladies. 'He was an amusing character,' said J.M. on one occasion. 'When we were trading in the "pits" together all Jesse could think about was screwing. And when he was screwing, the only thing he thought about was trading in the "pits". Jesse would have a phone to his ear while the rest of him was "in the saddle".'

There was one occasion when I was a few minutes late for a luncheon meeting that J.M. and I had arranged. When I arrived at the restaurant, J.M. was leaning against a wall in deep concentration, studying several columns of numbers he had written in a small notebook. On top of the list

---

'When we were in the "pits" together, all Jesse could think about was screwing'

---

of numbers were names like Courtaulds, British Petroleum, Imperial Chemical Industries and British American Tobacco. 'What are you up to?' I asked. 'Oh,' he replied, 'I'm just having a look at the past few hours' price movements of some of my holdings.' I took a closer look at the columns of numbers, noticing the absence of anything other than names and numbers – there were no dates. I said to him questioningly, 'You don't seem to have entered the price you paid for those shares in your book. Or when.' His reply was an example of the market wisdom integral to every iota of his waking being.

'No! Never, never! As soon as I buy a share, I try to forget what I paid for it. The last thing in the world I ever want to do is think about what I paid for these things. If I do, it might influence my judgment. The stock market isn't interested in what I paid for those shares. The only thing that counts is how the shares are behaving now!'

Sheep to the Slaughter

J.M. was really one of the best – he was worth any ten dozen stockbrokers the City of London has to offer. And that could be an insult to the wisdom of J.M., for the level of intellectual achievement in the London stock-broking community has never been particularly high! But the point is that even the wise and seasoned J.M. was taken in, along with practically everyone else who ever scanned the financial pages of a British newspaper during the early 1970s.

I remember the occasion as if it were yesterday. J.M. and I were lunching at the Savoy Grill. Our chatter turned to the whizz-kids and gun-slingers of the day – Jim Slater, Pat Matthews, Gerald Caplan, William Stern and their American counterparts like Jimmy Ling and the infamous Bob Vesco and Bernie Cornfeld. J.M. had seen similar characters in the past, and had little time for the new generation of this kind of operator. He readily recognized the serious flaws in their methods. J.M. had first-hand experience, having watched the collapse of the investment trusts and conglomerates on Wall Street, whose captains had borrowed to the hilt before the Crash of the 1930s. He noted how exactly the same circumstances mangled the conglomerates of the 1960s. In Britain, according to J.M., the high fliers of the 1970s would be no different. But in 1972, immediately before the roaring bull market in shares was to hit that final peak, the hot-shots and gun-slingers were amassing fortunes; and like sheep the fully fledged members of the flock were right behind. Any investor's portfolio that did not have a representative sampling of the shares that were being heavily promoted by the brokers and financial public relations agencies were seen to be sadly underperforming the rest of the market. Money managers and advisers who were not holders of the 'favourite fifty' – regardless of the investment merit, or lack of it, in these companies – were heavily criticized by their clients and other members of the investment community.

One of the masterpieces of mass psychology is a book called *The Crowd* by Gustav LeBon. In vivid detail LeBon describes the forces and seductive nature of unanimity of opinion regardless of how inept and uneducated that opinion may be: 'You can take the most brilliant and knowledgeable individuals you can find. Put them into a hysterical shrieking crowd and even they will immediately turn into blockheads.'

Sadly even J.M., with his five decades of experience and superlative investment wisdom, succumbed to the dictates of the mob. With steel-like fingernails sharpened to a razor's edge, it was as if the grasping hand of mass contagion had reached into his skull, squeezing his brain to a pulp. As the rise in share prices was reaching for its final hour, in the spring of 1972, I studied the holdings that J.M. had included in his list of investments. All the familiar names were there: Slater Walker Securities, British Bank of Commerce, London and County, First National Finance, London City and Westcliff Properties, Cedar Holdings. . . . J.M. had given in, adding to his holdings some sizeable stakes in the fashionable second-line banks, asset strippers and third-line property companies. If you were now to pick up a newspaper and look for these companies in the list of shares on the financial pages, you wouldn't find them. Not a single one of them exists today. The share prices of those companies did not just crash in the singular drama into which the City of London was plunged during 1973 and 1974. They were totally annihilated.

Financial Whitewash

During 1974 the crash of the London fringe bankers, those whose projects they financed, and shares on the Stock Exchange combined to create the most severe crisis the City has ever encountered. Yet it is often referred to as the Secondary Banking Crisis, suggesting a peripheral affair far removed from the core of the British financial system. An attempt to mute the severity of the situation was precisely the intention at the time. Whitehall and the press joined forces and rhetoric in an effort to shield the public from the truth. The concerted tactics of the Bank of England, the main clearing banks and other organizations at the heart of the crisis portrayed the affair as a financial problem that concerned only the less reputable newcomers to the august table of London's senior bankers. This was all whitewash. Although the crisis may have begun with the fringe banking sector, at one stage the whole of the British banking system was threatened – and the City of London knew it.

The barometer which many believe measures the pulse of the nation – the Stock Exchange – reflected the extent of the disaster in no uncertain terms. By the end of 1974 the *Financial Times* Industrial Ordinary Share Index, the British equivalent of the Dow Jones Industrial Averages, had fallen by 74% from its peak. Bear in mind that this is an index of Britain's 'blue chip' companies – the shares of many individual companies fared far, far worse. A somewhat broader measure of Stock Exchange activity in Britain is the *Financial Times* Actuaries All Share Index – the Ordinary Share Index has only thirty constituents, whereas the Actuaries All Share Index is made up of 714 individual companies. At the end of 1974 the All Share index – when adjusted for inflation – was standing at just one-sixth of its peak value two and a half years earlier. Such was the nature of the maelstrom.

180

The period of 1973–4 was one of world recession and falling stock markets. Yet no other stock market in the world suffered the same type of massacre as did the London Stock Exchange. The big shock to the system during the early 1970s was the OPEC oil embargo and subsequent quadrupling of oil prices. Many people believe it was the boost in oil prices itself that was the direct cause of the recession. But the hike in oil prices was nothing more than a catalyst, pushing a global economy that had already been teetering on top of an unsustainable boom into a cataclysmic tailspin. It should come as no surprise that the economic boom that preceded the recession was structured on a mountain of debt. But the economic excesses responsible for squeezing the last drop of strength from an overheated world economy were concentrated to white-hot intensity in Britain. In addition to the global recession there were two phenomena peculiar to Britain at that time which are directly attributable to the uniquely horrifying experience which resulted in the crash of the London banks.

Funny Money Rides Again

The common denominator of all crashes made a reappearance in Britain during the early 1970s. On that particular occasion it was called the Barber Credit Boom, after the Chancellor of the Exchequer, Anthony Barber. The other phenomenon was rampant speculation in commercial property. As in the past, a mania for speculation had been feeding on the credit explosion. Those who lived through the dark winter of 1974 in the City of London were marked by a memory they would never forget, the bursting of yet another credit-induced bubble – as had happened so many times before over the centuries.

Take one portion of political expediency. Mix with it five portions of unrestrained credit. You then have a cocktail capable of turning a whole society into zombies. The political element that preceded the Crash of the London banks took the form of Prime Minister Edward Heath's mind's-eye view of the economy in 1971, his first year in office. He didn't like what he saw, particularly the unemployment statistics that were soaring to record levels. The solution was obvious – just as it had been to John Law in the eighteenth century and to the German authorities during the 1920s. The Prime Minister adopted an easy money policy and set about injecting more cash into the banking system through the means available to him. No doubt Mr Heath had an eye on the type of economic atmosphere he hoped to create by the time the next election would be due in 1974. There can be no other explanation for the single-mindedness with which he set about the task of flooding the economy with money.

The policy of Edward Heath and his Chancellor can best be described as 'Get up and Go-Go-Go!' Enterprise was the cry, competition the watchword, and an export-led boom by manufacturing industry the target. All symbols of restraint vanished along with the former incomes policy that faded into obscurity with the abolition of the Prices and Incomes Board.

The Labour Party tended to argue that a further disturbing factor was the adoption of the European Common Agricultural Policy (CAP). According to Douglas Jay, academic *Times* journalist and one-time Financial Secretary to the Treasury, 'The adoption of the European Community's Common Agricultural Policy led to the steep and artificial forcing up of British food prices and the cost of living.'

When prices rise because money is losing value, you need more of it just to stand still

---

The events that lead to financial mania are multi-faceted. In the 1970s a common EEC agriculture policy was just another element that led to downward pressure on the value of money, as was seen in Germany in the 1920s. When prices rise because money is losing value, you need more of it just to stand still. But Mr Heath did not want the economy to stand still during his term in office. On 21 September 1971 the government published its White Paper on Competition and Credit Control, designed to lift the existing restraints on bank lending. A liquidity ratio of 28% was recommended, in place of the reserve ratio of 12.5%. Don't worry about the numbers or the technicalities. The important part was, in effect, that the lending potential of British bankers took a quantum leap. The floodgates were opened for John Law-type fiat money.

There was another element of a slightly more subtle nature that was to have a major impact on the unrestrained expansion in bank credit. What we can clearly see is that, even today, matters of state and issues of national importance can be swayed by the gentlest of pressure applied to the right person at the right time. The next stage in the funny money saga of the early 1970s was to emanate from the Bank of England.

Theoretically, the Bank of England as a body is totally independent of the government. On matters of monetary policy, its decisions can often override those of the Treasury or government. The Bank presides over the whole of the British banking system. British bankers were enthused by the policy adopted by the Heath government, and saw the opportunity for limitless profits.

To influence the powers presiding over the British central bank the most delicate brand of diplomacy was needed. The Chancellor of the day, whom Douglas Jay calls 'the amiable Barber', was clearly the right man. By all appearances he seemed wholly sympathetic to a profligate monetary policy in all its forms. The latest innovative suggestions were served to him at a private dinner party in January 1971.

The Governor of the Bank of England, Lord O'Brien, now placed the seal of approval on the removal of a further impediment to the unrestrained issue of credit. In the June edition of the Bank's *Quarterly Bulletin*, he explained: 'What we have in mind is a system under which the allocation of credit is primarily determined by its cost.' This statement was just the type of small, innocuous-looking atomic bomb that was dropped on Hiroshima. During the latter part of the 1960s and the early 1970s, the Bank was gradually moving towards the position where interest rates were determined by market forces rather than government intention. Since World War II the government, acting through the Treasury, had maintained a variable ceiling on the amounts the banks could lend to private borrowers. That ceiling was lifted dramatically with the White Paper on Competition and Credit Control. This meant, wrote Douglas Jay, that the authorities 'had held in check the natural urge of profit-making banks to expand their lending. . . . These ceilings were now to be largely abandoned in favour of "competition", market forces and so on; and the main restraint was to be . . . the rate of interest.'

Now if interest rates were to be the only restraining factor on the amounts banks could lend, and interest rates were to be determined by market forces, market forces would also determine the amount banks could lend. Quite simply, the banks could lend as much money as people wanted to borrow, at whatever interest rate the borrower was willing to pay. So the banks could lend as much as they liked!

Nothing could have sounded sweeter to the leaders of the New Conservatism at the start of the 1970s than the short message from Lord O'Brien. Subsequently, one move followed another in a blind effort to inject more and more funny money into the economy. The Bank of England decided to relax the regulations which determined who could operate as a bank, and a whole new range of financial intermediaries and 'banks' suddenly appeared (though they were not allowed to call themselves 'banks'

Napoleon described Britain as 'a nation of shop-keepers'. In the early 1970s 'a nation of bankers' would have been more appropriate

---

officially). Britain was once described by Napoleon as a 'nation of shopkeepers'. It would have been more appropriate in the early 1970s to describe Britain as a nation of bankers – albeit tiny bankers. The day of the 'second-line' banks was at hand.

Next came a massively expansionary Budget in March 1972. Consumption soared. Retail prices exploded as the value of money fell. In June there was severe downward pressure on the pound. Rather than boost interest rates in an effort to protect the level of the pound, the pound was allowed to move into free-fall, precipitating the Sterling Crisis of 1972, while the bank rate was stubbornly maintained at the low level of 6%.

That year inflation hit a national record of 23%. Was Britain faced with riots in the streets because of the high cost of living? No – the public were remarkably complacent, and for a good reason. When bank lending runs out of control, the greatest inflation is often seen in the price of financial assets. That meant not only roaring share prices but also a boom in house prices, to the joy of the three-fifths of UK householders who by then owned their own homes. During 1973, house prices rose by 52%.

In those days there was no ceiling on the amount of interest on mortgage loans that was tax-deductible. And the 1972 Budget had made *all* personal interest tax-deductible. The result was a scramble to borrow – the more the better. The high street banks were a bit stodgy about lending for share purchases, but not so the secondary banks that had sprung up like weeds in the wake of Competition and Credit Control.

Cannon Street Acceptances was one such bank, which after the March 1972 Budget lent out sums in £50,000 and £100,000 chunks to all comers for share purchases. The clearing banks – behind the scenes – were the source of the lending bonanza. William Stern, the residential property king, recalled that 'money in tens of millions was being offered and made available by a number of first-class banks'. His peer in industrial property, Ronald Lyon, told the same story: 'In my company, it is no exaggeration to say that we were having bank money thrust at us from all directions.' That money, as we shall see, was mostly to find its way to money heaven in the great debt liquidation to follow.

'In my company, it is no exaggeration to say that we were having bank money thrust at us from all directions'

Financial assets of every variety were caught up in this dizzy scenario – shares, works of art, antiques, and in particular residential property, offices, shops and industrial property. What had happened to the original idea of using funny money to generate an export-led boom through British manufacturing industry? Well, the idea was ill conceived to start with. A fiat money boom leads to rising prices across the board as money falls in value. If he is to make a profit, a manufacturer must always think of the cost of his end product. Easy money and low interest rates are only one element in that cost. Not so for the speculator in property or other assets, where the price of money and its availability are the only consideration. So long as the price of property – or whatever other speculative vehicle is chosen – rises faster than the cost of borrowing, the speculator is in pocket. This in turn leads to even more borrowing.

The failure of the Heath-Barber attempt to manipulate the economy through the issue of credit became so obvious that in 1972 the Bank of England was driven to make a public statement, calling on the first-line

184

major banks to cut back on their lending to property companies and the financial sector. Naturally that meant more business for the second-line banks.

The trouble facing any government which attempts to make political capital from a policy involving the abolition of controls should never be underestimated. In the final analysis, when it comes to a choice between getting egg on their faces or flying in the face of defeat, politicians usually go the same way. The outcome of the Heath–Barber episode was a foregone conclusion.

According to the official *Financial Statistics*, between December 1971 and December 1974 the total assets of British banks soared by 131% to £85,204 million. Advances rose by 160%, or £48,339 million. Excluding deposits held by overseas residents, UK advances and deposits doubled inside three years. Douglas Jay observed: 'More pounds sterling were created in these three years than in the whole of the twelve hundred years' history of the pound. . . . But the rise in the Government's borrowings . . . was in no way commensurate with the credit expansion . . . the *Private* Sector Borrowing Requirement was the trouble.'

The Saga of the Second-line Banks

The second-line banks were not banks in the true sense of the word, providing the type of facilities you get from your local branch of Barclays. Essentially they were money-lenders. Several had been in existence for many years before the debacle: they were the perfectly respectable subsidiaries and associates of the major British banking institutions and finance houses. Many were quoted on the Daily Official Stock Exchange List as 'Other British Banks'. The other variety, the Section 123 Companies, had come into being as the result of a judgment delivered by Lord Denning in 1966 in the case of United Dominion Trust (UDT) *v.* Kirkwood. UDT, for many years a leading finance house, was now claiming that it was a banker rather than a money-lender. His Lordship agreed. Lord Denning's judgment was enshrined in Section 123 of the 1967 Companies Act. With the shake of the legislative pen, all the money-lenders became bankers.

The formula they used was a relatively simple one. They would make loans that the larger banks were unwilling or unable to make for reasons of policy or because the financial risks were too high. They would pay their depositors – and the money market – a higher rate of interest than other deposit takers would. They would then charge their borrowers much higher rates of interest than the high street banks.

Many had started inauspiciously, adopting a highly individualistic lending pattern. Often they specialized in hire-purchase loans to consumers. There were those who lent only on the security of a second mortgage.

Many were prepared to lend on property development of a high-risk nature. A few specialized in discounting the accounts receivable of small businesses – known as 'factoring'. As more and more money was injected into the economy by the Heath government, the stature of the second-line banks grew along with the volume of their business. They went, for instance, into short-term 'bridging finance'. A borrower might discover that he could buy a particular property for £2 million and sell it a week later for £3 million. There would be a second-line bank ready and waiting to bridge that seven-day gap.

Prudence and caution were not strong points with second-line bankers. So much more money was always available, and there was so much competition from rival lenders. But there could be problems. It was all well and good to lend money for share deals, provided there was an ample margin between the amount of the loan and the value of the security against which the loan was made. But if the share market fell further than the margin of security allowed, the second-line bank would suddenly find that part of their loan was unsecured. The same held true of property deals. If a second-line banker lent £80,000 against a building valued at £85,000, it was fine as long as the value of the building did not fall below £85,000. If it fell to, say, £75,000, he could have a £5000 bad debt.

The Case for the Defence

There are several more positive features of the second-line banks and their involvement in share dealing and property speculation which should be looked at before we pass judgment on them – to fail to do so would be to take the attitude of a kangaroo court. Given the economic climate at the time, and the policies of the Conservative government, the secondary banks served a vital purpose. Whether it was a useful purpose is another matter. The point is that, had these secondary banks not existed, the big high street banks would probably have taken on their role – with even more disastrous consequences.

Many people criticize the second-line banks too harshly for attempting to behave like bankers but paying insufficient attention to the risk to which their involvement exposed them. But consider the manner in which over the past few years high street banks – including foreign banks of all kinds – insurance companies and pension funds have been rushing headlong into the residential property market in open competition with the building societies. Quite a few have gone so far as to buy themselves into the estate agency business – by acquiring whole chains they have become even more involved in the property game than the second-line banks and financial institutions in the 1970s. At the same time, British building societies have been launching excursions into corners of rock and roll banking.

186

Following Big Bang – the revolution in City practices that took place in October 1986 – the high street banks and other finance houses took on certain Stock Exchange activities which involve extremely high risks for a lending banker. All this has been piled on top of dubious lending to Third World countries, and off-balance sheet risk that is totally unquantifiable. When we reflect upon the nature and activities of the second-line banks in the 1970s in the light of what has been happening in the 1980s, the implication of their engagement in fly-by-night activities can be seen in perspective.

I have used the terms 'second-line bank' and 'fringe bank' for purposes of familiarity and reference. The 'fringe' epithet was not pejorative but related to the manner in which they operated, on the very edge of traditional banking practice. The second-line banks were highly geared – that is to say, a high proportion of their funds were borrowed through the money markets and other sources, and a lower proportion came from depositors, as in the case of the high street banks. Moreover they had some prestigious backers, including the bluest of the City's blue blood. Names such as Barclays Bank and leading insurance companies like Eagle Star and the Prudential crop up among their major shareholders. Even the government's paymaster, the Crown Agents, had substantial holdings. It is true that the Crown Agents came to grief in 1974, having invested in the same types of securities as the second-line banks. But in the early 1970s they still enjoyed an unblemished reputation and were regarded as one of the firm rocks upon which the British financial structure stood.

The Property Speculation Mania

The problems which were to emerge in the second-line banking arena were not attributable so much to the structure of these institutions, or to their mode of operating, as to the nature of the financial system itself. We live in a world in which speculative manias and crashes are endemic, but also one in which people are inclined to dismiss the lessons of the past. Unreasoned mass contagion is and always has been present in the very air we breathe. Like the bankers and investors who were falling over themselves to invest in railroads during the last century, so in the early 1970s the second-line bankers were falling over themselves to lend to those in the commercial property market. In so doing, they were over-extending themselves.

By 1970 property developers were suffering financially. Prices had been driven up by inflation, so that it was no longer possible to construct a building and meet the annual interest bill, given the level of rents which could realistically be asked. The developer could hope in most cases for a sizeable capital gain. The question was how he could afford to hang on to the building as an investment until current outgoings no longer exceeded annual income. One solution was to go for sale and leaseback. The lending body bought the freehold of the site and usually paid for the development. It granted a lease to the developer at a ground rent. The developer hoped to extract a higher rent from the tenant in due course.

The main risk for the developer lay in his being unable to let the building, or to obtain a high enough rent. But if he was successful, he was on his way to making his millions. As the market grew, the developer was presented with a further option. He could sell more developments to a lending body once they were completed, and use the proceeds to finance other developments which he could then keep.

From this point on, the risk escalated. As a rule secondary banks had to pay more for their funds, so the stakes were high. A complex sequence of operations had to go smoothly, which meant that the market needed to stay buoyant. Any decline in confidence could set off a chain of events capable of bringing down the whole house of cards.

The clearing banks came into the game when developers began to turn to them for medium-term – rather than short-term – finance. By now it was the company itself, not just individual projects, for which the developer wanted backing. It was an expensive way to raise funds, but so long as property values went on rising, developers could increase the proportion of borrowed capital in the company (called gearing) without fear that they would be embarrassed if they were called upon suddenly to repay their loans. With the co-operation of the high street banks and others willing to lend long-term, the gap between interest charges and rents would be bridged until rising prices had narrowed it. Moreover, as the value of their portfolio rose developers could borrow even more from the banks, using the new borrowing to pay off the interest on the older loans.

A Web of Speculative Finance

But what had made the banks willing to move into a risk area? For some years they had watched as property developers made huge personal fortunes while they collected a modest 'rent' for the money. It seemed to many bankers it was about time they were able to get hold of shares or share options. To put it crudely, as it was frequently put by the property entrepreneurs, the banks too wanted some of the gravy.

It became more and more difficult for developers to imagine there would ever come a time when property values or rents would stop rising. The trap into which many entrepreneurs and investors fell was to assume that, because the contracts bore the magic words 'property' and 'land', they were not actually speculating. They genuinely believed they were safer than if they had been dealing in Dutch tulip bulbs or John Law's paper promises. And property values were valid only so long as the auditor was prepared to believe whatever numbers the valuer put down. Unhappily, surveyors valued even holes in the ground on the assumption that they would be completed on time and let in full to tenants at current market rents. In short, it was a classic example of good, old-fashioned greed and self-deception.

To put it crudely, as it was frequently put by the property entrepreneurs, the banks too wanted some of the gravy

---

To an objective observer (a rare species at such times) Britain was beginning to look and act like Florida during the land boom, with a succession of eager but innocent suckers following the whizz-kids into the property market. There was also a new dimension – the intake stimulated by the secondary banks included Euro-currency deposits. These too were channelled into property and the stock market. This further increased the risk, since no one country can hope to control either the supply of money or the rate of interest in the Euro-market.

The explosion in lending to the property sector and to financial intermediaries produced some remarkable changes. In the two years after the introduction of Competition and Credit Control, bank lending to those sectors quadrupled from £1.5 to £6.4 billion, and it actually overtook lending to manufacturing industry. It accounted for over two-fifths of the growth in all bank lending over the period. Furthermore, about three-quarters of it came not from the major clearing banks but from 'others'. (As a rule of thumb, those figures from 1973 can be multiplied by five to get in line with today's pounds.)

What was going on? Basically, official interest rates were being held absurdly low in relation to inflation. Inflation, as reflected particularly in property values – also in the shares of property and financial companies – meant phenomenally high returns for companies and individuals speculating in these areas. So they were prepared to borrow to the hilt and pay well over the odds. The major banks would not accommodate them, but the fringe banks were falling over themselves to lend at high rates. And where did the fringe banks get the money for the loans? Ultimately from the major banks, who were quite happy lending to the so-called 'wholesale' market for big loans between banks and other financial intermediaries. Barclays, for example, would willingly lend to a huge hire purchase and finance house like UDT, which would lend on at higher rates to the fringe establishments with semi-banking status like First National Finance – to name one of the biggest.

During 1973 it was seen that, however fine the original intentions of the monetary policy of the Heath government, it was not working out along the lines originally projected. Retail prices were rocketing and beginning to cause alarm. Instead of stimulating business, the banks and city institutions were channelling the newly created money into the property market casino and similar gambling vehicles.

As the public began to become edgy pressure was put on the authorities. In July 1973 the minimum lending rate maintained by the big clearing banks was raised to a punitive 11.5% in the hope of moderating property speculation. The stated policy in 1971 had been to allow interest rates to seek their own level through market forces rather than be fixed by government. This volte-face sent shivers down the spines of those property speculators who paid attention to such matters. Most did not!

The hike in the minimum lending rate meant that borrowing would become more expensive and profit margins would be smaller. The amount of risk in comparison to the potential reward was drastically altered. The rate of property acquisitions slowed. So did the rise in values, and the property market began to teeter. Many deals rested on a pyramid of debt; often no collateral had been exchanged other than the promise of a rise in property values. If property values were to fall, someone, somewhere in the daisy chain of buying, selling, lending and borrowing was going to suffer a huge loss.

The Ball Starts Rolling Downhill

By autumn 1973 doubts were being entertained about the life of the commercial property bubble. Reason – and history – said the bubble must be nearing its limit. But, as usual, a chorus of reassurance was able to silence the voice of reason. Property prices peaked that autumn and began to slide. But the lending continued, albeit at a slower pace.

The momentum of the decline was given a shove by public indignation. Tales of the huge profits earned – or as some would say, unearned – by property speculators began to fall on the ears of those who couldn't necessarily afford the mortgage payments on their own homes. Such forms of quick-money endeavour were seen as the 'ugly face of capitalism'. The government was under pressure, even from members of its own party who were disenchanted with the Heath–Barber policies.

The Chancellor of the Exchequer now delivered what could be regarded as the final blow to the speculators. Bowing to pressure from the public – whose mind had been made up by the media – he introduced a tax on development gains. Nervous depositors at once began to withdraw their money from the second-line banks.

Now almost all the secondary banks had been breaking the cardinal rules of banking. The major banks get most of their money in the form of ordinary deposit accounts rather than from savings accounts or money deposited for a fixed term or on fixed notice. And, indeed, savings accounts can usually be drawn on at no notice. In theory, even the big

190

banks would be in trouble if droves of depositors withdrew all their money at a swoop. But, if they did, where would they put it? In another major bank, most likely. So there is no net withdrawal from the banking system; and any major bank that has a sudden influx of new deposits would normally be happy to lend it back again to a bank which has suffered a run. That is the great advantage of a national branch system: the only way the money can leave is if it goes abroad – which was not possible in the early 1970s.

It is a completely different matter with a secondary bank. In the case of a run of withdrawals, the fringe bank is by no means certain of getting access to funds from the banking system. That is why it was imperative for second-line banks to guard against a mismatch in its deposits and its loans. What were the secondary banks doing in the early 1970s? The vast bulk of their deposits were from the wholesale market, and the average maturity, or notice period, of these funds was a tiny nineteen days. Yet they were then lending that money to property companies and developers for one to five years. 'To lend it long and borrow it short/Is the quickest road to the bankrupts' court' goes the old rhyme. Some of the new 'bankers' seemed never to have heard it. They trod the predictable road.

Another Bubble Bursts – London and County Goes Under

In November 1973 disaster struck London and County, of which the then popular and respected leader of the Liberal Party, Jeremy Thorpe, was chairman. It was run by a man named Gerald Caplan, whose boardroom was later likened to 'the court of a medieval king'. London and County had come face to face with a run on its deposits.

On 29 November it was clear that L and C would have to suspend payments to depositors who wished to withdraw their money. That was not a risk that the Bank of England was happy about. L and C had depleted its own funds in a futile £5 million effort to support its own shares – which was at best irregular, at worst unlawful. It had also arranged an emergency loan from a bank called Keyser Ullman. The Bank of England decided that L and C's depositors should be protected at all costs because of the scale of the problem – about £400 million in today's money. On the 30th L and C's shares crashed from 80p to 40p, having been 200p at their peak at the end of October. By 3 December a rescue package was in place, calling for £20 million of new loans from L and C's institutional shareholders. First National Finance took over the management. The entire board resigned except for the nominee of Eagle Star and Jeremy Thorpe. Just what a can of worms London and County really was emerged over time. Its final collapse was staved off until March 1975, when it went down for a cool £50 million. In 1978 Gerald Caplan, then living in California, was charged with theft and other offences.

191

So began the Crash of London, 1974. When the next fringe 'bank', Cedar Holdings, got into trouble the Bank of England knew they had a crisis on their hands. It happened two days after an austerity budget on 17 December. Bank rate had by then soared to 13%. The *FT* 30 Share Index had tumbled to the low 300s from its May 1972 peak of over 540. The atmosphere in the City of London was fraught: there was clear danger of a domino effect. At a tense overnight meeting of top financial and industrial brass at the Bank of England, it was agreed – astoundingly – to refinance the whole of Cedar's £72 million deposit base. Barclays Bank was to provide up to £22 million and the shareholders the balance.

Within forty-eight hours of that meeting, however, share prices were cascading downwards again. Rumours of further bank failures proliferated, along with those of property companies. Everyone was stampeding to get rid of shares tainted with the provincial property/second-line bank stigma. The Governor of the Bank of England called another secret but more ambitious meeting with representatives of all the major City banks.

By the afternoon of 21 December a special bankers' committee had been formed. No less than £1000 million was earmarked for the rescue of any other secondary bank threatened with collapse. No one appears to have suspected it would take not months, but years, before the worst was over. According to Margaret Reid's book *The Secondary Banking Crisis 1973–1975*, by March 1975 aid given under the auspices of the committee totalled £1285 million. A further £1700 million was contributed by other banks and investment houses.

By the time the smoke had cleared and the officials began sweeping up the debris, the financial storm had necessitated the rescue of twenty-five banks. Of those secondary banking concerns that sought aid under the official scheme, one was scaled down and sold off; eight died in the hands of the Official Receiver; fourteen were taken over by other British banking institutions; and two became the property of foreign bankers.

Almost all the secondary banks had been breaking
the cardinal rules of banking

By early 1974 the Bank of England was able to breathe a sigh of relief that the crisis had been restricted to a comparatively small ring of bankers. Yet the money required to finance the rescue was equivalent to 40% of the capital and reserves of the entire British and Scottish clearing banks in 1974 – without taking into account the aid provided indirectly by the rest of the banking community. The authorities had gambled and won, but it was no odds-on bet. If fifty banks had failed instead of twenty-five, the gamble might not have paid off and the entire British banking system could have collapsed. It was that close!

Can such crashes be avoided in the future? And if so, should the public be made aware of the facts in advance? These are the questions many Americans are asking in 1988, as they watch their banks being subjected to one rescue operation after the other. The press statement issued by the Bank of England in December 1973 was a masterpiece of silent diplomacy: 'In recent weeks a number of so-called "fringe banks" have experienced a withdrawal of deposits obtained through the money market. . . . [So] the Bank of England has established . . . machinery whereby such cases can be promptly considered and the situation . . . kept under continuous review.' Had the recently appointed Governor of the Bank of England, Gordon Richardson, been an eye-witness in Rome when the

Has not the time come for the public to be given the facts about the financial world – as we have health warnings on cigarette packets?

Empire collapsed, one could imagine his authorizing a statement to the effect that: 'On the night in question, the Emperor Nero did not allow the smoke, the flames or the noise to interrupt his violin practice.' Has the time not come for members of the public to be indoctrinated in the simple, everyday facts of the financial world – in the same manner as we have health warnings on cigarette packets?

We know that the moment fat profits are promised, and the banks – or whoever – appear to be delivering the goods, there is no shortage of little pink snouts eager to get into the swill trough. Surely it would be reasonable to hope that adult human beings might be expected to show a little more sense? But upon reflection, perhaps this is not a reasonable expectation. Think only of the behaviour of stock market investors before the Crash of '87 – and also after the crash. Of course, no government in the Western world today would have it any other way. To take away the dreams of the people would mean an immense loss of political capital.

We are told that the deceptions and disinformation emanating from behind the closed doors in high places are intended to serve the public interest. The comforting words of President Hoover, that a major economic recovery was underway, certainly did not serve the interests of those investing in the stock market in the spring of 1930. His 'economic recovery' turned out to be one of the worst depressions the West has ever seen. Judgment Day for President Reagan's and Mrs Thatcher's solemn pronouncements is still in the future.

11

The Crash of '87

How I helped thousands of investors avoid the
worst stock market collapse since the Crash of '29

A Word to the Wise

The great inventor Marconi once tried to encourage a friend whose clever
innovation was being ridiculed. 'You must be prepared for the greatest
difficulties,' he said. 'But if you are an inventor of true mettle, you'll win
through – just as I did, against every form of stupidity, of which the
deadliest is the stupidity of doubt.'

The vehemence and venom with which mass opinion resists change and
any challenge to its preconceptions is not confined to inventors and
scientists. Roger Babson, who had accumulated considerable wealth in
his stock market activities and was one of the great analytical minds on
Wall Street in the 1920s, dared to fly in the face of popular opinion. In
1928 he insisted that the stock market could not rise for ever, and warned
of the strong possibility of a severe stock market crash at any time. Babson
made his forecast while the stock market was still rising strongly and his
reward was public ridicule, scorn, criticism, denunciation and disgrace.
Not many contemporary accounts recognized Babson as one of the few
who anticipated the Crash of '29 long before the event. The hero of the
1920s was the guru of the day, Professor Irving Fischer of Harvard
University. In September 1929 Fischer announced to the world: 'The
American economy has achieved a permanently high plateau.' This was
precisely what the crowd wanted to hear! They even applauded Herbert
Hoover when he said, 'The economy is basically sound' . . . during the
Crash of '29.

The 1960s saw the publication of J. K. Galbraith's *The Great Crash*. It
is without doubt one of the major definitive studies of the subject,
revealing the author's great understanding of the debacle. Although he
never predicted in so many words another crash similar to that of 1929,
many read into the book the suggestion that one could occur. A roaring
bull market was underway in America at the time, and the mere inference

that such a disaster was possible caused havoc. The author received letters threatening his life, and several people claimed that by writing the book he was attempting to induce a crash.

For decades the investment community the world over maintained that a stock market crash similar to that of 1929 in the United States could never happen again. Yet in October 1987 a similar crash *did* occur. In intensity it was nearly equal to its famous predecessor, and it occurred in about the same space of time. For me, the Crash of '87 has a very special significance. I predicted the likelihood of such a crash in my book *The Downwave*, published in 1983. As a result I suffered the same experiences as the many others throughout history who have dared to challenge popular opinion. I was ridiculed, lied about, became the victim of cruel jokes and made to appear 'hopelessly wrong'.

Early Warnings

During the five years preceding the Crash it was my view that both the US and UK equity markets represented an unacceptable degree of risk for investors. I recommended investment in the new bull market in US bonds that was just getting underway. It wasn't until October 1987 that I recommended taking action to exploit the Crash, which was the culmination of a movement that had begun several months before. During that summer, severe cracks had begun to appear in the market. I reported every one to my daily radio listeners over LBC, the London news radio station. Having watched the US and UK equity markets screaming skyward in early July, I wrote in the 18 July issue of *Investors Bulletin*:

> The formula for a financial holocaust of unbelievable dimensions is firmly in place. Deregulation, unquantifiable risk, the uninhibited use of credit, create a situation that is so hypersensitive that the slightest crisis of confidence could suddenly take on proportions of a magnitude beyond human comprehension. But what Unit Trust manager would dare take his clients out of this speculative orgy and expose himself to the wrath of the investor who believes this will continue forever?

It was during the week ending 18 July that the *Financial Times* 30 Share Index in London broke through the 1900 level for the first time, as institutional and private investors eagerly competed with one another to buy whatever shares they could afford. It caused the turbulence which is invariably seen before a major upheaval.

In *Investors Bulletin* on 18 July I warned:

> The continued turbulence has several implications. One is the tremendous level of volatility that is characteristic of this market due to

195

the nature of the participants. No matter what you think the future may hold, a highly volatile market is a highly risky market. There is no possible way to justify any alternative conclusion. On Wednesday we had a market that gained 18 points in two hours; lost 14 points in the next four hours; and then gained 14 points in one hour. On Thursday we had a market that gained 25 points in five hours and lost ten points in one hour. There are obviously large numbers of investors and speculators with sweaty palms and itchy telephone fingers who are anxious to jump in and scoop up profits in large quantities at the first sign of adversity. So far, this market hasn't really had any bad news to contend with. But sporadic injections of bad news are a permanent way of stock market life. When we do get a dose of bad news (which is inevitable) the market reaction is likely to be exceptionally violent as all the players head for the exits at once.

But I also concluded in that week's edition: 'It ain't over 'til it's over and it certainly doesn't look like it's over yet. During last week, the *Financial Times* 30 Share Index bobbed and weaved as it took shareholders on their one-way trip to money heaven, producing yet another blaze of speculative glory.' Actually it *was* all over, as I was completing that week's issue. All that was lacking was the confirmation.

On 16 July the *Financial Times* 30 Share Index had reached a peak of 1926.2 on an intra-day basis and then began to decline. A week later, in the 25 July issue of *Investors Bulletin*, I outlined what had happened:

If we look at what's happened to the UK equity market over the past week, once again we find all of the components that could act as a precursor to a 1929-type stock market crash. Sentiment was precisely the type that was found preceding the stock market crash of 1929. A glance at any of the newspapers told you that the prospects of a serious market decline were inconceivable. The general feeling was that shares could only go up . . . not go down. The only problem for investors was . . . what to buy. Those who were considering selling were virtually non-existent.

Last week we saw one of the worst declines over the shortest period since the bull market began in 1975. It is too soon to tell whether or not the rise in the *Financial Times* 30 Share Index to an all-time high of 1926.2 on Thursday the 16th July was the death-knell that sounds the collapse. It is also too soon to determine whether or not the recent panicky decline could be the precursor to a secondary rally that indicates the long and laborious bull market has run its course. The decline was only four days in duration. A decline of a much more extended duration would be required to produce the technical foundation needed to confirm the likelihood of a subsequent bear market following the first major rally in the bull market.

In sum, if the recent market slash is going to subsequently develop into a full savage bear market, that bear market is likely to be in full swing during the autumn.

Into August share prices on the London Stock Exchange continued to decline. By the 7th the *FT* 30 Share Index had fallen by 231 points from the summer peak. But during the second week of August share prices were once again moving higher. In the 22 August issue of *Investors Bulletin* I reported:

If a bear market began from the 16th July peak, the structure of the nature of ensuing rallies and declines would have to take a form which had previously not been seen during the big bull run. Any rallying action would have to be limited to two-thirds of the downward drive that preceded it. Downward drives in themselves would have to develop a series of five components, as opposed to three, which is the nature of corrective action. The second and fourth components . . . the rallying phases . . . would have to be of approximately equal duration and amplitude. To date, none of the declines that have developed since the bull market began in 1975 have met the aforementioned criteria which are an integral part of the two major analytical tools for the anticipation of future secular trends, Dow Theory and the Elliott Wave Theory.

'The indications that we are now in a bear market are stronger and more pronounced than anything witnessed in the past twelve years'

After carrying out a thorough analysis of the various elements involved in the structural behaviour of the British equity market since the July peak, I wrote the following concluding paragraph to my market summary in that issue:

On Thursday of last week, the *Financial Times* 30 Share Index crashed through the 1700 support area. A strong rally should now be expected from a level which is marginally below the 1700 area. This rally can be expected to be larger than any of the rallies that have interrupted the downward drive that began on the 16th July. The rallying action should be limited to 66 per cent of the downward drive that began on the 16th July and whose terminal juncture lies immediately ahead. Ideally, the rally will abort at the 50 per cent retracement level. During the next rallying phase many investors will believe the bearish forces are expended. Most will hold the view that the bull market is once again underway. Large public participation can be expected during the latter part of that rallying phase we see ahead. It will be at the terminal juncture of that rallying phase subscribers will be advised to commence their short selling and 'put' option trading. The indications that we are now in a bear market are stronger and more pronounced than anything witnessed in the past twelve years.

So far as I am aware, no one else in the UK dared suggest a bear market was underway. For the rest of the summer and into early autumn, the rally took a classic form. The momentum of the upward rise in prices slowed considerably. By mid-September the *FT* 30 Share Index was still nowhere near a level consistent with a normal bear market rally, but by 3 October the rally had finally reached the target I had been anticipating back in the summer. Then, on Monday, 5 October, volume suddenly swelled and heavy selling pressure appeared, while the *FT* 30 Share Index made an attempt to move beyond the parameters normally associated with a bear market rally. That was my cue. I shouted the message loud and clear on the radio on Tuesday morning, during my pre-opening stock market commentary:

During today's session the market will be in the hands of the bears. Given the behaviour of the *Financial Times* 30 Share Index when it moved into the 1880s, you could easily see a 'crack', targeting yesterday's drive at the terminal juncture of the rally that began in the low 1680s back in August. If that turns out to be the situation, then you'll have a 300 point decline staring you in the face, and it will be time to put your short selling strategy and 'put' option strategy into motion. . . .

The 'crack' appeared on cue. In the 10 October issue of *Investors Bulletin* I made the following recommendation: 'After many long months of patient waiting, the technical position of the market over the past week has resulted in triggering the operation of our short selling and "put" option strategy. In this week's Portfolio Review, for the first time you will find our high risk trading portfolio with this week's recommendation.' The forecasts and recommendations that were made would have placed traders in a position to exploit the bear market within 3% of the peak of the bull market and nine days before Meltdown Monday. I then stepped back, looked the market square in the eye and said, 'Make my day!' It did.

The Brink of Chaos

On Friday, 16 October 1987 occurred an eerie event. The hurricane that hit London early that morning took the weather forecasters completely by surprise. It struck me as foreboding at the time, but I did not consciously appreciate its ominous nature until later. Sparked by freak atmospheric pressure patterns in the Bay of Biscay the previous night, it drove north, cut a swathe of ruin through Brittany and unleashed most of its remaining fury on south-east England. Countless centuries-old trees were prostrated; thousands of houses damaged; gas, power, telephone and water connections cut; immeasurable miles of roads blocked; and the entire railway network in the south-east brought to a standstill. Offices were empty, the Stock Exchange closed and the City of London deserted. A few underground trains were still running. In the long pauses between trains, empty beer cans rolled to and fro, and wisps of waste paper were blown hither and thither by fragments of wind that had somehow penetrated below ground, compounding a weird scene.

The weather records contained no close precedent for a hurricane like this over London, so it was at least strange. But why was it ominous? For some days I had been watching the world's stock markets with increasing apprehension. Clearly the action in stock markets was taking place in America and really big trouble was in store. That was where it would start. The Dow Jones Industrial Share Index had peaked on 25 August at 2722. After a break in September it had recovered to around 2640, paused, and then on 6 October suddenly plunged over 90 points. What was sinister was that there was no recovery on the following day, and then a further slide of nearly 80 points into the Monday of the following week. I was expecting a decline of about 300 points in the London market. What seemed to be looming ahead was much more menacing.

There was a rally on the 13th, but from there on the move began to speed up – too fast for most observers. Subsequent commentaries show that few managed to follow the events, let alone explain them. This is not surprising, for those who understand what makes share markets move are seldom the same as those who explain the movements. Besides, what was in the process of developing was chaos. I use the word in a special sense – in the same sense as the process of chaos by which freak pressure patterns turn into a hurricane.

The Butterfly Effect

Thanks to the work of a gentle and visionary American physicist called Edward Lorenz, we now know that the weather is literally unpredictable. Before you die laughing, let me enlarge. Ever since the days of Isaac Newton, scientists (and the rest of us) have approached questions of natural physics with the assumption that they have finite answers. The answers might be elusive; but with patience they could be found. It was on this assumption that the great mathematician John von Neumann decided to apply the electronic computer to the study of the weather. It was, he assumed, just a matter of throwing enough time and calculations at the problem and in due course he could come up with enough answers, not only to forecast the weather, but to be able to change it. Needless to say, he failed – which is why the efforts of the TV weather pundits are still a source of endless mirth.

In the early 1960s Edward Lorenz came up with a different theory – that the factors that create the weather are in fact infinite, or as near infinite as makes no difference. And he produced a lovely example to illustrate his meaning. The world's weather balance is so delicate and sensitive, according to Lorenz's theory, that the flap of a butterfly's wings in the Gulf of Mexico could be a decisive factor in an immense chain of events leading to a cyclone in the South China Sea, or somewhere. It came to be called the Butterfly Effect.

Gradually Lorenz's work won acceptance, and much more than that. It is generally regarded as the seed of a new scientific school of thought, and a new approach to certain natural phenomena which scientists had been at a loss to explain over the centuries. Deepest of all, perhaps, was the apparently random chaos of turbulence. So deep that Werner Heisenberg, the great quantum theorist, is supposed to have said that when he got to heaven he would have two questions for God: 'Why relatively? And why turbulence? And I'm sure He'll have the answer to the first.' Following in Lorenz's footsteps, the 'chaos' school – for so it came to be called – cracked the problem of turbulence in the 1970s.

Stock markets seem to have much in common with complex systems like the weather (or turbulence). There are some probabilities in both. At times, forecasts can be made about stock markets just as they can be made about the weather – with varying degrees of certainty in each case. Yet both remain relatively unpredictable. Both contain fluctuations within fluctuations – minute-by-minute, hourly, daily, weekly and so on. So perhaps are the combinations that go to produce a given outcome – such as a warm dry westerly breeze or a 6.56 rise in the *FT* 30 Share Index. Both, it seems, are capable of suddenly disintegrating into apparently random chaos. Which is why the timing of the hurricane on Friday, 16 October is so striking. For Friday, 16 October was the day when Wall Street crossed the threshold from relative order into progressive chaos.

Things had been getting unruly in the two preceding days. The trouble was the bond market. Bonds (or fixed-interest stocks) are safe investments, guaranteed by the government or large companies, mostly held by institutions like insurance companies. Bond prices had been falling sharply since August. That meant that bond yields had risen. In fact, by the week beginning 12 October bond yields had climbed over 10% whereas the average yield on shares was down to about 2½% – about the lowest on record. At a certain stage, big investors looking at the difference between yields on shares and on bonds say: 'Enough is enough! If we can get over 10% on the dead safe stock of the US Government and only 2.75% on risky shares, we're going to sell out of shares so that when the time is right we can get into bonds.'

That is what happened that week. In fact, it had been happening in a more modest way since the peak in US share prices on 25 August. For it was precisely *then* that bond prices had started to plummet, and yields to rise. But that week in October the flow of money out of shares became a torrent.

On 14 October the bond market was further upset by a bad set of US trade figures. The following day bond prices plummeted – pulling share prices down with them. In those three days alone, the Dow Jones Industrial Averages plunged over 150 points; and since 5 October the loss had been just short of 300 points, or 11% – something never seen before in the long bull market that stretched back to 1982. So by Friday, 16 October, as the hurricane blew itself out over the City of London, the stage was set for the onset of chaos.

The New York market was down from the opening. Gradually during that day Wall Streeters and share-watchers around the country started to get the feeling that things were going wrong. It was irrelevant that the bond market was steady. An inexorable process had been set in motion in New York. It was like the process that had started the night before in the Bay of Biscay. The science of chaos had discovered that the conditions under which a smooth flow is transformed into turbulence are both infinitely complex and inescapable. In mathematical terms, they abide by the rules of a number of equations which are elegantly simple but can be repeated ad infinitum. Even though there were billions of possible variations to the outcome of share trading in New York that Friday, the eventual outcome was in a way inevitable. The Dow fell a record 108 points in an unprecedented torrent of selling totalling 385 million shares.

The chairman of the US Reserve Board, Alan Greenspan, described events as 'an accident waiting to happen'

Yet, that was derisory compared with what was to come. The hurricane that blasted its way through the world's stock markets the following week was also, in a sense, inevitable. The causes were too complex to grasp in detail, but we can trace the broad outlines of the gathering storm. With hindsight, the chairman of the US Federal Reserve Board, Alan Greenspan, described events as 'an accident waiting to happen'. With hindsight, hadn't J. K. Galbraith made a similarly shrewd observation – that the causes of the 1929 Crash were all in the speculative orgy that preceded it?

I had been busy with various matters that day in the eerie wake of the London hurricane – just checking now and then to register how the slide in US share prices was proceeding. Before I headed home it was still well under control. Around eight o'clock, however, a friend arrived breathless with the news that the Dow was off 80 points, and the fall had been accelerating. At that moment I knew with certainty that the crash I had been expecting for so long had actually begun. I also knew it would unfold with great violence over the following weeks.

Day by day, month by month, year by year the speculative orgy in stock markets had been building. In London the build-up had been almost uninterrupted since 1975; elsewhere, it only began in earnest in 1982. But by 1986 and 1987 the markets in Scandinavia, Italy, Spain, Greece, all the

---

Surely it was crazy to keep money in a bank or building society in such times!

Americas, Australasia, Japan and the 'four tigers' – Hong Kong, Singapore, Taiwan and Korea – the stock markets *everywhere*, were in the grip of an intensity that had not been seen – and never on a global scale – since shares were first exchanged in Amsterdam in the seventeenth century.

The last time anything comparable had occurred on the international scene had been in the late 1950s and early 1960s. Even then, the only place where the speculation had reached such crazy proportions was in the stock markets of continental Europe. It arose on the back of a flood of American money, betting on boom times in the newly formed EEC. Even then the public wasn't present in such great numbers. Continental investors had paid dearly for that mini-mania. Indeed, in several markets share prices did not regain their early 1960s' values until the 1980s.

That, maybe, was the biggest change that took place in the 1980s. Millions of newcomers began investing in shares. In America the number of investors climbed in 1987 from some 30 million to over 50 million. In Britain, the increase was proportionately more dramatic – according to some estimates the number rose from some 3 million to around 8 million. There was a special reason in Britain's case – privatization. Everywhere, including Britain, an increasing number of women began to own shares. In Japan they had 'Mrs Watanabe', with her shares in the newly privatized Japanese telecom company NTT, as a figure of caricature.

Shares are inherently risky. Over the centuries they have risen and fallen in cycles. In 1974 share prices in Britain had plummeted to little above a quarter of their peak values in 1972. But what did the newcomers know about this? That plunge merely made the recent record look even better. Between the start of 1975 and the Crash average share prices rose ten times. Surely it was crazy to keep money in a bank or building society in such times! Besides, a huge industry had grown up with a vested interest in selling shares to the public – not just stockbrokers, but unit trust companies too, who would invest and manage your money in shares

selected by them. Insurance companies had either to see themselves beaten
by the unit trusts or join 'em. Naturally, it joined 'em! The government,
too, had a vested interest in rising share prices, for that ensured the success
of its privatization issues.

There was also the psychological angle – there are few joys as intense as
that experienced by those who hold large quantities of shares in a swiftly
rising market. There was a further bonus: a seductive bonus. People are
seduced into thinking they are clever. 'Financial genius', it has been cutely
said, 'is a short memory in a rising market.' But the truth of that gem is
only apparent when the market starts turning down.

So millions of new punters came to believe that rising share prices were
the norm. Those warnings in the promotional literature, urging them to
remember that 'share prices can fall as well as rise', were strictly for the
birds. They may have been true in theory. But in practice the warnings
seemed to be no more valid for share prices than for – well – for house
prices. If they fell a bit, they always came back up again. Perhaps
the warnings were really just a kind of propaganda designed to keep
the ordinary man away from this haven of the privileged. It was only after
the Crash that we learned what unbelievable follies some of these
brand-new capitalists had been permitted to indulge in.

Over three years, from 1985 to 1987, Vernon Smith at the University of
Arizona and Arlington Williams at Indiana University ran experimental
stock markets in their labs. They would pit a bunch of students or
businessmen against each other in a competition in which the punters
would trade shares with one another in a simulated market place.
Invariably, newcomers to the experiment would bid shares up into a
raging boom, which would be followed by a bust. This would frequently
happen again on a second session. But after the guinea pigs had grown
really accustomed to the game, the pattern of trading would calm down to
a gentle see-saw.

---

*The stockbroking houses, the institutions and the
banks were full of young men and women who had
never experienced a bear market*

The newcomers were not confined to the public. The stockbroking
houses, the institutions and the banks were full of young men and women
who had never experienced a bear market. The share industry boomed as
never before, and huge salaries were offered to promising young people. It
was the mid-1980s that saw the introduction of the term 'yuppie' – young
upwardly mobile professionals. The expression came from America to
Britain – and at first usually denoted a share trader. The yuppies did much
to encourage the get-rich-quick spirit. Hear the sheer exhilaration of Jay
Thomas, philosophy graduate turned trader and a young man wiser than

his years – wiser because he understood that he was just lucky. He was speaking to *Business* magazine just days before the Crash.

> Sometimes before I fall asleep at night I laugh out loud and kick my feet in the air at the absurdity of all this good fortune. . . . When else in the history of mankind could a young man . . . become genuinely wealthy without taking personal risk or possessing unusual talents? No doubt one day it will all be outlawed. But for now I will enjoy the occasional, intense feeling that I've won some sort of sweepstake.

His sentiments were shared by those hundreds of thousands of speculators who did take risks, as well as professional traders – not all of whom were as bright as Jay Thomas. The real losers among the risk takers were the LBO crowd – LBO standing for leveraged buy-out. This was the gobbledygook invented for a familiar concept – the company takeover or merger – when some genius decides that the whole thing, more or less, can be paid for with borrowed money. The game was started by individuals like Boone Pickens and Carl Icahn and their ilk in America. They bid for multi-billion dollar companies with what amounted to the company's own money – something which in many countries is illegal. The borrowed money came in the form of what were rightly known as junk bonds. Naturally, the fees paid to the investment houses that arranged the LBOs with their attendant junk bonds were in no way small change. In one recent case they were put at 500 million dollars! But this didn't matter, because in the end they were probably paid for by the company that was being taken over or bought out. (Such a company was said to be 'in play' – in the fun-loving spirit of the game.)

'For now I will enjoy the occasional, intensive feeling that I've won some sort of sweepstake'

The British version of the game tended to be conservative by comparison. It usually involved a large company, rather than an individual – a brewery, for example, bidding for a spirits producer. Sometimes, admittedly, a few corners were cut, or participants were excessively 'economical with the law'. They tended to end up in a dialogue with the relevant enforcement authorities. But in America the typical bidder was an individual, and the high fees involved meant that the investment houses were constantly in search of suitable parties who could be inveigled into bidding for General Motors, General Foods, Bank of America or other suitable candidates. An idea of just how good all this was for share prices can be gleaned from the example of James I. Freeman, a strategist with the American bank First Boston. In a client circular he enthused that 17.5 billion dollars had been raised in buy-out pools. But 'that is just the beginning'. With leverage (borrowing), pool managers could buy out 140 billion dollars' worth of shares – a veritable 'freight train of money coming down the tracks'. So the question was not *if* the market was going up, but how much and how soon. In the month the market peaked it was generally agreed, even by the 'wets', that 3200 on the Dow was a minimum figure.

Some in the trade alleged it was pique at not having been approached by First Boston for a multi-billion LBO which led David Herrlinger to make his 6.8 billion dollar offer for Dayton Hudson Corporation. On the contrary! He seems to have been a shrewd observer who had carefully, and accurately, sussed out the whole business. His bid sent the shares soaring, adding a billion or two to the value of Dayton Hudson. Then people began to realize they had not the slightest idea who David Herrlinger was! Dayton Hudson lost its billion or two again, and the reporters honed in on Herrlinger, an investment adviser from Cincinnati. Was it a hoax? 'It's no more a hoax than anything else,' replied the bidder perceptively, from the safe haven of his front lawn. It was only later they admitted him to the local hospital. Life's real mean when you're the only one in step!

Meltdown Monday

The Land of the Rising Sun toughed it out: Tokyo shares gave up just 2.3% on the morning of 19 October. So did Australia, where shares lost a modest 3.9%. Retribution there was to come on Tuesday. Hong Kong was more realistic: shares crashed 11%. And so was London. The Stock Exchange had been closed on Friday, and so the shock of Wall Street's ominous break that day came undiluted. London was in for a grim day, and right at the start of trading shares were down 6%. But that wasn't nearly enough – that was just for openers.

The world's stock markets today are all linked by a system of instant communications. What happens in any other major market is available on the screen at the stroke of a key. The US trade figures and other key economic news items, for instance, are known all over the world within seconds of their release. Dealing instructions whizz from London to New York or Chicago in seconds via direct phone links. London is particularly important as a financial centre for international dealings because, apart from anything else, it stands mid-way between Tokyo and New York on the clock. Meanwhile the futures markets allow investors to make bets on share prices or interest rates with almost unlimited credit. If you feel that shares may fall, within seconds you can place a bet on the futures markets that the shares will drop.

The speed of communication and all these new dealing facilities long ago raised fears that in tricky times things could get out of control. Back in

March, the Chairman of the New York Stock Exchange had written of his worries about a 'meltdown' in the stock market – a sort of Chernobyl effect – should the selling of shares and futures produce a self-feeding spiral. 'You could get a steamroller effect in a bear market,' he wrote, 'for which there is no safety effect in the system today.' He didn't hedge his views: 'At some point in time you are going to have a first-class catastrophe.' Vernon Smith at the University of Arizona would say the new dealing facilities were a red herring. His experiments showed you could achieve catastrophe provided the stock market was full of freshmen.

As if programmed, the big brass did all the wrong things

At lunchtime in London on Monday, 19 October, things went very quiet as observers waited to see how Wall Street would open at 3.30 p.m. It could only be down, deeply down. It was later revealed that the stock market regulatory authorities were so worried by Friday's action that they had been busy right through the weekend sounding out the position of the big institutions. Their findings were described as 'frightening'. The question was whether the Stock Exchange might have to be closed. The atmosphere in the brokerage houses emerged from newspaper accounts. At the early morning conference at Merrill Lynch, chief stock market analyst Robert Farrell told president Daniel Tully that he thought the market could be down 200 points. Donaldson, Lufkin & Jenrette had been so deluged by 'sell' orders that they brought in a fistful of security guards to line the dealing room in case of an invasion by anxious clients.

Within the first hour, 140 million shares had been sold – a full day's trading in normal quiet times. Within that same hour, the fall in the Dow had exceeded Friday's record 108 point plunge. What this meant was that anything could happen. Among the millions of observers that day there were many – even if they represented a small minority – who were fully prepared for a repeat of 1929. Still, no one was quite prepared for what did happen. The best form of defence was humour. The story goes, according to Mihir Rose in *The Crash*, that when one senior trader in London learned at 4 p.m. that the big index was down 302 points, he croaked feebly: 'That's a record.' 'Sir, this is a golden album,' retorted a younger colleague.

As if programmed, the big brass did all the wrong things. Margaret Thatcher happened to be in Dallas that day, visiting her son. Her contribution was: 'The underlying Western economies are strong, and growth prospects are good. That is what matters.' Ronald Reagan came up with: 'All the economic indicators are solid.' At once thoughts turned to President Herbert Hoover's equally unfortunate reassurances in 1929. Worst of all were the efforts of David Ruder, head of the Stock Exchange

206

Commission, the market's regulatory board. In response to journalists in Washington he said: 'There is some point, and I don't know what that point is, that I would be interested in talking to the [Exchange] about a temporary, very temporary, halt in trading.' That, as Richard Lambert put it in the *Financial Times*, was like shouting 'Fire!' in a crowded theatre. It was certainly good for a further 100 point fall in the share index.

The chairman of the Federal Reserve Board, Alan Greenspan, also flew in to Dallas that never-to-be-forgotten day. His first question, on being greeted by a Fed official, was how the market closed. His reaction was a double-take worthy of Oliver Hardy. Initial relief was followed by incredulity when he heard the answer: 'Down five-oh-eight.' Even though 5.08 would have struck him as improbably lucky, 508 was clearly inconceivable. That was a fall of 22.6 per cent! It was a loss of some 700 billion dollars – or 3000 dollars for every single citizen of the United States. From St Louis it was reported that the chairman of one of the city's leading investment firms, Elliot Stein of Stifel Financial Corporation, had taken the unprecedented step of leading his employees in prayer.

And Worse Was to Come . . .

What still remained to be seen was the reaction of the other stock markets to Wall Street's catastrophe. The world-famous international fund manager George Soros, head of the 2.6 billion dollar Quantum Fund, had been appallingly wrong-footed by the New York Crash. His widely shared view had been that it would originate in Tokyo.

Tokyo had of late been whirled up in an astonishing mania. Its rather dull, partially privatized telephone company NTT, for example, was valued at more than the recent national income of West Germany, even though its profits were relatively tiny and only growing very slowly. The total value of shares quoted in Tokyo was higher than those quoted on Wall Street. This mania was paralleled by an even more mindless boom in property. According to official figures, the total value of Japanese real estate, mostly in Tokyo, was over 10 trillion dollars. This was two and a half times the figure for the whole of the USA. So you could say there was unusual interest in the news from the Orient that morning.

Tokyo's stock market is fixed by all sorts of rules and customs designed to protect it from panic. But still it fell about a sixth, or 15%. Hong Kong threw in the towel and closed its Exchange. When it reopened the following week, it was down 46% from its 16 October level.

The *Sydney Morning Herald*'s headline screamed: 'Sell, sell, sell – the panic hits!' Australians sold, and shares lost a quarter of their value that day. The chairman of FAI Insurances, one Larry Adler, who has made something of a name in Britain, defined the fall as a 'crash'. 'A correction is when you lose money; a crash is when I lose money.'

In Britain, Chancellor of the Exchequer Nigel Lawson described Monday's events as 'an absurd over-reaction' and urged investors to keep calm. They did: the fall in the big index was no worse than Monday's, just another 250 points. In two days shares had fallen 22%, and nearly £100 billion had gone to money heaven – about £7000 per British household.

In New York, before the markets opened, the Fed announced that it was 'ready to serve as a source of liquidity to support the economic and financial system'. That was a considerable relief, for a shortage of ready cash was the real nightmare. Then the market learned what chaos really meant. Of all the big banks in America, J. P. Morgan is the bluest of the blue. On Monday it closed, its shares down one-third, at 27¾ dollars. On Tuesday it opened at 47 dollars, and then plunged back below 30 again.

The chairman of one of St Louis' leading investment firms took the unprecedented step of leading his employees in prayer

---

At its low point, below 1620, the Dow was 900 points – or more than one-third – below its level of the week before. At noon, it was trading just above 1700, 120 points below the previous close. But the Chicago futures market was pointing to a level of 1400. In Chicago, officials thought the New York Stock Exchange was on the point of being closed, and they decided to act. At 12.15 the Chicago Mercantile Exchange stopped trading. In New York there was an uncanny hush. 'We just didn't know what was going to happen,' said one trader. Later Felix Rohatyn of merchant bankers Lazards – the architect of the rescue of New York City's finances ages earlier – was to say this: 'Tuesday was the most dangerous day we had in fifty years . . . I think we came within an hour of a disintegration of the stock market.' But at 1.20 the market turned.

Once the panic was over, gentle jibes were once more in order. The wit Mort Sahl told a story about an armoured car that was robbed of 2 million dollars' worth of securities – with a street value of 29,000 dollars. So, of course, began the search for rationales, scapegoats – whatever you like to call them. Some people blamed computers. Others blamed index futures and other devices that had been invented to make life on Wall Street more fun and more rewarding. The jargon included toys such as 'portfolio insurance', 'program trading' and 'index funds'. But really these were just components in the mechanism through which chaos was brought about, rather than the cause of anything. They may have contributed to volatility, but the causes were already in place in the market before the Crash.

Not least of these causes was the pervasively short-term nature of the punters' time horizons. Never mind if it's going to fall twenty points – so long as it'll rise five before it falls, buy it. Same thing on the way down, of course. The genial columnist of the financial weekly *Barron's*, Alan

208

Abelson, struck the right note. Writing at the end of that nuclear week, he cited various possible precipitators of the Crash. His selection included 'the Japanese' in an argument it was 'tough to counter . . . since everyone knows the Japanese are to blame for everything. . . .' he continued: 'Our own suspicion is that it's the fault of short-sellers who, as is their nefarious wont, will stop at nothing, including disguising themselves as computers and indulging in wanton program selling.' The joke for insiders was that short sellers had been the scapegoats of the 1929 Crash.

Taking Stock

In a sense, that was the end of the Crash of '87. The Dow never went below 1700 again that year. On the Tuesday it closed above 2000, and it spent much of the following months around that number. On average the stock markets of the world bottomed in late November – typically a third to two-fifths of their 1987 peak levels. Vernon Smith's experiments in Arizona suggested that the punters would be drawn back in again for another mini-replay of the big bubble.

That was what happened in 1929, and already in Tokyo this time around – though the property bubble in Tokyo seemed to have been pricked. Property prices by the spring of 1988 were reported to be about 25% below their September levels. At that time Akio Mikuni, president of the Mikuni Jimusho credit rating agency, thought that a '70 to 90%' fall would get things into line. It was generally agreed that the market would never be the same after the Crash – certainly not for the tens of thousands of traders who lost lucrative jobs in the sackings that followed.

Meanwhile, we waited in vain to see investors jumping out of Wall Street windows. One Miami investor, Arthur Cane, was more inclined to blame his stockbrokers than himself. The precise nature of his grudge against Merrill Lynch was never revealed. According to a bystander, Cane 'came into the building with a briefcase, indicating that he had a cheque with him, walked into the office with the two brokers, opened the briefcase, took out a gun and shot the two of them and himself'.

In London, a twenty-three-year-old trainee accountant named Anil had begun trading in the speculative options market in February 1987, when he was introduced to County NatWest Securities by the Holborn branch of the National Westminster Bank. Although the stated policy of this branch is mainly to cater for professionals, Mr Gupta's application to deal was accepted. Later he told the *Daily Telegraph*:

I had no idea that I could lose so much. They always gave me credit. Within a few months I was allowed credit of £100,000 and I did quite well making £20,000 to £30,000 on options.

The credit built up because I found that, when County NatWest owed me money, they never paid on the due date. So, once I was in debt, I did not pay either, and I found they carried the balance forward.

My margin account went £100,000 into the red and I was asked if I could pay. When I said I could not, I was encouraged to buy shares with more credit to back my existing liabilities. My debit and credit balance increased to £750,000 but they did not seem to be worried.

A trade initiated in September, several weeks before the Crash, was responsible for a loss of a cool million for Mr Gupta! In effect, it was a bet that the *Financial Times* Stock Exchange Index would be above the level of 2250 at the end of October. The youthful Mr Gupta truly believed that markets operate within well-defined limits, which was all that his limited experience had taught him. Like so many others, he was not aware that markets can do anything they like, any time they like. There are no clearly defined limits. Mr Gupta explained the reason for his confidence: 'I stood to make about £36,000 and even on 15 October it looked as if I was going to be all right. The *Financial Times* Stock Exchange Index was standing at 2300. As far as I knew the maximum movement on the 100 Index in one day up until Monday, 19 October 1987 had been fifty points.'

On Friday, 16 October there was no index calculation on the Stock Exchange due to the power failure caused by the hurricane. When dealings began on the Monday following, share prices in London collapsed. In one day the *FT* Index fell by 249.6 points, five times what Mr Gupta had learned to expect. But his problems didn't end there. The following day, Tuesday the 20th, the *FT* Index plunged by a further 250.7 points. In two days it had lost over 20% of its value.

Now, you may well think that allowing a £6400-a-year trainee accountant a credit line of £750,000 borders on the absurd. But what about the fifteen-year-old schoolboy who was given a credit line of £100,000, and who lost £20,000 in the process? A pupil at a school in Derbyshire, he would carry out his speculative activities when he returned home for

---

You may well think that allowing a £6400-a-year trainee accountant a credit line of £750,000 borders on the absurd

---

lunch. He placed his orders to deal by telephone to stockbrokers in Wolverhampton and Scotland, who had allowed him to open accounts but because they never saw him had no idea he was so young. The comment of one senior partner in the Wolverhampton firm, which lost money as a result of the boy's speculative dealings, was: 'He has been very naughty. . . . Perhaps we are now seeing one of the problems of wider share ownership. . . .'

A crazed investor who shot two stockbrokers and then shot himself; a fifteen-year-old boy whose only experience came from his school economics classes; and a trainee accountant – these were the big speculators in the stock market boom that ended in July 1987. Can we honestly say that our leaders and the investment community have become more sophisticated than the Dutch, whom we have been pleased to deride for their somewhat bizarre behaviour in gambling all on the price of a tulip? Surely we are bound to admit that our society in the 1980s is no less susceptible to crashes than any other society has been since primitive man first put up a wild beast's pelt or stone axe on the outcome of some simple wager.

Nigel Lawson went so far as to say that the Crash of '87 was the 'non-event of the year'

Is the Crash of '87 now ripe to become a mere memory, to be preserved in the annals of history as yet another example of man's folly? Or is there more to come? Since the collapse which they said could never happen happened, many people have been comparing the Crash of '87 with that of '29. We tend to forget that the worst of the Crash of '29 occurred after the initial massacre. That's why the Crash of '29 is primarily linked with those fateful days in September and October when shares on Wall Street were tumbling with a ferocity comparable to what we saw during October 1987. Between November 1929 and April 1930 shares on the Stock Exchange enjoyed a revival and recovered about half the ground lost during the initial crash. But from late April 1930 onwards the decline began again. This time it was far more devastating in the end than the first familiar phase of the Crash in autumn '29. By the time it was all over in 1932, the Dow Jones Industrial Averages – the blue chip indicator of the US stock market – had lost 98.8% of its value. But that was merely the beginning. America now had the Great Depression to contend with.

Since the Crash of '87 apparently reached its nadir in November 1987, there has been a conscious and concentrated effort on the part of the authorities – and of vested interests within the financial community – to convince the man and woman in the street that it was nothing more than a temporary aberration. Indeed, Nigel Lawson went so far as to say that it was the 'non-event of the year'.

But there remain several ominous parallels between the two crashes. There was a substantial massive expansion of credit prior to both. One of the most worrying features of the Crash of '87 is that ample warnings had been issued to the effect that credit was running wild. Yet those warnings were not heeded. As late as May 1988 credit creation in the UK was still running rampant in an orgy of lending and borrowing.

Felix Rohatyn of Lazard Freres provided a most useful perspective on the aftermath of the Crash of '87 in the December 1987 edition of *International Currency Review*:

The securities markets may recover temporarily and the crisis may appear to be behind us. But the fundamental problems have not changed – on the contrary. All over the world, tens of billions of dollars have been spent by central banks to stabilise the markets, confidence has been eroded, and a huge amount of paper wealth has been eliminated. We have had a very severe warning. We cannot afford another one!

Of one thing you can be absolutely certain. No one alive can tell you, with any degree of accuracy or reliability, that we will not experience a re-enactment of the 1930s during the years ahead. A crash is a primal shriek for the hard of hearing!

12

Crashes ... Why They Happen ... What We Learn

The reason crashes happen is because we learn nothing, which is why they will continue in the future just as they have in the past

The Nature of Speculation

Why do crashes continue to occur? What sets in train these colossal tumours of boom and bust? Why do we never profit from the experience of the past? Before attempting to answer any of the questions, it would be wise to examine the nature of markets themselves. The very nature of speculation is one of those brain-breaking paradoxes we keep tripping over as we muddle through the minefields of uncertainty.

The notion of enrichment through speculative endeavour is built on a necessary foundation of error. The only way you're going to come out with a vast profit will be at someone else's expense – his error. You will achieve profits in your dealings mainly by living from the errors of the other players. You become a predator, in fact, a carnivore, a beast of prey. Others must die, so that you may live and thrive. Like nature's own great engine, which works partly by means of an eternally repeated cycle in which the big keep eating the small and the smart keep eating the dumb, markets require an endless supply of losers to keep on functioning.

The motive for playing the game to start with is the single most interesting aspect of the game. On the surface, it may appear to be the desire to get rich. But it's more than that. The seductive nature of speculation lies in its promise not only to make you rich, but to do it quickly and with a minimum amount of effort and energy. Men have been willing to risk everything in pursuit of this alluring objective.

There is, of course, another way of getting rich – the hard way, through care, determination and effort. It is the way parents usually teach their children; it is the way taught by convention; the way that society encourages; it is the straight and narrow ... the long path urged by the Judaeo-Christian ethic and touted in most schools.

213

But who am I trying to kid? That idea is about as exciting as a stiff dose of castor oil. And it's boring. It's paralysingly boring to the general run of mankind because the long, hard path to wealth and riches may not always be achievable. The idea is only really interesting in the egregious cases – those that stand out from the flock, in the original meaning of the word. By definition, those who stand out or excel in this way are few, and their achievement is beyond the ordinary run of mortals.

The 'easy way' is far more seductive and within easy reach . . . even a fifteen-year-old schoolboy or a trainee accountant can play. We stand at the hub of a wheel surrounded by spokes to quick, easy riches. It is the sweepstake, the football pools, the national lottery. It is the killing in the stock market, the rapidly built property empire, the swiftly amassed shipping fortune. And make no mistake, getting the jackpot on the football pools is not much different from the fortunes that have recently been carved out of what is perceived to be the bedrock of our society, bricks and mortar!

An individual's approach to life itself will often determine whether or not he or she is likely ever to become a victim of speculative mania. There are those who attempt to control their destiny and those who allow destiny to control them. The man who attempts to control his destiny will usually attempt to quantify the risks involved in any particular venture. He will rarely enter into a venture where the risks cannot be quantified. If he's in business, before launching a product he will carry out a market survey or a trial run. Before establishing a price for his product he will compare the prices charged by his competitors. Before embarking on an expansion programme and, say, building a factory or launching a promotion, he will get more or less precise costing. He'll have a budget prepared.

There are those who attempt to control their destiny
and those who allow destiny to control them

By contrast, the individual who lives his life by the seat of his pants will court risk on the somewhat vague assumption that the bigger the risks he takes the greater will be his rewards, without really knowing what his risks or his rewards are. All he knows is that somewhere over the horizon, and at the end of the rainbow, there is a pot of gold that will transform his life, with which he may not be particularly enamoured.

There are many aspects of living over which none of us is able to exercise any influence. These can be the forces of nature, the forces of society and trivial items such as interest rates and prices. Here, the risks cannot be measured. Nor can the rewards. The man who attempts to control his destiny will try to keep his exposure to these factors to a minimum. The will o' the wisp will hardly be concerned and will adopt a 'Be what may' approach.

The man who holds the reins of his life tightly will control his enterprise. He will have measurable goals which he can alter and modify to suit changing conditions. He will control his rewards and his risks – more or less. He is in control of his destiny. The will o' the wisp, whether he is a property tyro, amateur stock market player or football pools winner, will float at the whim of winds that are knowable. He is the breeder of crashes. There is a bit of him in all of us – at some times more than at others.

Given the slightest opportunity, we will attribute
any perceived success to our own efforts

The easier road, the road of the will o' the wisp, is the broad road that leads to destruction. But what a way to go! 'Eagles with our own wings in the topmost dome of heaven.' The operative word in that phrase is 'our'. Given the slightest opportunity, we will attribute any perceived success to our own efforts. Such is the nature of our self-delusion.

If a man makes a killing at the races, he has achieved a measure of success. He certainly hasn't failed. He has been lucky. But on hearing the news his good friend might say: 'Congratulations!' rather than 'Christ, what luck!' The winner will almost certainly feel that in some way he is personally responsible for his good fortune. If he studies racing form, he may even think the credit is all his. The same thing will often happen with a lottery or sweepstake winner. After all, they chose the number, they had the hunch and they backed it. They did it. And it certainly happens to the player of markets over and over again. Only more so! I can tell you that from first-hand experience.

During the years I spent as a stockbroker, there were winners which I would recommend to my clients and there were losers. If I gave a client a loser, I never heard the end of it! 'You made me buy those shares,' Moishe Goldfarb once said to me. 'You knew I didn't want them. You'd take the blood out of my dying mother's body to earn a commission, wouldn't you, Beckman? I'm going to take the gas pipe.' Honestly, that was the conversation. I'll never forget it. A few weeks after that I gave Moishe a winner and he trebled his money in six weeks. I certainly heard the end of that one fast enough . . . as soon as he got the cheque in his grubby paws. In two seconds flat he was telling his colleagues about the painstaking research he had embarked upon before deciding to buy the shares. And there was also his deft timing, which he demonstrated with a chart he had just torn out of somebody else's chart book.

You think fishermen tell tall tales about the one that got away? You should hear some of the tales told by stock market losers who try to convince themselves they're winners. Should they get one winner, after a string of ten losers, the exhilaration and imaginary riches grow to the sky.

It's something that has to be experienced to be believed. The speculator is an eagle sailing with his own wings in the topmost dome of heaven . . . a god even. This rich tapestry of continuous mass self-deception is the stuff that manias are made of.

Have you heard the one about the two stockbrokers, Grabbitt and Runn, who meet in a lunatic asylum?

Grabbit: 'I'm better than mortal men! I can see the future!'
Runn: 'Where did you get this great gift?'
Grabbitt: 'The Lord gave it to me!'
Runn: 'Like hell I did!'

That story has been floating around financial circles for a long time along with others of a less friendly tenor. The claims made by the practitioners of the black art of speculation in terms of their special prophetic gifts frequently confuse the more hard-headed denizens of the financial world. What is even more amusing is that many of these prophets actually believe in their own advertising. It should be obvious to anyone who thinks about it for a while that, like almost everything else involving human emotions, markets cannot possibly be predicted with the accuracy claimed by those who have the savings of others in their charge. Markets are like wild hurricanes, subject to random events that no one can predict. It is sadly true that those responsible for advising others on their savings are also primarily responsible for perpetuating the many fantasies that fuel the manias which lead to panic.

---

*Markets are like wild hurricanes, subject to random
events that no one can predict*

Back in the 1960s an American nightclub dancer called Nicholas Darvis wrote a book called *How I Made Two Million Dollars in the Stock Market*. The book told of how the dancer – while pirouetting on the dance floors of the world's most fashionable nightspots – amassed a fortune between engagements by using a simple system. He described it as the 'box system'. Copies of frantic cables between Darvis and his stockbrokers were reproduced, showing the companies he was dealing in, the price paid for the shares and the price at which they were sold. There were also heated conversations between Darvis and various film stars of his acquaintance, wanting to know more about his great gift as a stock market speculator. The book combined the razzamatazz of showbiz, the glamour of Hollywood, the nightlife of the international jet set and a formula for quick, easy riches. Woweeee! What a formula for a best-seller! Indeed it was a best-seller, appearing week after week and month after month at number one in the book charts. Millions of copies were sold all over the world to the financially washed, the financially unwashed and the financially unwashable.

The book fired the hopes and imagination of millions of people in the United States and elsewhere. In their eyes, with a judgment totally undeflected by thought and reason, Nicholas Darvis was the new Messiah of the financial world, willing to spread the commandments which would bring great riches to all who followed. Darvis had found the touchstone –

Nicholas Darvis was the new Messiah of the financial world

---

the Midas touch – which was within reach of anyone able to count and perform feats of simple arithmetic. The subliminal promise of the book was that anybody could make a fortune in the stock market. After all, if a nightclub dancer could do it by spending a few minutes a day on the telephone between jaunts of terpsichore, even a migratory fruit-picker should be able to do it by sending hand signals from a tree.

So, in the 1960s, yet another myth was added to help fertilize the seeds of mania that were already sown. Of course, there were a few who could still remember the Crash of '29. But they were mere grains of sand on a beach of billions, ready and willing to be mesmerized by the allure of easy riches, as their ancestors had been so many times before.

Not too long after Darvis's book was published, a public inquiry was instigated by Louis Lefkowitz, then US Attorney General. The purpose of the inquiry was to ascertain the validity of the claims made by Darvis, given the influence the book was exerting over what could be a dangerously gullible public. The investigation strongly indicated that the overall claim of the book could be totally fictitious. There seemed to be considerable falsification by omission. While Darvis proudly wrote of the profitable trades he had made, the investigation revealed a number of loss-making trades made by Darvis which never appeared in the book. If the loss-making trades made by Darvis – which never appeared in the book – were deducted from the profit-making trades – which *did* appear in the book – it was difficult to see how Darvis had made 2 million dollars in the stock market . . . if he had made anything at all! Furthermore, the 'box system' which he claimed to have discovered bore a strong resemblance to a system advocated by the king of all speculators, Jesse Livermore, in his one and only book, *The Livermore Key*. One of the reasons that Livermore took his own life was the fact that the methods outlined in his book were no longer feasible in the United States following the introduction of the Securities and Exchange Commission and the imposition of various restrictions on share dealings. By the time *How I Made Two Million Dollars in the Stock Market* was published, people had forgotten all about Jesse Livermore. Livermore had become the anti-hero of a bygone era – along with the Crash of '29.

After studying the findings of the Darvis investigation the Attorney General launched a criminal action against him, alleging that certain statements he had made were fraudulent. Darvis's legal advisers countered with an action against the Attorney General and the United States for defamation of character. Lefkowitz decided the public interest would not be served by embarking on a long, tedious and complicated trial that was likely to give Darvis even more attention than he had already received. He therefore decided to drop the criminal action on condition that Darvis withdrew his action, giving an undertaking never to transact any type of securities dealings in the United States, or to become in any

---

The lawyers wanted to know if I could help them find Darvis. They had a bankruptcy petition against him

---

way involved in the US securities industry. Darvis agreed. He then left the United States to become an exile in Europe.

Whether or not Darvis actually made 2 million dollars in the stock market has yet to be proved. It is a matter of public record, however, that he made several million dollars from the sale of his book. But by the time I met him in 1976 in the Dorchester Hotel in London, there was every indication that most of the royalties had been whittled away. There had certainly been no profitable share dealing using the 'box system'. At the time, Darvis had very little to say about the stock market. By this time he was trying to make a personal comeback with a new book he was writing. It was called *How to Be Your Own Doctor*.

We met on several occasions after that. The man fascinated me. I really wanted to know what made him tick! I've known several successful stock market operators over the years, all of whom shared certain characteristics. Darvis was a showman and a promoter of the highest order. But the qualities which comprise the successful stock market operator were nowhere to be found in my assessment of his character.

A few months after our initial meeting Nicholas Darvis checked out of the Dorchester Hotel without leaving a forwarding address. It was to be several years before I heard the name again. The last occasion his name came up was the result of a telephone call I had from a firm of lawyers. It seems I have acquired a reputation as a central information bureau for every stock market operator coming in and out of London. The lawyers wanted to know if I could help them find Darvis. They had a bankruptcy petition against him. It was long overdue for service!

Credit – Without Which Crashes Would Not Be Possible

Credit is the genesis of all crashes. By borrowing money you can make limited resources perform feats which are limited only by the amount you can borrow. Credit is the lifeblood of any boom. Easy credit is the harbinger of manias. In mid-1988 I saw an ad in a newspaper which exemplifies the crazy era of easy credit in which we live. 'Hurry! Hurry! Hurry!' the ad said. 'Now you can borrow all you need to get completely out of debt!'

You can also borrow money in the United Arab Emirates. It is no different in that respect from anywhere else. The difference rests in the security you would have to give for the loan, and the interest you would have to pay. The law of Islam will not allow a lender to charge interest on a loan. A borrower cannot be required to provide security for a loan in the form of a mortgage on property or any other item that could lead to penury. In some respects, Islam is considered an inhumane religion, with its calculated punishments for wrongdoing – a finger for this, a hand for that, a left arm for one thing, a right arm for another . . . and off with his head for the more heinous crimes. But in other respects, particularly in the case of 'usury' – as it tends to be translated in Arabic – Islam is notably humane. In fact, to Moslems the very origin of the word 'mortgage' is repugnant, with its connotation of enslavement unto death. The revulsion felt for the Western 'mortgage' system really hits home when you reflect on the suffering of the farmers during the Great Depression. Those were members of society responsible for producing the very first basic necessity of human life – food. Yet burgeoning farm loans – the produce of a system that had been tossing out loans like confetti – meant mass dispossession in the agricultural community. Farmers lost their land, their homes and their livelihood.

In practice the line drawn between the men who decide to shape their own destiny and those of the will o' the wisp persuasion is not well defined. There are also many transgressions. On occasions, the planner

---

'Now you can borrow all you need to get completely out of debt!'

---

may be seduced into becoming a will o' the wisp – less often the other way round. For the sight of easy riches in abundance is often a bitter test of the planner's resolution. The case of property is a classic one. There is no area of financial endeavour that has produced more zillionaires than property. Immediately following World War II, there was a genuine need to be filled. This the entrepreneurially minded property developer was quick to exploit. Bomb-scarred London was in dire need of renovation and new accommodation. The property developers of the 1940s and 1950s had the

219

vision, drive and fortitude to take on the calculated risk of development. They were mostly Jewish, members of the hardest-working race.

With hindsight, the strategy looks as simple as selling lemonade from a box stand on a street corner. The property developers could borrow at 5–6% in those days. At the same time, it was possible to prelet new developments at a return of between 8 and 20% of development costs. Although such margins don't make you a billionaire overnight, the return was satisfactory, and quite sufficient to compensate for the risk involved. Soaring property values provided the extra layer of icing on the cake.

If property development was so profitable back in the 1940s and 1950s, why wasn't there a stampede of investors scrambling to get on board? There was in the 1960s and 1970s, when property development and property speculation were becoming a mania. The answer is quite simple – adding a further component to the nucleii of manias. Property investment and property speculation were perceived as involving a calculated risk during the 1940s and 1950s. For quite some time property values had been considered to be subject to fluctuation. They could rise as well as fall. The war years saw property values falling, as had the period of the Great Depression. Those in pursuit of easy money are not interested in involving themselves in a calculated risk. The easy-money crowd are always looking for the certainty, the sure thing! Once the stock market, the property market, the gold market – or whatever other market you can think of – acquires the reputation of being a sure thing (reinforced by the associated 'proof'), further substantial rises in the price level are an absolute certainty. That's when the mania develops – the precursor to a crash.

High-Rise Can't Go On for Ever

Property prices soared throughout the 1960s and early 1970s. There was a Florida land boom-type bonanza. The boys who joined the property game in the early 1970s were nothing like the developers of the 1940s and 1950s. They were playing the property game with a totally different set of rules. Rental incomes were no more than 3–5% of the value of the underlying property. Borrowing costs had escalated to 12% and more. Obviously, in the absence of a rise in property values – or a fall in money values – the developer stood to lose 7% on capital employed. This was a far riskier equation than that confronting the property developers of the 1940s and 1950s. But there was one major difference which altered the equation decisively in favour of the property speculators of the 1960s and 1970s. That was the general perception of future property values. Good old bricks and mortar were considered an absolute certain investment in the 1960s and especially the 1970s. Bankers of all stripes were anxious to lend to property developers against the security of virtually any form of property. All you had to do was appear before a banker with two pieces of timber and a bag of nails. You were an instant property developer. You now had limitless access to easy credit terms against the security of something which had not yet been built – or, in many cases, even conceived. Lending to the property developer was considered as sound as lending to the lesser developed countries – which were also willing to pay interest rates that were slightly above the going rate for the 1960s.

The property game in the 1960s and 1970s was played on the basic, mindless assumption that property values would continue to rise indefinitely, and at a sufficient rate to absorb interest charges and development costs. Moreover, the property speculator would be left with a spectacular profit to boot. That happened for a time – then it stopped. The result of all of the players attempting to jump off the merry-go-round at the same moment was a collapse in the British banking system and a widespread fear in the City that it was 'the end of the capitalist system as we now know it'. All of this was attributable to the enormous debt burden the property developers had allowed themselves to incur, while they were gambling on what was generally considered to be a 'cert'.

The great fortunes made during the run-up to the Crash convinced the high-rollers that the higher they rolled, the better. Given their unshakeable faith in the divine right of property prices to rise and rise forever, it followed that no level of borrowing could ever be too high. Those whom the gods would destroy, as I quoted in the chapter on Nelson Bunker Hunt and the silver bubble, they first make mad. Well – if not mad, at least imbecile. Consider the blind unreason directed towards property in the late 1980s. Are current attitudes to the residential property market in Britain any different from the mad assumptions that led to the collapse of the factory, office and shop property market in the early 1970s?

I am now renting an apartment in Monte Carlo which costs 2½% per annum of the capital value of that apartment. I am earning 10% on the capital I have invested, without considering potential capital appreciation. If I were to buy the apartment instead of renting it, I would suffer an immediate loss of income of 7½%. In other words, property values will

---

Were I to buy the apartment instead of renting it, I would suffer an immediate loss of income of 7½%

---

have to rise by at least 7½% per annum for me to break even. In order to profit from buying this apartment, property values will have to continue rising by more than 7½% per annum.

Were I to obtain a mortgage to buy the apartment, it would cost 10%. The cost of 'renting' money is four times the cost of renting the property. The apartment is a place for me to live in and enjoy. I do not consider it a gambling token. Quadrupling my expenditure in order to achieve ownership will certainly not make the apartment any more enjoyable. I'll let the owner assume the risk of fluctuating values, while I enjoy the view of the sea and the mountains. To my mind, buying the apartment seems absurd.

I have a similar situation in London. I live in a three-storey penthouse that I rent for 4% of its capital value. If I want to borrow many hundreds of thousands of pounds, my bank will duly oblige at the knock-down-for-quick-deal rate of 9½%. With only a small down payment I can be the proud owner of a long-term lease at more than double what it costs me to rent. I would also have the added benefit of incurring the various maintenance and insurance costs which are not applicable to my current tenancy. I would have to be a lunatic to buy it!

If house prices in Japan fell 70–90% it would bring them into line with what people can actually afford

---

As yet, there is no shortage of lunatics. Since the publication of my book *The Downwave* – in which I described the possibility of a collapse in residential property values spanning ten to fifteen years – property prices have fallen sharply in Ireland; they have been decimated in Aberdeen, where at one time one out of every ten properties was on sale; in Wales property prices have also fallen; and in Corby residential property was actually unsaleable for a time.

In Tokyo, according to the Yasuda Trust, property prices peaked in September 1987. Akio Mikuni of the Mikuni Jimsho credit rating agency maintains the move has still done little to bring house prices into line with financial and economic reality: 'If prices fell 70–90% that would make a difference. It would bring housing prices into line with what people can actually afford. It would bring debt service costs on property investment down to a level where they would be covered by rental income.'

Throughout America, property prices have been tumbling and mortgage loans have been turning sour. The plight of the US savings and loans associations, which have been falling like ninepins, provides ample evidence of the state of the US property market. The speciality of the savings and loan associations is advancing loans secured by property.

Yet in spite of the overwhelming weight of evidence to indicate that the property boom is well past its prime, my forecast on property has been described as 'hopelessly wrong'. The reason? Property prices are still expected to rise strongly in the south of England, and have been doing so since my book was published. But that – remember – is still only five years ago! The behaviour of so many people is just like trying to convince the world that the Crash of '29 never happened. And why? Just because half a dozen shares didn't collapse! But the astonishing part of it all is that people are still being convinced, and bankers are still falling all over themselves to advance mortgages on residential property. This is the type of lunacy that prevails during the early stages of a crash. It will continue to

222

prevail until the crash becomes so ostentatiously obvious that opinions of this type have lost all credibility. But by then it will be too late for anyone to do anything about it.

In Britain and elsewhere, a house can be rented for about 3–6% of its capital value. Borrowing costs in Britain range from 9% to 12% depending on the borrower and the nature of the property. Those who have been defaulting on their mortgages have been doubling in number every year for the past four years. Yet consumer credit – most of which has been directed towards housing – has been reaching all-time record levels month after month.

Many have taken their life savings to make a down payment on the house they are buying. In several cases this amounts to no more than 5–10% of the credit-inflated purchase price. I had a young unskilled clerical worker in my office who bought an apartment but had no life savings to put down as a deposit. Nor did she have enough for the legal costs of buying or even the first premium for the endowment policy with which the mortgage was linked. But she did manage to find a friendly local lender willing to give her a personal loan at an interest rate of 25% per annum, secured by a third mortgage on the apartment. (She had already taken out a second mortgage for the deposit!)

This borrowing and lending orgy is no different from that which allowed a £6400-a-year trainee accountant £750,000 worth of credit. Or that which enabled a fifteen-year-old boy to obtain a credit line of £150,000.

Now what is going to happen to all those home owners if property prices start to fall . . . and fall . . . and fall, as they did in Florida in 1926 – as they're doing now in many parts of Britain, and in various parts of the world? What will happen to the savings of those who have sunk all their money into property? If property values fall by, say, 10%, what will happen to the life savings of those who were able to put together no more than that 10%? What will happen to the many people who have made commitments that they could afford to repay only if property prices continued to rise? But . . . does anybody care? Rampant apathy is another characteristic of the terminal stage in the greed cycle.

---

*Rampant apathy is another characteristic of the
terminal stage in the greed cycle*

Most of you should fully understand the mechanism of a crash by now. The basic message of each single crash is exactly the same. There has been one inexorable common denominator of every crash I've told you about. There has never been a crash without an explosion of credit – credit which was extended on the assumption that prices would continue to rise indefinitely. It was tulips at one time, railroads, canals, the stock market and holiday homes in Florida at others. But the unalterable fact of the matter is that prices have never – nor will they ever – rise to the levels expected of them. You have to be blind not to see it. When men are especially blind, credit creation leads to unserviceable debt, which in turn leads inextricably to a crash. The circumstances which led to the crashes of the past have seldom been as obvious as they are today. As we approach the twenty-first century, the debt levels of the West have no parallel in recorded history.

The Tao of Greed and Fear

The reasons crashes happen should no longer be a mystery. We have many object lessons to guide us that the ancients never had. In matters of money, greed and fear are the all-conquering emotions. They are the two faces of Janus. Between them they wait in constant service upon every arena of speculation. It has often been said that fear is a more powerful emotion than greed in financial markets. But that type of judgment obscures the Janus-like nature of the creature. Alongside the greed of the holder of any speculative vehicle in a rising market is the fear of 'missing out' in the heart of the bystander who has yet to join the crowd. Running in tandem with the fear of a shareholder in a falling market is the greed of the bargain hunter, anxious to see prices fall further so he can buy more cheaply.

The majority of the time, markets will fluctuate within relatively narrow bands, and the overall trend will not be unduly pronounced. The normal exposure to fear and greed under such conditions will have little effect on the psyche of the layers other than the odd bout of insomnia. But once a trend begins to accelerate the adrenalin starts flowing, while the emotions become more dominant, exerting an increasingly powerful influence over the mind's ability to think rationally. We know instinctively that, if we are to make a profit by buying and selling things, we must try to buy as low as we can. What could be more simple? As Will Rogers once said: 'All you have to do to make a lot of money in the stock market is buy stocks before they go up and then sell them before they go down.'

But given the inimitable perversity of the marketplace, rapidly rising price levels induce people to behave in precisely the opposite way to the one which good judgment would advise. As the momentum of a price rise accelerates more and more, people want to buy. This can easily be seen from the volume of Stock Exchange transactions during the course of any upward movement in the market. It can be seen that the higher the price level, the greater the volume of business. If the rise proceeds, still more buy. It goes on that way until right at the peak price level. Just before the crash there are more people buying than ever before. This was readily apparent in the London Stock Exchange in the summer of 1987 before the

224

Crash. Never in British history had so many people been buying shares, nor had share ownership been so widely spread.

Surely the old-timers, like my dear departed friend J.M., know better? The old-timers have seen it all before. They know that price rises can go into a spiral that goes well beyond reason. There are no quantifiable limits to unreason. But the old-timers also have to live in the financial world, so they join in too. They can't afford not to – not if they are to be seen as pragmatists. They have a dread of 'missing out' and being dubbed a dodo by their contemporaries. I know what that's about. I can live with it. Many old-timers can't.

The Need for Fresh Blood

Left to themselves, the more astute professional investors seldom send a market spiralling into the realms of utter nonsense. Markets require newcomers – the financially unwashed and financially unwashable. A market needs that fresh virgin blood money which doesn't know that shares, property, gold bars or works of art are supposed to maintain certain historical relationships, and that when those relationships are violated all sorts of horrible things can happen.

As a speculative boom reaches maturity, the vehicle of speculation, whether it be gold, silver, antiques, stamps, tulips, shares or property, will pass from the experienced veterans into the hands of the newcomers. The seasoned veterans will have bought low at prices which seemed to offer good value at the time. They will then sell at unexpectedly high prices to the 'pros'. The 'pros' will pass on the vehicles to newcomers at undreamed of prices, inviting more sales from the seasoned veterans . . . and so on and on it goes!

The Point of No Return

Language will compound the process of the speculative spiral as the point of no return is approached. As the vehicle approaches its maximum angle of ascent, people will say, 'Prices are rising' or 'Prices can never come down.' Professor Irving Fischer made a statement to that effect just before the Crash of '29, if you recall. As expectations rise to equal and exceed the prevailing price trend, so too does the temperature of the market.

A speculative boom will begin with a general mood of doubt, rising like a phoenix from the ashes of a previous crash. Doubt soon becomes hopeful optimism. This is then followed by a tussle between greed and fear. Don't worry about the outcome – greed always wins! The next phase of the emotional gamut is unshakeable confidence. Finally euphoria, which represents the ultimate triumph of wishful thinking over all elements of experience, logic and reason.

That brings me to the most excruciating paradox of all speculative manias. The moment the outlook for tulips or canary seed has 'never looked brighter', when the reasons for holding on – and maybe buying more – have never seemed more convincing; when the prospect for gain looks the most promising to the greatest number of people – that moment is the point of no return. It is precisely at the peak of the market – the moment when prices can go no higher – that, in truth, the outlook is hopeless. The reasons for holding whatever the masses may be holding have evaporated, and the prospect of loss is absolutely certain. That is the split second when a boom turns into a crash.

This paradox is a manifestation of the great mystery of nature, which has been felt and touched on by the more visionary Western philosophers and savants from the ancient Greek Heraclitus to the atomic physicist Nils Bohr. It has been central to the oldest philosophies like greed and fear. The pinnacle of hope is in fact the incipient stage of despair, while the slough of despondency is, in reality, the birthplace of hope. If we continue to travel north we must ultimately start travelling south.

In the wider world, darkness is but the absence of light: where one ends, the other begins. Male is the complement of female in the same way. What seems to be fixed is in constant flux (Heraclitus). All that is fixed is constant flux (Beckman). Mass is energy, space is time (Nils Bohr et al.). This view of nature is enshrined in the Yin and Yang of the ancient Taoist philosophy. The Yin and Yang are exquisitely depicted in the ancient symbol called T'ai-chi T'u, the symbol of the supreme ultimate – a creation of indescribable elegance. A crash can be a creation of indescribable elegance – provided you get out in time!

Price No Object

Now for another paradox common to all crashes. When the crowd is swept up in a speculative craze, the object of that craze can command any price you care to name. No matter what the price, the object of that craze will be unanimously considered to be undervalued. The higher the price goes, the greater will be the perceived undervaluation. Is that paradoxical enough for you? Price is simply no object when a mania is in full swing. The logic is simple. It goes as follows:

Sam the Bat-winged Hamburger Snatcher: 'Hey, Charlie! Did you know the price of glinks is going up?'
Charlie: 'No! You got any glinks?'
Sam: 'Yeah, I got one. I'll let you have mine for 1000 dollars.'
Charlie: 'What did you pay for the glink?'
Sam: 'I paid 900. But, I told you . . . the price is going up!'
Charlie: '1000 dollars is a silly price to pay for a glink.'

Sam: 'Take it or leave it. It'll be 1100 tomorrow.'
Charlie: 'Are you sure?'
Sam: 'Sure as the beef in a hamburger!'
Charlie: 'Well, I'll give you 975. The glink has a spot on it.'
Sam: 'Done!'
Charlie: 'Hey! You across the street. You wanna buy a glink for 1000 dollars? It's going up to 1100 tomorrow!'

In the old days, that type of bargaining would be representative of what was called the Greater Fool Theory. That is to say, however foolish a purchase might seem during boom times, there would always be an even greater fool willing to pay more. 'That's the price, £500,000,' says the property agent. 'There's no risk. You'll get £650,000 in a year's time. They don't make out-houses in Chelsea like this any more, do they?'

The price-no-object syndrome goes over very well in Japan. There's a story they often tell about a Westerner visiting Tokyo who was puzzled by a somewhat prodigious rock sitting in the corner of his host's office. On asking what the object was, he was told it was a rock. 'Very beautiful, isn't it?' said his host. 'And valuable also. It's probably worth £6000.' Though it was a handsome rock from certain angles, the Westerner thought, he was still puzzled. He was naive.

That was some time ago and rare articles like Japanese rocks, a share in NTT or a square foot of Tokyo land have become appreciably dearer. Maybe the rock would fetch £60,000 today. Who knows? There is a fiendish logic in the process. If you sincerely want a glink, or an out-house in Chelsea, or a Japanese rock – whatever the price – if it will cost more tomorrow you'd better buy today . . . if you have the money.

The moot point, of course, is whether the price *will* actually be higher tomorrow – or in a year, or in five years' time . . . or ever. The price of tulips, if adjusted for inflation over the past three hundred years – or even if unadjusted – is nowhere near the price levels of the seventeenth century. Back then, you could cash in your tulip and buy a house. You can't do that any more. There was one point in 1853 when US shares didn't cost more the next day. Nor the next year! Nor the next twenty-seven years! The same held true for shares for many years after the Crash of '29.

At one point in 1837, land in Chicago cost less the next day, the next year and for the following sixty years. It would seem that for sixty years many people felt owning a home in Chicago would not bring the blessing that home ownership is supposed to provide.

The history of crashes shows that price levels of all things move like a pendulum, not like a rocket into space. But, then again, could it be that this time, *really* this time, we have moved into a new era and all that history is bunk? You may wish to believe that. Many do. Many have. That's why we continue to have crashes.

As we've seen, every speculative craze that I've written about was accompanied by the irresolute conviction that what was happening then was much different from anything that had ever happened before; that things really, really *were* different this time round. Think of them – one by one – up to and including the Crash of '87.

If there is one singular characteristic of this craze that stands apart from any other, it is the extent of global price inflation since World War II along with the attendant expansion of money in circulation. Rather than being different from those areas which were crash-prone, this era could be used as a prototype for a crash-prone environment. There is certainly nothing whatever categorically different about the way the world works in the twentieth century, compared with the nineteenth, eighteenth or seventeenth. That's because people still think the same way.

The Object Lesson

We can see why crashes happen, but what do we learn from them? At this point it would be possible to end this dissertation with one word – nothing! Doesn't the hiatus of October 1987 prove this to be so? Why do we learn nothing? Why are we unable to profit from the lessons of history? I've already touched on one reason: people always think it will be different this time round. In the 1870s it was the railroads that were supposed to have permanently changed the face of America and its commerce. In the 1830s it was believed the canals had permanently changed the face of America and its commerce. But from the vantage point of the 1870s it was all different. The railroads really did change America. A barge could barely move faster than a horse, and besides you couldn't build a railroad just anywhere. The railroads brought many changes. A change that was never delivered by the railroads was a crash-averse economy.

If there was any era that was capable of bringing about major changes it was the 1920s. It had the motor car, aircraft and much, much more. The radio, which was in millions of homes by then, carried the message of a new era loud and clear, as only mass communication can do. President Hoover gave many talks on the radio, telling of a brave new America which was conquering fields that were incomprehensible to the grandparents of his listeners. Hadn't Lindbergh shown that people could fly across the Atlantic Ocean? The mind boggled – but the stock market buckled and crashed just the same.

Here, in the 1980s, we have silicon chips and global communications; along with the power of governments to deliver us from evil, recessions, depressions, inflations and crashes before they run out of control. At least that was the perception before Meltdown Monday. I'm not sure what it is now. It's probably the same!

228

We know how people tend to nullify the lessons of the past. But many people seem simply to forget. How can they forget the lessons of catastrophe? The philosopher Descartes once remarked that education is often, and perhaps necessarily, painful. That which hurts, teaches. We all like to dismiss anything that may be painful. With time, we can forget just about anything we choose.

The Depression of the 1930s touched a generation that could not forget. It left our grandfathers with a legacy which meant they could scarcely bear the thought of going into debt, or borrowing for anything. The exhortation of Polonius was a patch of Shakespeare that was treated with the utmost reverence – as they understood it:

> Neither a borrower nor a lender be,
> For loan oft loses both itself and friend,
> And borrowing dulls the edge of husbandry.

Modern ears have extreme difficulty in grasping that subtle concept.

J. K. Galbraith made an interesting observation on the manner in which 'the suicidal tendencies of the economic system' have occurred with some persistence every fifty to sixty years for as long as reliable records have been in existence. He concluded that the interval was 'perhaps roughly related to the time it takes for men to forget what happened before'. In *The Great Crash* Galbraith saw his task as 'to keep the memory green'.

The 'oblivion interval' seems to be about two generations. So the grandparents, who could not forget, constantly reminded their children, who could not remember. True learning must come from experience. The children never passed the message on to the grandchildren. Or if they tried, they found it fell on deaf ears – the strictures appearing irrelevant or incomprehensible to young people living in utterly changed times. Meanwhile, the older generation – who were old enough to have experienced the lessons of the past – were too old to remain at the centre of financial matters and exert any influence.

Above all, the eagles whirled up in a cyclone of hugely profitable speculation have better things to do than worry about a catastrophe that never comes – despite many cries of 'Wolf!' And even if over the long run – by which time we are all dead – it does end in tears, the poet's cries of 'Seize the day' and 'Gather ye rosebuds while ye may' seem far more pragmatic. It also seems much more fun!

A Short Course in Crash Aversion

What do you think? Is a crash just around the corner? If so – will it happen next week? Will it happen next month? Will it happen next year? Or is it happening already?

Will your home soon be worth merely a small fraction of what you paid for it? Will you lose your job and be unable to meet your mortgage repayments? Are the life savings you plunged into your home about to go to money heaven? Have they gone to money heaven already?

Is the stock market about to plunge and plunge and plunge, leaving you with worthless bits of paper in bankrupt companies? Or maybe it's the value of the currency that will plunge and plunge and plunge, leaving you with a pension that won't be enough to purchase a box of matches . . . a bank account that won't contain enough to buy a crust of bread? Will

---

*'They don't make out-houses in Chelsea like this
any more, do they?'*

---

your neighbourhood be ravaged by rioting in the streets, while you're subjected to the attacks of sexual perverts in your public parks and theft and vandalism in your home – while some of your neighbours drink champagne?

Will you be able to cash your pay cheque next month? Or will the bank upon which the cheque has been drawn have closed its doors? Are you about to find your only means of survival will be the crumpled notes in the biscuit tin and the small change in the piggy bank?

As you are fully aware by now, every one of these things has happened to people before. Are they about to happen again? Are they about to happen to you?

If you would now like me to provide you with some definitive answers to those questions, I'm about to disappoint you. Making predictions that are set in stone is neither the intention nor the function of this book. I do not deal in absolutes. I deal in possibilities and probabilities, supported by fact and evidence. So far you have been presented with fact and evidence – along with a hint of possibilities, probabilities and eventualities.

If I were to predict a menacing crash within the next year or so, some of you – on the basis of that prediction – would take action. A large number of you may already have taken action, studying the various elements of crashes to fortify your existing convictions. But a far, far greater number would ignore such a prediction in favour of being brainwashed by the many vested interests which insist that the Crash of '87 was a non-event; by the vested interests so desperate to convince us all that life would be a perennial bowl of cherries if people would only continue to accept their guidance. To the victims of mass mind control – the major victims of all crashes – the prospect of a crash is probably inconceivable. I am fully aware there is absolutely nothing I can do or say to convince these people otherwise. They really don't want to know. They are the financially unwashable!

There are, on the other hand, the perennial pessimists – nature's worriers – who have been preparing for a crash of one kind or another for most of their lives. They've erected their bomb shelters. They have a stock of tinned food and long-shelf-life biscuits on hand. Safely stashed away, out of sight beneath the bed, is the sub-machine gun. There's a bag of gold coins buried in that secret spot in the garden. Any prediction I might make would simply fortify their personal apprehensions. But it would bring them no closer to achieving the kind of flexibility that is required to cope with a rapidly changing world.

What I am about to give you is a short course in crash aversion, based on the facts and evidence that have already been presented. On the bottom line, the fact is that crashes have repeatedly attacked an enormous number of vehicles and caused hardship to billions of people over the past few hundred years. The evidence strongly indicates that this phenomenon is continuing unabated. In other words, it is not simply the product of times past. . . .

An analysis of the various crashes that have punctuated history reveals that certain common factors have been responsible for bringing speculative manias to their inexorable conclusion – a crash. Whether or not what we've seen over the past few years falls into the category of a speculative mania is up to you to decide. Whether or not the common factors that have produced crashes in the past are present today – and are of sufficient magnitude to suggest a crash is imminent – is also a decision that you alone must make. If you do make these decisions yourself, rather than abdicate responsibility for them by relying on the advice of a third party, it is far more likely that you will take the appropriate course of action – and stick to it – than would otherwise be the case.

Should you now have decided there is insufficient evidence for you to consider embarking on a course of crash aversion, there is really nothing for you to do. You will find the newspapers, magazines, investment advisers and stockbrokers eager to advise you how to prepare for prosperity in perpetuity – as the violins of a thousand political Neros all over the world accompany the tunes they play.

---

*To the victims of mass mind control the prospect of
a crash is probably inconceivable*

On the other hand, should you now have decided there is cause for concern and some defensive action is called for on your part in order to protect you and your loved ones from the elements of a serious financial dislocation, read on! I think I can offer you some useful guidelines and a well-grounded formula to protect you against the collapses which have plagued investors throughout history.

My career as a financial adviser has spanned three decades. During that time I've witnessed the collapse of Australian mining shares; the London bear market from 1969 to 1971; the fall of the London banks; the plunge in the price of gold; and the Crash of '87. Although I was active on every one of those occasions before the crash, none of those who took my advice were devastated by any of those disasters, nor were the clients whose funds I managed. This is not the experience of the average investor. He finds himself virtually bereft of his savings by the time the crash is over. He is so psychologically demoralized that he vows never to become involved in any market again. In this way he is depriving himself even of the opportunity of recouping what has been lost.

I'm certainly not about to tell you to get a supply of tinned sardines, a pocketful of gold coins and a sub-machine gun, the advice of one well-known stock market operator in the early 1970s. If that's what you're looking for, try reading C. V. Meyers, who forecasts a fascist state rising like a phoenix from the ashes of the inevitable economic chaos that lies ahead. Or you might try Howard Ruff, who predicts riots, mass looting and rampant crime. Ruff's advice is to find an isolated country retreat and stock it with canned food, powdered milk and well-oiled shotguns to fight off the marauders who will be on your doorstep in search of food as the nation starves. Franz Pick too might be to your liking. He thinks that all currencies will be worth less than the paper they're printed on. Everything you own should be in gold bullion. You must wear a bullet-proof vest at all times, he says, barricade yourself in your home and expect mass rioting in the streets twenty-four hours a day for the foreseeable future. Get the picture? Well, you won't find any of that here.

I certainly don't believe we're going to see the destruction of our social system – not by a long shot. Over-riding the peaks and troughs of social and economic activity is a steadily rising trend in man's achievements, which I believe will continue. Man's greatest achievements will probably be reached during the twenty-first century, with the development of artificial intelligence, life extension, genetic engineering and a wide range of innovations which will raise the standard of living the world over. But before we arrive at this exalted position there are risks to be considered. Chronic paranoia is not the answer – making personal, physical and psychological adjustments to changing circumstances is.

Building a Shock-proof Crap Detector

The great philosopher Schopenhauer said, '90% of everything you see and hear is crap.' When it comes to dealing in financial markets, quite a bit of leverage is involved. The crap count probably works out at more than 90%.

It was Ernest Hemingway who said, 'What everybody needs is an iron-clad shock-proof crap detector.' Again, when dealing with financial markets this will be your most useful item of defence equipment in terms of crash aversion. Bullshine is OK. Everybody indulges in it. Husbands do it to their wives. Wives do it to their husbands. Children do it to their parents. Salesmen do it to their prospective customers. Politicians do it to gain electoral capital. It's at the point where bullshine starts to affect your future and your savings that it begins to be dangerous. You're going to need a pretty solid crap detector to protect you against that.

A financial analyst by the name of John Magee used to operate from a room in a house in Pittsburgh, Pennsylvania that had only a door and no windows. The only source of power was an electric cable coming through the ceiling with a light bulb attached. Magee refused to have a telephone or a radio and would not read the newspapers. His only source of information was the price lists of the securities traded on the New York Stock Exchange. He felt that normal information sources were likely to be biased, out of date and inaccurate, and served to distort the judgment needed to make a totally objective assessment of the price action of the market and its securities. The windowless room was John Magee's personal shock-proof crap detector.

If your shock-proof crap detector is to be effective, and give you the advance warning you need when it looks like a crash could be looming, you're going to have to be certain that, when installed, it points in the direction from which the crap may be coming. Most people are aware which that is! But they don't want to admit it. Admission means an information vacuum. But an information vacuum is better than misinformation or disinformation. You all know the major source of pusillanimous piffle, don't you? It's the politically degenerate, sales promotion-oriented mass media.

In Aldous Huxley's *Brave New World* people are provided with what are called 'somas'. The 'soma', like a tranquillizer, would make people more susceptible to suggestion while permitting their attention to be continually diverted from reality. Through listening to constant transmission over the mass media, the minds of the masses would be kept occupied and deflected from any form of serious thought. The idea was to keep them laughing, crying, excited, hating, loving, wanting, buying – anything at all!

C. V. Meyers forecasts a fascist state rising like a phoenix from the ashes of the inevitable economic chaos ahead

---

In contemporary society, that means engaging people's attention not only with guilt- and envy-oriented news stories but also with sitcoms and soaps, whose intellectual level never exceeds that of an eight-year-old suffering from arrested development. It means an unending flow of minutiae and trivia dressed up as booms and calamities: human degradation and personal denigration of those we love to hate. It embraces

233

sensationalism, sex, violence, football, darts, snooker, basketball, boxing – anything to induce vicarious involvement, distracting the minds of the people from the notion that our leaders and other prominent vested interests may be less omnipotent or well-meaning than they would like us to believe they are.

It should be recognized that governments, multinational manufacturing corporations, banking institutions and the media share a common interest – that common area is to maintain confidence, whether justifiable or not. Obviously it is in the interest of all of them to tell people what they perceive to be popular at the time, in this way securing the favour of the greatest number. If people like what they see on a particular TV programme, they'll continue to watch that programme. If too many people don't like what they see, they'll switch to another channel. Then the producers and presenters will be booted out and the programme will cease to exist. What is it that people want more than anything to be told? They want to be told that their past, present and future are just hunky-dory, reachy-peachy – a never-ending orgasmic journey. So the media duly oblige – throwing in the odd harmless item here and there to suggest 'balanced reporting'. That's supposed to enhance their credibility.

A popular political line in every age – under every type of regime, in every corner of the globe – is to promise people they're going to have more of everything, regardless of the state of the economy: everything from a chicken in every pot to every man a house owner. A car in every garage!

---

*An information vacuum is better than misinfor-
mation or disinformation*

Three TV sets and a radio in every home! A deposit in every bank! Shares in all the country's enterprises! The right to become a baby factory at the expense of the state – should you so choose! Not only do politicians promise people more of everything, but in recent years they have tried to convince people that more of everything – regardless of circumstance – is their inalienable right. It is the government's duty and obligation to make certain the people receive more of everything. In this respect, the government makes testimony and the media swear to it.

What the media avoid like poison – and the authorities will censure at every opportunity – is the presence of any one of the many rational, intelligent economic experts who might possibly have a clear understanding of the fiscal distortions that are bankrupting the nations. Prophets have never been popular. This is primarily because most individuals do not take kindly to forecasts that suggest they are about to pay for their apathy and licentious endeavours. This makes it easy for the media to convince people of the things of which people want to be convinced, while dismissing any notion that could be contrary to the popular view.

A few years back, when Mexico was having its debt problems, there was a concentrated effort among media sources to convince the man in the street that all was under control. At the time a man named Christopher Storey consented to do a live interview on national television. Christopher Storey is the genius whose work appears in *International Currency Review*. He is considered to be one of the world's leading authorities on international debt crises. Well, Storey told it the way it was: the debt crisis was certainly not under control. In his view an 'accident' could bring the entire global financial system to its knees at any time. This was not what the TV channel was expecting to hear. There was a furore. Christopher Storey has never appeared on that channel again, nor on any other British radio station or TV channel for that matter.

---

*What the media avoid like poison is any one of the
rational, intelligent economic experts*

It should come as no surprise that I have considerable experience in this area. Several years ago I appeared on a radio programme, having been asked to comment on the effect that a recent rise in mortgage rates might have on house prices. It was at a time when there was not one individual anywhere who imagined that house prices could ever fall. When I mentioned that the rise in rates could trigger a fall in house prices which might last quite some time, the presenter looked as though he was going to have heart failure. My broadcast was followed by a sharp letter from the Secretary General of the Building Societies Association, who decried everything I had said. The radio station in question is one of Britain's commercial stations. They rely on advertising to survive. A not inconsiderable portion of their revenue comes from building societies and property agents. The people at the station quickly assembled a panel of 'experts' for a broadcast to be transmitted on the evening after mine. The 'experts' included a lawyer, who earned a considerable amount of his income from acting in house purchases; a property agent, who earned his entire income from selling houses; and a building society spokesman, whose income was directly derived from granting mortgages to house buyers. They were there ostensibly for the purpose of giving their 'objective' assessment of my views. They spent a full half-hour in unanimously refuting what I had said in about thirty seconds. Surprise, surprise! Their 'objective' opinion was that there could not be a fall in house prices. I was never given the opportunity to counter this 'objective' view, nor have I ever been invited on that radio station again.

Just after the publication of my book *Into the Upwave* in April 1987 I was invited to appear on a television programme. I was told the programme would be filmed at my apartment during an entire morning, and they would give me between ten and fifteen minutes to talk about the book. Whenever I'm asked to appear on radio or television I invariably study the format to determine the thrust of the programme. What I discovered – after looking at a few tapes of the programme in question – was that no individual ever had more than a two- to three-minute spot. They may have intended to devote ten to fifteen minutes of the programme to discussing my book. But I would be allowed to speak for no more than two to three of those ten to fifteen minutes.

Any semi-skilled TV director can make an Einstein look like a baboon

---

I'm thoroughly familiar with most of the tricks the media get up to. Any semi-skilled director can take three minutes out of a two-hour tape and make an Einstein look like a baboon. Or, if so required, make the average elephant appear like a ballet dancer. The entire affair was beginning to look somewhat suspicious. So I contacted the public relations firm that my publisher was using to promote the book, asking them to find out who else was going to be on the programme. They said they were informed that it would be the financial editor of the London Broadcasting Corporation – LBC – and a few investors. I had my own programme with LBC for twelve years, so the presence of LBC's financial editor was comforting. But then again, in the course of a taped interview he might say I was the Nostradamus of the financial world, but it could sound like he'd said I was a babbling idiot once the editors had finished with the tape. I didn't like the sound of those 'few investors' who were going to appear. I remembered my previous radio experience. It sounded too much like a set-up to discredit my views on the British economy before anyone had a chance to read them.

That being so, I told the PR firm to contact the presenter of the programme and say that I would be absolutely delighted to come on the show – but only if I appeared live. 'Make sure,' I said to the PR man, 'that you stress the words "absolutely delighted".'

So far as the TV presenters were concerned, that was the end of the game. In no way were they prepared to give me the opportunity of countering the impression that they were preparing to create. They refused to allow me to appear live. But that didn't stop an attempt at character assassination. When the programme finally appeared, there was a brief mention of the book and a dissertation from Ivan Fallon of the *Sunday Times*, who appeared to be reviewing me rather than my book. Once again that was the product of a doctored tape. But best of all was the punch line. The presenter told viewers that I had refused to come on the show if Ivan Fallon was going to appear – as though I considered Fallon to be some sort of ogre and arch enemy, which wasn't and isn't the case. You can be certain the media will thwart any attempt at changing or modifying the images it intends to put across to the public. The truth must never be allowed to deflect them from their predetermined objective, particularly when that predetermined objective involves the City fathers of the British Establishment. It has been said that 'One man with the truth is an army.' Nothing has ever been said about the ability of such an army to win battles!

Most radio and TV stations have an 'approved list' of commentators on whom they can rely to tout the views of their masters in high places. Those masters can be either the City institutions with direct links to government, or multinational corporations which also want to be certain that the public are exposed only to the view which is in their best interests. Think about it! Whenever you see or hear what is supposed to be an independent view of a particular economic event, or a sudden development in securities markets, ask yourself where that view comes from. It will usually be someone from one of the securities firms who is prattling away. Now, do you mean to tell me that only stockbrokers are privy to economic knowledge? What about the many independent economists who are not on the government's – or any broker's – payroll? What about the professors of economics at the universities? Why is it that you are permitted to hear only the views of stockbrokers? Why not the others? You know the answer, don't you? A stockbroker can always be relied upon to give the view which will help him peddle the shares he wants to sell to the public. That view will always be an optimistic one. You'll hardly ever hear a stockbroker say the market could crash, or that shares are going to go down – regardless of how ominous the background. Get the picture?

Do you mean to tell me that only stockbrokers are
privy to economic knowledge?

In addition to the panel of 'experts' maintained by individual members of the media, the government is ready to provide one or more of their own standing army of 'experts', any of whom will be ready to deny what some heretic – some blasphemous prophet – might have to say that is incompatible with the party line. From time to time, a major economic mind will slip through the defensive network and tell it as it is. When there is a threat that people like Christopher Storey, John Eatwell, Sidney Pollard, William Keegan, Andrew Gamble, Andrew Glyn, John Harrison, Ralf Dahrendorf, Milton Friedman or Friedrich A. Hayek are about to make an impression on the minds of the masses, the media will waste no time in devoting editorial space to the government's standing army of powerful economic puppets, who are given free access to homes all over the nation. They will quickly assure members of the public that the forecasts of these economic 'alarmists' are nonsense. The assurances they give will usually prove quite effective since the economic elite has absolutely no means of countering the propaganda that is delivered.

A few years ago, a body of international economists (numbering no fewer than 411) came to the unanimous conclusion that the British economy was heading for hell in a hand basket. Britain's Chancellor of the Exchequer was quick to appear on the boob tube. 'All economists are charlatans,' was his sweeping reply. He then proceeded to deliver his economic predictions. Commenting on the Crash of '87 a few months

---

A large body of international economists agreed that the British economy was heading for hell in a hand basket

---

after the event, once again Nigel Lawson made headlines by stating: 'The October crash was the non-event of the year.' I'm sure the Chancellor's statement was a big hit with a fellow I know who lost 70% of his savings in that Crash. During the early stages of the Crash, there was a parade of unit trust managers and institutional investors on the boob tube making soothing noises designed to calm people down and deter them from selling their shares. A Stock Exchange study published some time after the Crash revealed that most of the damage was done to the private investor. It seems that the institutional investors bailed out in time – by encouraging people over the boob tube to hold or buy while they were already sellers.

The news and information circulated in most countries – and published domestically for the rest of the world to see – are determined by the editorial policy of a frighteningly tiny handful of individuals. If these vested interests want you to see something in print, you see it. If they don't, you won't. It may be that the manipulators decide that their best interests would not be served by telling you about the true state of affairs – such as the deterioration in the external economy; the state of mortgage delinquency; the burdens of consumer credit; the impending failure of a building society; the shaky state of a bank; the dire straits of a company such as Chrysler or British Leyland; the problems the authorities may be having with transfer payments; the artificiality of invisible exports, etc., etc., ad infinitum, ad nauseam. If that is the case, then either that information will go on 'the spike', relegated to obscurity, or be sold to the underground press, subsequently to be denied should too much attention be drawn to a publication with too small a circulation. Before you are permitted to read or hear an alternative view, it is likely that efforts will have been made to detract from the credibility of the source where that alternative view appears.

So the very first step in becoming crash-averse is to approach what you read in the press, hear on the squawk box and see on the boob tube in the same way that porcupines make love – very, very carefully!

A Crash Spotter's Guide

Without a shock-proof crap detector, you won't see the various signs that indicate a crash is coming, because they'll be obscured by the smokescreen continually being generated by the mass media. The message will be muted by the din of consensus opinion. But once you've got your shock-proof crap detector in place, you'll be able to see the signs more clearly.

Actually, the media itself can be helpful in your crash-spotting endeavours. It should be recognized that all forms of media tend to reflect general interest rather than create it. During the final stages of the boom which precedes any crash, there will be a proliferation of investment magazines and books, along with a plethora of investment advice. Once the crash starts, a desperate effort will be made by the media to convince everyone how inconsequential the fall in the price level actually is. The more serious the decline, the more desperate the effort. When there seems to be more interest focused on investment than usual, and when the attempts to promote investment are more heated than usual, you may be certain that this is a sign that a crash is in the making.

Has speculation become rampant? Has public participation in the stock market, the property market or any other market been especially active? Are an inordinate number of people employed in the securities industry, the property market or other forms of speculative endeavour? It is a sure sign of an emerging crash when there is exceptional activity in these areas.

If speculation has become rampant; if there is an inordinate number of new people being employed in the securities industry; if investment advisory services have been sprouting like weeds – these are the tell-tale signs. When public participation in the stock market becomes over-active, this is the kiss of death. When every taxi driver begins chatting about the stock market or property values the moment you get into his cab, you know trouble is brewing. When the lift attendant in your building, the girl

Is women's swimwear now the equivalent of two sequins and an elastoplast?

at the supermarket checkout and the cootchy dancer at the local businessmen's club all begin talking about shares or property, any boom that's been in place cannot possibly have much further to go. When otherwise astute businessmen begin looking for tips and start gambling thousands of pounds on speculative endeavours; when people who have studied for years start leaving established careers to become investment advisers, stockbrokers, share dealers or unit trust salesmen – that's another very powerful clue.

What is the general attitude of the public? Are they optimistic? What are consumer spending patterns? What is the trend in fashion? Has there been a heavy demand for luxury goods? Do you see more sumptuous limousines than usual on the streets? These are all signs which indicate that a crash could be on the way. Rising personal borrowing and heavy consumer debt, accompanied by a feeling that the economy is booming and will continue to do so, are also indications that the economy is about to exhaust itself and crash. Heavy consumer purchases, bigger, faster and more luxurious cars, demand for exotic imported consumer goods, foreign travel, holiday homes – these are all characteristics of the death knell that is heard before the collapse. Have fashions become more

---

Working and saving are a totally outmoded ethic during the latter stages of the boom that precedes a crash

---

flamboyant? Have hemlines become crotch lines? Have necklines become nipple lines? Is women's swimwear now the equivalent of two sequins and an elastoplast? Have the lapels on a man's suit become wider? Does the shoulder line on his suit make him look like Arnold Schwarzenegger? These consumer trends too are indicative of the final stages of the boom, the precursor to the crash.

Markets invariably reflect people's attitudes. Markets that foster excesses are, in general, the product of a permissive attitude. There is a significant connection between fashion, standards of morality, sexual permissiveness, alcohol abuse, drug addiction, gambling and excessive speculation. Once it is perceived that we live in times of plenty without end, mass psychology will take an Epicurean turn and members of the public will steadily and en masse shed the cultural and moral standards that keep society stable. Interest will be centred on secular humanism, materialism and free sexuality.

As life becomes easier during the boom years, people become increasingly self-indulgent. The individual will just not be prepared to tolerate the slightest inconvenience or mild deprivation. Obesity becomes a major problem. If life – for a short while – fails to live up to expectations, people will turn to drugs and alcohol in their quest for instant gratification. When the conventional faiths no longer satisfy, people turn in large numbers to alternative religions. We have seen the growing success of Scientology, the Moonies, the Hare Krishnas, transcendental meditation and a host of lay preachers all over the United States – some of whom exploit the masses as they search desperately for instant gratification.

What holds true for alternative religions holds just as true for alternative medicine. And for similar reasons. Individuals are dissatisfied with the prolonged treatments associated with normal medical practice. In their search for instant gratification, people turn to herbalists, iridologists, acupuncturists, faith healers, naturopaths and eventually to any one of a wide range of crackpots offering instant results. Instant gratification is the order of the day in a crash-prone society.

Working and saving are a totally outmoded ethic during the latter stages of the boom that precedes the crash. Speculation is the norm. Areas that were previously considered speculative are treated as sound investments. People have very little interest in long-term savings or anything else that fails to provide instant gratification. A work ethic ceases to exist. Even though unemployment may be high immediately before the crash, a seller's market develops for those whose skills are still in demand. Workers will hop from job to job with impunity, regardless of the qualitative or quantitative value of their labours. The only thing that counts is the size of the salary and benefits offered – nothing else. An employee may enter a firm at a higher salary level than in his previous firm, and immediately begin to scan the Appointments pages of the press and contact employment agencies to see if he cannot obtain an even higher salary elsewhere for the same work. Productivity diminishes. Jobs are treated lightly by employees. Employers are forced continually to offer larger incentives to attract workers. Job security is regarded as a minimal consideration when accepting an offer of employment. The length of paid holidays, number of fringe benefits and frequency of automatic non-production-rated salary reviews are given a much higher priority by the average employee. A close scrutiny of the trends in the labour market will provide a clue to the likely proximity of a crash, as will the extent of permissiveness in society generally.

This study of crashes began in the seventeenth century. But the phenomenon that I've been outlining was prevalent long before then. Waves of sensual excesses marked the peaks in the Roman, Greek, Spanish and French civilizations, as Oswald Spengler noted in his historical study *The Decline of the West*. During the early 1920s alcoholism was seen as

---

Is it a coincidence that the last decade in Britain has seen the proliferation of pornographic films?

---

so great a threat to American society that Prohibition was introduced. Yet this didn't stop the circumvention of the law any more than the heavy penalties for drug trafficking do today. The Roaring Twenties was the time of nationwide bootlegging in America, while speakeasies – where alcohol could be consumed illegally – flourished mightily. New sexual freedom was marked by a wave of women's lib in the wake of the success of the suffragettes, by scantier swimsuits and rising hemlines.

Is it simply a coincidence that the last decade in Britain has witnessed the proliferation of pornographic films, of masturbation booths in London's seedy Soho girly-mag shops, and the sudden flowering of sex shops offering what they describe as 'marital aids'? We have seen publicly advertised prostitution featuring a variety of sexual perversions; child pornography; and 'sauna' services offering 'assisted showers' and 'special' treatments for customers walking in off the street. Are we living in a crash-prone society? Think of all that has happened in recent years and decide for yourself!

Although Western society may not have reached the depths of degeneracy witnessed in Germany during the 1920s, personal morality is certainly heading in that direction. Clearly, the standards of accepted morality have undergone a dramatic change. Divorce is steadily on the rise. It is almost chic in some circles. Virginity is considered outmoded. It has almost become a taboo among some younger women.

What about business morality? A spin-off in the decline in business morality is an increase in the number entering the legal profession, prepared to cope with an explosive rise in litigation. In the United States the number of lawyers has risen to 617,000. Japan has only 12,000. The state of California today has no fewer than 79,000 lawyers, representing one lawyer for every 310 people. In Japan there is only one for every 9800 heads of population. The number of lawyers may have increased, but the standards of service have decreased. US Chief Justice Warren E. Burger is on record as stating his belief that lawyers generally overcharge their clients – especially for simple transactions – and that law schools and bar associations ignore professional ethics.

Experience has taught that as the boom enters its final stage business ethics and morality follow in the same direction as personal morality, and to such an extent that dishonesty becomes the norm. In his book *How You Can Find Happiness during the Collapse of Western Civilisation* Robert J. Ringer makes this comment: 'I do not say that most people think that they lie, steal, cheat and deceive; they simply do lie, steal, cheat and deceive, regardless of whether or not they are conscious of it. On the contrary, you would be hard-pressed to find someone who really believes that he is guilty of these actions.'

A philosophy of destruction is inseparable from a crash-prone atmosphere

---

As morality drifts downwards to the lower levels consistent with the generally declining values endemic to an easy-money, anything-goes society, people will lie, steal, cheat and deceive – personally and professionally – without once admitting it to themselves. This is because a low standard of morality has become the norm. Dishonest actions are seen as honest – part and parcel of normal commercial practice – during a period

242

when morality is stood on its head. Turn your mind back to the 1950s and 1960s if you can. What were your experiences in business then? How do they compare with your experiences now? Do you yet detect the signs of a crash-prone society?

Polarization is another element in the crash-prone environment – the widening gulf between the 'haves' and the 'have nots'. As the nineteenth-century historian Alexis de Tocqueville noted: 'There exists also in the human heart a depraved taste for equality, which impels the weak to attempt to lower the powerful to their own level, and reduces men to prefer equality in slavery to inequality with freedom.'

Football hooliganism is a familiar example of re-pressed class warfare

---

As a boom reaches its final stages, before the curtain is drawn and the crash occurs, there is a yawning chasm between the fortunes of those who have profited during the boom and the static or declining resources of those who have not. Synonymous with the early stages of a crash – and helping to perpetuate the crash – are class wars. Class wars – or wars between the 'haves' and 'have nots' – have been a fact of life throughout recorded history. As a society becomes more crash-prone, class wars intensify. At its worst, class war manifests itself in bloody revolutions, such as the US Civil War. More notably there was the French Revolution of 1789 – a class war of the purest kind.

The human emotions that culminate in class war are the same emotions that serve to generate the excesses which demand the cleansing effects of a crash. These emotions are covetousness, greed and envy. The 'haves' want more of what they have, while the 'have nots' want what they see the 'haves' as having. Eventually the 'have nots' will come to the conclusion that attainment of the level of materialism that the 'haves' enjoy is unachievable. This is when class war breaks out. The 'have nots' then declare hostilities in an effort to bring the 'haves' down to their miserable level. A philosophy of destruction is inseparable from a crash-prone atmosphere. As an increasing number of individuals begin to feel they will never achieve the success that others enjoy, they will tend to find comfort in merely seeing the possessions of others confiscated and their achievements destroyed. Under such conditions, crime rates soar – particularly crimes against property and wanton vandalism. Minority groups become restless and violence-prone. Football hooliganism is a familiar example of repressed class warfare.

While a crash-prone society reveals itself in many psychologically disturbed symptoms, there are also many physical symptoms which relate to the health of the nation. During the 1930s a health craze developed in the USA, not unlike the recent jogging fad, the running marathons and the

243

Jane Fonda-inspired aerobic exercise mania. The sudden interest in health in the 1930s was a reaction to the upsurge in stress-related diseases during the boom years of the 1920s. Booms are accompanied by many wonderful things. Yet the things that money can buy and the atmosphere that prevails in an acquisitive environment tend to increase the level of stress. In its various forms, stress has been recognized as one of the most insidious and subversive killers known to mankind. The consequences of stress are far-reaching. Not only are they physical and emotional, but also psychological, biological and biochemical.

The most obvious physical and psychological manifestations of stress include heart disease, certain forms of cancer, high blood pressure, a host of gastric malfunctions, poor nutritive distribution, alcoholism, drug abuse, a wide range of psychiatric problems and even psychopathic behaviour. The most significant stress stimuli are frequently related to financial problems. While it may be obvious that the failure to 'make ends meet' creates stress, the desire to acquire more and more wealth is even more stressful and can lead to the most serious consequences. There is stress associated with the amassing of wealth, and the attempt to protect it during a boom. Another form of stress is the product of personal alienation and the deterioration of personal relationships in the harsh, competitive, unforgiving context of a materialistic society which is itself the product of the boom.

In recent years, it is probable that more emphasis has been placed on the elements of stress than at any time in history. Literally thousands of books have been written on the subject. Numerous stress management courses and hundreds of medical procedures have been devised to prevent, detect, modify and manage the manifestations of stress. It is important to recognize that a stress-prone financial environment is a crash-prone financial environment. If you spend a great deal of time thinking about your investments, you may find you suffer such bodily symptoms as ulcers, colitis, headaches, heart palpitations, general tiredness or malaise, difficulty in sleeping, frightening dreams, hormonal changes, impotence and high blood pressure. At the same time you may suffer an inordinate increase in errors, defective judgment and a diminished ability to tolerate small setbacks and failures, along with such heightened psychological symptoms as temper, aggression, depression and frustration. If that is the case, you may be certain of one thing: every time you look in a mirror, a potential victim of this crash-prone environment could be looking back at you.

Much of what I have discussed so far relates to the broad symptoms of a crash-prone environment. These broad symptoms can persist for quite some time before a crash becomes imminent. So they don't necessarily mean that a crash is about to land on your doorstep. These broad symptoms are also difficult to quantify, in the sense of attempting to judge the period of nadir. So let us consider a few of the phenomena which are usually present during the course of a crash or in the run-up to it. Once again, we can turn to the media for assistance. But not in the way people normally turn to their newspaper for advice.

Whether you're gambling in tulips, gold, silver or the stock market, commercial or residential property, you will find during the latter stages of a boom – before a crash – that every time there is a news event of particular significance there will be a sudden, vigorous increase in the intensity of speculative activity. But when there is a news event of a relatively negative nature, that occurrence will often be ignored. Frequently we find that news items which in every other way would be

---

During a boom, bad news does not sell newspapers

---

considered negative are in fact treated as though they were positive. For example, if a company has a bad second quarter and its profits fall, its shares may go up because investors feel the news was 'over-discounted'. In other words, it was not so bad as expected. Let us say a rumour is circulating which might be bad for the price of gold. Although there may not be any response to the rumour in the sense of the gold price falling, the moment the rumour is proved false the price of gold could well rise quite sharply. During a rising trend, investors tend to accentuate the positives, remaining oblivious to negatives. The truth is that news tends to follow the market, rather than vice versa.

There is always a fair spread of both good news and bad every day. During boom times, you will find the good news splashed across the front pages with the bad news tucked neatly away inside or dismissed in a couple of column inches where few will see it. During a boom, bad news does not sell newspapers. But when a market is about to crash, the process is reversed. Markets will tend to become quite oblivious to the more favourable news headlines. They will continue their downward drift even though the background news might be positive. You will also see a pronounced change of emphasis between the amount of good news and bad news featured prominently in the paper.

By now you will have noticed the almost total absence of any economic indicators or indicators of market activity which I have recommended you to include in your crash spotters' guide. There is a sound reason for that. Crashes are not economic or financial phenomena. They are social phenomena. A market becomes crash-prone because the individual tends to go on participating in a boom long after that boom has ceased to be financially or economically viable. Crashes come like a bolt from the blue, once the factors I have mentioned are firmly in place. There really are no reliable indicators to tell you precisely when the crash is going to start. The best you can do is to attempt to determine how far a particular market or financial environment has already become crash-prone.

Having said this, there are a few more pointers of economic significance that could be useful. One is the long wave cycle of economic behaviour, which I have described in considerable detail in my books *The Downwave* and *Into the Upwave*. The long wave cycle of economic activity spans forty-five to sixty years between the peaks that precede the crash. Precision timing is out of the question. We are not dealing with a railway timetable. We can say only that the average duration of this cycle is about fifty-four years. What this theory can tell you – with a reasonable degree

---

Markets become crash-prone because individuals go on participating in a boom long after they are financially or economically viable

---

of reliability – is that a market that has spent sixty years without taking a dive is more likely to be crash-prone than one that has spent only thirty-five or forty years without a crash. After fifty-four years, you should assume that the market is on borrowed time. For what it's worth, the sixtieth anniversary of the Great Crash on Wall Street will be upon us in October 1989!

There are a few further economic indicators that you can watch which will tell you at last when a recession is likely to occur. While a recession may not necessarily lead to a crash, the more crash-prone the economy the greater is the likelihood of a crash. All these factors must be considered in the overall picture. It should also be remembered that before the economic cancer is detected, most economic indicators are going to be looking good and there will be a never-ending chorus of experts saying how well the economy is doing. The signs that the economy will not be doing all that well for much longer are that interest rates start to rise, unemployment starts to rise again, retail sales begin to look less buoyant, consumer credit slackens, property prices start to fall, and, finally, orders for capital goods begin to drop. Yet I must tell you that a crash could well be underway before any of these signs appear. So it would be most unwise to postpone your crash aversion tactics until you see these signs if you feel in your bones that we are in a crash-prone situation.

There is also an occasion which occurs every four years in the United States that can render an already crash-prone environment even more crash-prone. That event is the presidential election year. Major troubles have a way of crystallizing immediately after the January inauguration of a new President following the November election – as history has shown. The second phase of the Great Crash took place during the year after an election year. The closure of the banks also took place during the year after an election year. The stock market crash of 1969–70 in the United

246

States followed an election year. The actual year of the presidential election is generally good for stock market investors. That is because politicians are especially adept at short-term manipulation, and naturally the party in power will do everything it can to provide at least the appearance of prosperity by pumping up the monetary aggregates during the year of a presidential election. Several studies have been made to show the correlation between monetary growth and the election cycle. During the four-year cycle the highest levels of monetary growth have nearly always been recorded during the presidential election year. The lowest levels of monetary growth are generally recorded in the year of the inauguration, as the party in power in the White House attempts to reverse the potential damage that monetary excesses can cause. While election years typically favour investors, post-election years tend – on balance – to be crash-prone years. The next post-election year is 1989, coinciding – as I said earlier – with the sixtieth anniversary of the Great Crash on Wall Street.

It may surprise you to discover that the British stock market was actually the first to crash in 1929. But it's a fact. The US stock market followed. The British stock market was also the first to crash in 1972. The US stock market followed. During the 1980–2 recession, the contraction in the British economy was far greater than that in the US economy. With the passage of each year the multinational trading countries become more and more interdependent, as do monetary systems and political alignments. While the United States economy has given the appearance of being more vulnerable than the European economies during the late 1980s, this has more to do with its global economic visibility than anything else. More information is published on the US economy, and with greater frequency, than on any other economy in the world.

---

*More information is published on the US economy
than on any other economy in the world*

In recent years the British economy has been portrayed as something of a miracle, booming along while growth outstrips both the rest of the European economies and the US economy. This is a false picture. It ignores the fact that, whatever the level of economic buoyancy in Britain, it is the product of a fiat money policy. During 1987 the vulnerability of the British economy was finally revealed. During the October Meltdown, the fall in the British stock market was greater than the fall in the US stock market. The USA is rich in natural resources, its economy is far more stable politically than those of other Western countries, and it has an exceptionally mobile workforce along with a high standard of technology. At the same time, the US economy is inexorably tied to the economies of western Europe; and Europe's economies could rapidly become disaster areas before the next global crash. Britain and Italy are probably the most vulnerable, and it would be wise to watch the economies of both nations very closely. Unfortunately, the information available on both economies is less reliable than one would normally expect.

The Tactics of Crash Aversion

You should by now have a fairly good idea of why crashes happen. You should also have a pretty good working knowledge of the conditions that prevail prior to a crash. Here comes the really big question. What do you do about it?

Probably the first thing is to engage in some careful introspection: examine your fears and motives within the context of our contemporary social and financial environment. People are a strange lot. They will scream the rooftops down when subjected to the slightest personal discomfort. But within a short time of being relieved of their initial misery they will show little or no interest in devising a way of avoiding the same degree of discomfort in the future. The Crash of '87 is a prime example. There was panic everywhere during the days following the Crash. A similar experience was shared by investors during the 1929 Crash. Following the 1929 Crash and the 1987 Crash, shares moved up again – for a time. In 1930, they began crashing again. In May 1988, after being relieved for a few months of the misery associated with the Crash, investors were sitting with the same share portfolios that they had before the October Meltdown, much as their 1930 counterparts did.

Are you a victim of 'psychosclerosis'? That's a term I invented a few years ago to denote hardening of the brain – mental paralysis – an extremely common affliction among people involved in financial markets and not all that uncommon among people in general. Ironically, many people who seem to understand the somewhat perilous and precarious state of the world in which we live remain unwilling to face the possibility of a crash and to take whatever action is needed to become crash-averse. The reason can often be traced to confusion and fear. Sometimes a person's knowledge of the facts, coupled with the lack of any viable solution, can make him so fearful that psychosclerosis sets in. A common self-justification for psychosclerosis is the notion that the timing never seems quite right. If you are among those who are waiting for the timing to be just right before taking crash-averse action, I can give you my absolute personal guarantee that the time will never be just right. Moreover, you are the holder of an absolutely foolproof recipe for becoming a crash victim. Nothing could be more certain. But if all that is holding you back is a viable plan which is not going to expose you to a complete change in lifestyle – and which will not get you out of the frying pan into the fire – if a crash never happens, I think I can offer you a reasonably sane approach to the future.

The first and most important rule of all is, whatever you do, keep it simple. The disaster theorists will often come out with extraordinary strategies that involve buying gold, burying coins in your back garden or trading in Mongolian fruit bat futures. I have no use for any of those strategies when it comes to recommending crash-averse tactics for the average person. He won't be able to make use of them, and probably couldn't handle the risk associated with such tactics even if he could. Furthermore, people would find themselves gambling with their futures to

---

The disaster theorists' strategies involve buying gold or trading in Mongolian fruit bat futures

---

the same extent that they would be were no crash aversion tactics implemented. I'm going to confine my recommendations to the suggestions which I think will be the most useful, and the most helpful, to the greatest number of people: suggestions which do not involve speculation of any kind.

First and foremost, get out of debt if you can. If you can't, place that among your highest priorities. If you do have liquid funds and can get out of debt, use them for that purpose. It is highly unlikely that the return you're going to get on your investments will be equal to the interest you're now paying on outstanding debt. It would be ludicrous to have investments in government bonds that are giving you 7–9% while the interest charges on mortgage debt or credit are anything from 10 to 25%. If you were to sell some shares to repay your credit card debt, this would be the equivalent of getting a risk-free 25% return on your investment. Very few investments have ever offered a return of that nature.

Once you've achieved your first objective – reducing your debt to the absolute minimum – the next step is to bring your liquidity level up to the absolute maximum. If you are reasonably convinced that a crash is on the way, all you have to lose by turning everything you have into cash is some last-gasp profits. Nothing more! If you buy gold, you could lose if the gold price falls. If you buy long-term government bonds, you could lose if interest rates rise. If you simply move into cash, you can't lose unless the currency collapses. The way to protect yourself against a currency collapse is by simply keeping your funds in two currencies – 90% in the home currency and 10% in the currency of a country where interest rates are high.

Of course, if you move into cash you run the risk that the bank or building society may close its doors in the event of a catastrophe. But you can bring the risk on that particular aspect down to rock bottom. When it comes to investing your cash, you must confine your investments to only the biggest and most formidable institutions. You will probably be able to get 1% or more extra interest in one of the smaller institutions. These should be avoided like AIDS. In the event of a financial catastrophe, such as was witnessed in Britain during the early 1970s and is now being witnessed in the US savings and loan areas of banking, you can be certain the government will direct all its resources to those institutions that have attracted the largest numbers of depositors and are harbouring the biggest bulk of ordinary people's savings. The biggest and the best should be your criteria in terms of selecting a bank or building society with whom you want to deposit your cash.

When the crash is beginning to appear mature and recognizable, you are likely to be bombarded with sales literature encouraging the purchase of 'capital protection' plans, or promising you the chance of investing in those areas that will do well while markets are crashing. These plans should be avoided – not even remotely considered. There is always a cost involved that will result in you either increasing your risk profile or getting a return that is less than your bank or building society can offer. The numbers will look convincing. In the field of finance, figures don't lie but liars sure as hell can figure! Aside from building cash you must also build liquidity. Items which are called 'cash equivalents' will not be so liquid as cash in the bank.

When and if a crash hits, most markets will become highly illiquid. Property will be difficult to sell. Shares will also be difficult to sell. The market for investments, such as stamps, rare coins, antiques, strategic metals, precious metals and all of those other alternative investments that were being touted as beneficial to a well-diversified portfolio, will become nearly impossible to deal in. If you find you need cash, and the only way for you to raise it would be through the sale of any of the aforementioned, you may find you have to dump your collection of fine wines or gemstones at a small fraction of the values that existed during the pre-crash days. If

---

*In the field of finance, figures don't lie but liars sure
as hell can figure!*

---

you are harbouring an illusion that by holding on to investments of this type they will eventually recover to pre-crash value levels, you have a very, very long wait. Individuals who were buying gold and gold-related assets in the 1930s had to wait forty years before such assets returned to their 1930s' values. Obviously their funds would have been far better simply sitting in a bank during that forty-year period.

The next step in your crash aversion programme should be to make a careful study of your assets and consider truthfully why you own them. Let's take your home, for example. Is it the home that you want, or are you living in a property which was acquired for its 'investment potential' and is actually surplus to your requirements? If the latter is the case, get rid of it quickly and buy a home which is in keeping with your residential requirements rather than your perceived investment objectives. What about those paintings and objets d'art you may have acquired? Do you hold those items for their aesthetic appeal or for their investment potential? During a crash, they will have no investment potential. They

---

A crash is a vortex, sucking virtually everything down into it

---

represent nothing more than the potential depreciation of your wealth, which could otherwise have been enhanced by simply converting them into cash and holding that cash in a safe haven.

Most people fail to appreciate the value of holding cash during a period of declining values. During a crash, cash is king, for two reasons. The most obvious reason is that, instead of sweating through every miserable moment of a crash, watching your wealth evaporate as values decline, you'll have the stress-free comfort of knowing that the value of your assets has been frozen – at least in nominal terms. Equally important is that, during a crash, the value of your cash will rise in two ways. It will be enhanced by whatever interest is paid, and will further increase in value by the rise in its investment-purchasing power. By maintaining a large cash reserve you will be in a position to snap up the many bargains that are likely to be on offer. They will come from the less prudent individuals, forced to distribute their assets to repay debts secured by those assets when they stood at their inflated levels. It must be recognized that a crash will affect not only the major host vehicles such as the stock market or the property market or whatever else has been the major area of speculative activity. A crash in one market will excite sympathetic calamities in a host of other markets. A large liquid cash position will allow you to pick up property at depressed levels, along with works of art, antiques, wine or whatever else has become the victim of over-inflated price levels. A crash is a vortex. It sucks virtually everything down into it – some things sooner, some things later. But everything goes in the end! To quote the quaint colloquialism of an old stockbroker friend of mine, 'When the cops raid the whorehouse, they take all the whores!'

In my crash aversion therapy I have concentrated until now on the subject of investment. But there are other threats to your wealth and wellbeing – besides being in the wrong investments at the wrong time – that should also be considered. The tail end of a boom is, as I have said, accompanied by a general lowering of standards, morality and business ethics. Cheating and dishonesty become the norm in an 'anything goes' society. This is particularly true among certain members of the legal, medical and accountancy professions who adopt a fee structure on the basis of what the market will bear. In many cases, you could find yourself with an open-ended commitment and with absolutely nothing to show for it. Win or lose, the fees charged by those professionals must be paid. During periods of financial strife there is a proliferation of crimes relating to fraud, most of which fall under the jurisdiction of civil rather than criminal courts. Someone may owe you money; someone may have cheated you out of some money. But you must think very, very carefully before allowing yourself to become involved in litigation. You could find that what you have been cheated out of can swell to several multiples of the original sum when amplified by legal costs. In many cases you would

During the period of easy money associated with a pre-crash condition, legalized thievery has no parallel

be far better to write off the debt and put it down to experience rather than compounding your problems – and your losses – through the courts. As a general rule, if possible avoid using the services of a lawyer and the open-ended commitment that you may take on.

What holds true for the legal profession is equally true of the accountancy profession. Cheating and overcharging have in some cases become the norm with even the biggest firms. As taxation becomes increasingly complex, many people will be tempted to turn to someone other than the accountant they may have been using up until now, because they feel they want more 'expert' advice. The cost of that 'expert advice' could easily exceed the value of that advice by several multiples. Once again you can become involved in an open-ended commitment, since it has become the norm to make an accountancy mountain of a fiscal molehill – accompanied by a correspondingly exaggerated fee structure.

Professional services that you may require which involve payment on a 'win or lose' basis, whether or not you're satisfied with the results, should be avoided wherever and whenever possible. These also include the services of architects, designers, surveyors, builders and a wide range of others where the results are unquantifiable, and whose charges are limited only by the imagination of those who are doing the charging. During the period of easy money associated with a pre-crash condition, legalized thievery has no parallel. Your business affairs must be conducted on extremely well-defined lines at all times. You must make certain that all agreements are made in writing and all undertakings spelt out in the minutest detail. The full extent of your financial commitment must be confirmed well in advance. Protecting yourself against dishonesty and cheating is likely to be a monumental task. Constructive paranoia may not be a bad thing. I was talking to my good friend Harry Schultz – the internationally renowned investment analyst – a while back. The manner in which wealthy people have become the target for cheating and

252

dishonesty by professional bodies came up in conversation. Harry said, 'Just because I'm paranoid, it doesn't mean they're not out to get me!' Robert Ringer's comments about the legal profession are probably the most damning of all: 'If you're holding out hope that the situation is going to improve, forget it. It's getting worse each year. These cock-roaches in three-piece suits breed rapidly, and they're immune to all known insecticides.'

As part of your crash aversion strategy, it would be wise to maintain a relatively low profile and keep yourself to yourself. Conspicuous consumption, which is likely to incite greed and envy in direct proportion to the increasing number of losers during the crash, must be considered a no-go area. This certainly does not mean you should live in a shack and drive a twenty-year-old junk box. It does mean you should place your affairs in perspective. If you have a burning desire to impress others, consider carefully whom you want to impress and why. Careful introspection could show that your efforts might be counter-productive.

In 1987 I introduced the term 'uppie' as the counterpart of the conspicuously consuming 'yuppie'. The uppie is an unpretentious, privately individualistic egoist. It is my assertion that only the uppies will be the crash survivors. Only they will be in a position to act as the front runners to establish the foundation for the prosperity emerging from the ashes of the next crash. The virtue of self-esteem cannot be purchased from a property agent or car salesman.

During a crash, the atmosphere will become desperate. During desperate times, desperate people do desperate things. There is no need whatever for you to make yourself a target for the desperate. Affluence can be enjoyed and savoured away from the prying eyes of those affected by adversity. One spin-off of a crash will be depressed economic conditions and rising crime rates. Part of your crash aversion strategy should include a close inspection of your personal security, insurances, alarm systems

---

Affluence can be enjoyed and savoured away from the prying eyes of those affected by adversity

---

and so on. People who live in big cities are more vulnerable to crime than those who live elsewhere. There is a greater concentration of wealth in big cities, while population density is also greater.

A few years ago I used to live in a building that was known throughout Europe for its wealthy inhabitants. Criminals from Spain, France and Italy would make day trips for the specific purpose of carrying out burglaries in that particular building. Having arrived in London on a morning flight, they would proceed to ransack as many apartments as possible in the time available, taking only cash and jewellery. They would then return home on the evening flight, arriving in their respective countries with the booty even before the unfortunate victims were aware of what had happened. When I lived in that particular building I once made the mistake of parking my Ferrari outside the front door instead of putting it in the lock-up garage. I was anxious to get to a business meeting and felt my car would be safe for the short time it would take me to change my shirt and brush my shoes. When I returned to my car twenty minutes later I was confronted with an empty space. I reported the car as stolen to the police, who asked me when I had noticed the car was missing. I told them it had been about half an hour before. 'Oh,' said the policeman on the other end of the phone. 'It's probably on its way to Calais or one of the other European ports by now.'

Potential tax burdens are unquantifiable and can bankrupt you in certain countries

---

Declining economic conditions in the aftermath of a crash will also mean declining government revenues as individuals' income and corporate profits decline. It will also mean rising government expenditure as welfare and unemployment payments rise. The outcome should be a foregone conclusion – higher taxes, particularly in the higher income brackets but spread amongst all brackets. The worse the situation is, the more punitive is taxation likely to become – and the fewer your chances of tax efficiency, as tax-gathering techniques become more sophisticated in this age of undetectable surveillance and high-speed computers. Potential tax burdens are unquantifiable and can bankrupt you in certain countries. In Britain retroactive, arbitrary taxation is within the boundaries of the law. An individual may think he has met his tax obligations in full, only to find that a massive liability of which he was unaware suddenly appears.

This brings me to my next recommendation as part of a crash aversion strategy. It's one which I mentioned earlier when I recommended you to get out of most investments and into cash. You should have a bolt-hole – not for the purpose of evading tax, but merely as an escape route to protect you from the possible adversity of a crash in your home currency and a government that could get out of hand. Your bolt-hole should be an account with a large bank domiciled outside your country of residence. The funds should be held in a currency which is less likely to be subject to debasement than that of your own country of domicile. The bolt-hole should be in one of the many tax havens. My recommendation, as I said earlier, is that 10% of your liquid assets should be kept in your bolt-hole.

As an afterthought, I also recommend you to give careful consideration to your current occupation. If a devastating crash does occur, millions of individuals will be trapped in urban nightmares because they allow their occupation to be the major determinant of their lives. Whether it's your job or your business, it would be unwise to be too emotionally and financially dependent on your current source of earning a living. This may sound like extremely unpalatable advice, but it's an area worthy of considerable thought. In the first instance, if you're a stockbroker, commodity broker, property agent or commission agent for the sale of luxury items, in the event of a crash you may find there is absolutely no demand for your services. Unless you have substantial savings or an alternative method of earning a living, you could find yourself on a breadline.

Secondly, crashes occur with sudden and unexpected violence. Economic conditions change very rapidly. Governments, which are always changing the rules, will be changing them fast and furiously during a crash as the situation becomes progressively more intense and the party in power is under threat. Under such conditions your business or profession could be destroyed overnight. No trade or profession, no industry or business, is immune to emergency legislation. A crash and depression can lead to a state of national emergency involving the imposition of exchange controls and the nationalization of companies and banks, along with an unimaginable range of aggressive action that governments may impose to the detriment of the wealthier class of citizen. Needless to say, a severe economic calamity will set off a chain reaction that will destroy jobs and businesses in a wide variety of areas.

It would be highly constructive for every individual who fears that the prospect of a crash is more than remote to begin establishing the foundation for a second course of income. I would not recommend that such a venture should be at the expense of an existing fruitful source of endeavour. My recommendation is that people should begin sowing a few seeds, employing minimum capital and maximum effort as a further means of insurance and flexibility.

No trade or profession, no industry or business, is immune to emergency legislation

---

If the history of crashes teaches us anything, it is that most people do what everyone else is doing – according to the psychology of the moment. People play follow the leader from one calamity to the next. The lemming instinct is devastating. Those who keep their own counsel, who act as individuals and refuse to join the dance of the blind, comprise an extremely small minority. My final recommendation is that you make immediate arrangements to join that small minority. Victor Frankl's words are indeed worthy of a permanent mental implant: 'Everything can be taken from a man but one thing: the last of the human freedoms – to choose one's attitude in any given set of circumstances, to choose one's own way.' If all around you are losing their heads while you remain calm, it could be that you don't know what is going on – but it could also mean that you have chosen your own way and acted on it!

Acknowledgments

The task of thanking all those who contributed to a work such as this is a prodigious one. The number of individuals who have helped feed my fascination for the historical background of markets over the years is incalculable. Many of their names appear as authors of the various source materials I have drawn upon to produce this compendium of crashes. I am grateful to all of them. I am even thankful to the Moishe Goldfarbs of the securities industry who have helped contribute to the many rich personal experiences I have had during my career in the industry. Broadly, dogs do not thank their fleas nor primates their ticks, but a crab can thank the securities industry for the ocean of material provided by its friends and relations.

Of course, some special acknowledgments must be attempted. This book would simply never have come to fruition if it were not for Robert Smith of Sidgwick and Jackson who conceived the idea of an anthology of crashes, chose me to write it and then lent his expertise and encouragement to the various stages of its creation. I am indeed grateful to him for his conception and flattered by his choice of author. Once again, I must acknowledge the invaluable assistance of Bob Finigan of the BBC who assisted with the research for the book while discouraging my incessant mutilation of the English language. If it were not for Bob Finigan the book would be far less readable than it is and those elements which are of dubious literary merit, far greater in number.

Conceptually, philosophically and materially, I remain indebted to my friend of some 25 years, John Percival, the editor of *Currency Bulletin*. John Percival also contributed to the research and helped lend a sense of direction to those psychological elements of human behaviour in capital markets which are so difficult to comprehend but which are vital to any study of the subject.

I must also take this opportunity to thank the members of my staff: Betty Stabler who assisted with the typing of the manuscript; Nick Stabler who helped dig through the piles of old newspapers in order to retrieve much needed material; and John Lawlee whose assistance in managing the affairs of my clients was so invaluable during periods when I was otherwise engaged. As far as my efforts are concerned, all errors of fact, judgment and lack of readability are attributable to me.

In conclusion, I want to earnestly and lovingly thank my wife Penelope, to whom this book is dedicated, for willingly subjecting herself to the cacophony of our existence.

Index

Aagra and Mastermans Ltd, 52
Abelson, Alan, 208
Abdullah ibn Abdul-Aziz, Prince, 160, 162, 166
Adler, Larry, 207
advertising, 1, 126–7
Advicorp, 162
agriculture: EEC policy, 182; *see also under* United States
Aislabie, John, 16–17
Allen, Frederick Lewis, 93, 96
Ames, Oakes, 54, 55
Amsterdam, Bank of, 29
Arizona, University of, 204, 209
Australia, 50, 74, 136, 205, 207, 231
Austria, 2, 57, 71, 136
averting effects of crash, 78, 229–55

Babson, Roger, 131, 194
Bache, 163–4, 169, 170
Balestier, Joseph, 88–9
Bank of England, 13; and South Sea crash, 17, 23; and 1830s slump, 48–9; and Overend Gurney, 52; and secondary banks, 45, 180, 182–3, 184, 192, 193
banking; by building societies, 187; credit, 140–41; fractional reserve, 140–41; Law and modern, 31
banks: central, 31, 35, 45, 140–41; *see also under names of banks and*: Britain; United States
Banque de Lyon et de la Loire, 71
Banque Générale, 33, 35
Banque Populaire Suisse, 162, 163
Banque Royale, 35, 37, 39, 41–2, 43–4
Barber, Anthony, 181, 182, 190
Barclays Bank, 192
Beckman, Robert: education, 172–5; predicts 1987 crash, 195–6

Belgium, 48, 57, 71, 135
Bernard, Samuel, 32
Biddle, Nicholas, 84, 85, 86, 87, 89
Big Bang, 187
Blainville's Travels, 9
Blunt, Charles, 23
Blunt, Sir John, 19, 23
Bohr, Nils, 226
Bombay, Bank of, 51, 52
bonds: and crash aversion, 249; government, 16, 30, 193; 1870s US railroad, 57; junk, 204; in 1929 crash, 135; and 1987 crash, 200–201
box system, 205–7
bridging finance, 186
Britain: 1773 property crash, 89; 1830s: (slump), 48–9, 88; (railway boom), 49, 50; 1857 crisis, 50; 1866 collapse, 52–3; 1870s slump, 70; 1885 depression, 72; 1890s property crash, 89; 1920s slump, 125; 1929 crash, 135, 247; 1930s, 125, 135–6
    1960s–70s: (inflation), 103, 163, 165; (recession), 181; 1970s, 180–93, 250; (credit boom), 181–5, 189; (inflation), 163, 165, 184, 189; (market build-up, 1975–87), 194–8, 202, 223; (property), 181, 184, 187–91, 223; (unemployment), 181
    1980s: (Euro-currency deposits), 189; (LBOs), 204; (privatization), 202; (property), 204, 220–23; (1987 crash), 205, 207, 247; (1980–82 recession), 247; (Third World loans), 187
    banks: *major clearing*: (funding), 191; (and secondary banking crisis), 180, 184, 185, 187, 189, 192; (1980s expansion), 186–7, 188; (Third World loans), 187; *second-line*,

257